THE BEST OF THE BEST

THE BEST OF THE BEST

The Yacht Designs of Sparkman & Stephens

FRANCIS S. KINNEY

AND

RUSSELL BOURNE

W. W. Norton & Company

NEW YORK · LONDON

Printed in the United States of America.

First Edition

The text of this book is composed in Bembo.
Layout and composition by Gina Webster.
Manufacturing by The Courier Corporation.

Photographic Credits:
p. 37, 48, 66, 82, 94, 128, 136, 160, 166, 168, 192, 213 © Peter Barlow
p. 220 © Billy Black
p. 241 © George Kuznecovs
p. 39 © Benjamin Mendlowitz
p. 208, 239 © Dan Nerney
p. 16, 33, 41, 45, 47, 50, 57, 59, 61, 65, 73, 74, 88, 164, 178, 195 © Rosenfeld Collection, Mystic Seaport, Inc.
All rights reserved

Library of Congress Cataloging-in-Publication Data

Kinney, Francis S.
The best of the best / by Francis S. Kinney and Russell Bourne.
1st ed.
p.   cm.
Includes index.
1. Yacht building—United States—Designs and plans. 2. Sparkman & Stephens. I. Bourne, Russell. II. Title.
VM331.K558   1996
623.8'223—dc20   94-48999
CIP

ISBN 0-393-02495-4

W. W. Norton & Company, Inc., 500 Fifth Avenue, New York, N.Y. 10110
W. W. Norton & Company Ltd., 10 Coptic Street, London WC1A 1PU

1 2 3 4 5 6 7 8 9 0

Dedicated to Olin and Rod Stephens

Acknowledgments

This book would not have been possible without the help and cooperation of the good folks at Sparkman & Stephens. Both Olin and Rod read the manuscript and made helpful suggestions, as did Alan Gilbert and Bill Langan. Rochelle Speiller was most helpful with the preparation of the manuscript.

Perhaps the most arduous and important task was performed by Howard Pierce, ferreting out details and checking facts on all the great S&S boats, and providing the invaluable appendices. Morris Rosenfeld and Peter Barlow kindly provided their wonderful photographs. To all our grateful thanks.

The Authors

Contents

Foreword

The death of Rod Stephens was announced on the day I sat down to write this foreword. It seemed a sad coincidence. Rod was a giant in the history of sailing yachts in our time. The story of the firm of naval architects known as Sparkman & Stephens delineates that history. We think back to early yachts designed by Olin and Rod Stephens, yachts like *Dorade, Stormy Weather, Edlu,* and that long line of gorgeous craft that flowed from the drawing boards of Sparkman & Stephens. To be sure, there were great yacht designers before Olin and Rod—the Herreshoffs and John Alden stand out—and there will be others who will follow them. None, however, are likely to surpass them. Some of the best, like German Frers, who apprenticed under the Stephens brothers, and Bill Langan, who stepped into their shoes when they retired, carry on the brothers' dedication to the creation of craft capable of swift, safe passage through whatever the sea may present. In doing so, they designed yachts of unsurpassed beauty—objects of envy and imitation across the seagoing world.

Rod Stephens's death on January 10, 1995, instantly brought from the well of my memory my first meeting with him. It was early in the summer of 1974. I had just taken delivery of a Swan 44, superbly built by Nautor of Finland from lines drawn by Olin Stephens with rig, deck layout, and accommodations by Rod Stephens. Rod came on board for a trial sail on Long Island Sound. I was awed by the fact that he would take the time to sail with me. After all, I believed—and still do—that he and his brother Olin were the world's greatest yacht design team. During our sail, on all points of the wind, Rod poked about, made a few notes, and, after we returned to harbor, departed with thanks but without substantive comment. I had enjoyed his company but wondered what it all had been about. Three days later I received a letter from Rod, enclosing a list of twenty-three suggestions for improvements. He was a totally practical perfectionist and a delightful human who will be sorely missed by the seagoing community around the world.

Another meeting took place in 1979, when he asked me to report in detail our experiences on my Swan 47 during the notorious Fastnet Race of that year. He was pleased to hear that we were able to keep going into 70 knots of wind and 25-foot seas with no breakage except the toilet paper holder in the after head (it gave in to the crashing about of one of our 200-pound crew members), and Rod agreed that to keep going is better than to heave-to—especially with the Irish cliffs looming to leeward.

The Best of the Best, then, has personal meaning to me. Not only did I know Olin and Rod Stephens, I had owned, raced, and cruised three of their designs: an Allied-43 (a centerboarder designed mostly for cruising, but raced under the old and much-loved measurement rule promulgated by the Cruising Club of America we won the Vineyard Race in her and "easily" survived the two-day force-10 gale that enlivened the 1972 Bermuda Race) and two Swans. And Frank Kinney, himself a fine designer, who conceived this book and worked on it until interrupted by death, was a friend. Fortunately, his pen was picked up by Russell Bourne, a writer and lifelong sailor. Frank and Russ and all those at Sparkman & Stephens who opened their files and memories have produced a book which truly records the wonderful work of this extraordinary firm. Chronicled here are the stories of yachts that stand out in the history of modern yacht design of the past three-quarters of a century. The Stephens brothers' yachts brought joy, and much silver, to two generations of sailors. I myself have won races in S&S yachts, and I have been beaten by them. I have cruised the coasts and crossed the Atlantic in them. I have survived great gales in them. I have loved them all.

The oceans of the world are dotted with Sparkman & Stephens yachts—always swift, always sea kindly, and always of great beauty. Truly they were and are the best. Here are the best of those best.

Eric P. Swenson

Introduction

Over the years so many of them have sailed before our eyes: since 1929, some 2,600 Sparkman & Stephens yachts of various rigs and descriptions. With all these to consider, it may seem impossible to single out the truly superior designs—the famous and recent winners which deserve to be remembered for their excellence. Not impossible, actually; a worthy challenge.

These triumphant *Ranger*s and *Lightning*s and *Intrepid*s have, at various times, and for good reason, stirred national pride. But they also represent—these S&S winners of the Bermuda Race and the Fastnet, of the Whitbread Round the World Race, of races from New Zealand to the Mediterranean—high points of what's become a truly international sport.

So it's in the spirit of worldwide recognition of a significant cultural asset that the authors have undertaken this research. Within the pages of this volume they have sought to set forth some 100 of the most beautiful, most beloved S&S vessels. Those designs by Sparkman & Stephens during the years since 1929 range across a surprisingly wide arc—not just ocean racers but everything from production one-designs to customized mega-yachts.

In this volume the boat is hero, quality of design the theme. With each selected yacht, the authors have suggested why that design was of special importance, either because of a technical breakthrough it made, because of silverware won or long life achieved, or simply because of the pleasure given by its lines to the eye.

For most of these boat biographies, interviews with and remembrances of the Stephens brothers and their successors have served as the authors' guides. In other cases, owners and rivals of the yachts have been tapped for their recollections. Occasionally subtle, the case for superiority has been made in the case of each boat; yet the authors must admit that the final criterion for selection is quite subjective.

Some brilliant campaigners or power craft or far-sailing cruisers or favorite one-designs may have been left out—either because of lack of surviving documents or because of the squeeze of other contemporary competitors crowding across the finish line. In an effort to make up for this, the authors have included an appendix (which may itself have gaps, such being the nature of yacht history).

Certainly no single volume, however capacious, could distill the essential elements of yachting in the twentieth century; the subject is too diverse for that. Nonetheless, the hope here is that the presentation of these selected Sparkman & Stephens designs will serve as a particularly revealing volume in the expanding library of international yacht racing and naval architecture.

The Stephens Brothers

Olin J. Stephens II and Roderick Stephens, Jr., have been called the best "seamen and designers of all time," two skills and two brothers unbreakably linked. That was their practice for five full decades (1929-79). Now that their design firm is being carried on by a new generation of seamen and designers, the accomplishments and breakthroughs of the brothers stand forth as all the more fundamental and remarkable—both to the firm and to the development of marine design.

The family commitment to sailing began in the early 1920s when Olin and Rod taught themselves how to sail amid the sandflats of Barnstable Bay, Massachusetts. Their boats were a series of balky day-sailers and small cruisers. But the groundings, the late arrivals, the discomforts simply made the boys dream more actively of what might float better and sail faster.

Olin's dreams took the shape of doodles and improving sketches in a number of notebooks filled while at Scarsdale High School, in New York State. For Rod, captain of the high school football team, the dreams were more physical, less cerebral. And as soon as he could persuade the family that the move was career related, he left Cornell to go to work at the mud-bottom level of the Nevins boatyard at City Island, New York. Olin, in the meantime, had had to return home from MIT to overcome a jaundice attack; after recovery, he felt disinclined to toe the line along with his would-be-engineer classmates. During an MIT interview he had seen the half-model of a hull designed by one of his professors, and he had recognized (out loud) that the boat lacked punch. He could do better, he knew.

Olin therefore went to work as a draftsman, first at Henry J. Gielow's office (where the super helmsman Sherman Hoyt ran the sailboat department), then for the renowned yacht designer Philip Rhodes. The brothers' father, in the meantime, believing in their talents and their dedication, engineered a partnership for them with the successful yacht broker Drake Sparkman. Thus was Sparkman & Stephens born, with Olin as chief designer and Rod (who joined the firm some three years later) in charge of all construction and rigging and testing.

But Roderick Stephens, Sr., was not finished with his support of his sons; he financed the construction of an experimental offshore racer, a design that all the family hoped would capture attention. Named *Dorade* after the French word for dolphin, this 52' 2" yawl cost $28,000 in depression-era (1930) dollars. And the magnificent gamble paid off: *Dorade* won the highly publicized 1931 Trans-Atlantic race, winning for the Stephenses a ticker-tape parade on their return home. Nor was that the last of the deep, narrow yawl's victories—see *Dorade*'s listing in Chapter 3—a gleaming string of trophies that would continue for many years.

Dorade's true value lay more in her potential as a concept, however, than as a silverware producer. It was not only that she contravened the prevailing wisdom for ocean racers—that they must be blunt-bowed, broad-beamed schooners, in the tradition of offshore fishing boats. It was that she applied the keenness of meter-racers to the challenge of transatlantic competition. In the words of the then-ruling sage of blue-water yacht design, John Alden, *Dorade* was really "an overgrown 6-meter!" It was a time to try new shapes at sea. From now on the risk of experimenting with radical hull forms and innovative rigs would be eagerly taken by new generations of yacht owners here and abroad. These skippers recognized Sparkman & Stephens as the premier designer who would get them to the finish line first, stylishly and safely.

Principles under Pressure

The late 1920s and early 1930s spun along in their own club-by way, with an odd mixture of Vanderbilts who could spend hundreds of thousands for J-boats and workaday sailors who had to contemplate yachting without paid hands. That was the era when the young Stephens brothers succeeded in keeping their design firm afloat, with major assistance from the well-connected, businesslike Drake Sparkman. There was, to be sure, the depression, but Olin recalls that because "most new building was then in smaller boats, it was a good time for a young yacht designer to gain experience."

The brothers also won their reputations in rather personal ways. It was expected that they would participate in campaigning whatever boats they produced for their daring clients. Olin, it was decided, should generally be the helmsman, ever keeping his eye on the tactics and the sail trim; Rod, nicknamed "Tarzan" by Harold Vanderbilt, would range about the boat in his red trousers, repairing this, suggesting that. It was a winning and charming team, with Rod supplying an accordion for after-hours songfests.

Characteristic techniques and principles of design began to emerge. Olin developed his technical skills, working with Ken Davidson at the new testing tank (former swimming pool) at the Stevens Institute of Technology in Hoboken, New Jersey. "One of the greatest breaks of my life came when Ken walked into our office (then in a store on City Island Avenue)," Olin wrote later. The Stephens brothers' 34-foot S&S sloop *Gimcrack*, designed in 1933, served as the first full-scale test subject for this program; the model of a 6-meter whittled by Rod (for purposes of experimenting with her sail plan) was also brought into service as a test subject.

By carefully observing and recording *Gimcrack*'s performance under certain conditions at sea over a three-year period, Olin and Rod were able to provide director Davidson with a data base. Thanks to that work, Davidson could then relate the resistance of 3- to 4-foot-long models towed in the tank (a resistance of about three-quarters of a pound) to the far greater resistance experienced by the hulls of full-scaled boats.

Although no "eureka!"-worthy observations came forth from these tests, lots of interesting numbers did. And these, considered and applied, led to the improvement of Vanderbilt's J-boat, *Ranger*, on whose plans Olin was invited to work in company with America's ranking designer, Starling Burgess. Three test models for this record-breaking, 135-foot sloop were prepared, one of which was Olin's. Many decades later came more elaborate testing devices and computers that provided far more sophisticated studies of a hull's underwater profile.

Yet, for all his belief in testing, Olin Stephens stressed from the beginning that a tank was nothing but a tool, a tool by which could be gauged the effectiveness of somebody's three-dimensional design; a tank would never provide the design. "In those early days," he's fond of saying, "yacht design was 10 percent science and 90 percent intuition or talent. Now it's about fifty-fifty." Nonetheless, by scientific method and rational experiment (such as with aluminum hulls), certain principles of S&S design asserted themselves.

For Rod Stephens, inventiveness and "seat-of-the-pants" pragmatism were the key factors. He was always the stalwart advocate of the yawl rig, *Dorade*'s rig, trusting in the efficiency and adaptability of this sail apportionment. As such capable yawls as *Stormy Weather*, *Baruna*, and *Finisterre* sailed forth from the S&S design boards, few doubted that his case against the traditional, American schooner rig had been won.

Rod also sharpened the rigging of S&S racing craft, perfecting the use of aluminum spars and stainless-steel rod rigging for *Ranger* (designed in partnership with Starling Burgess). Joining Rod in this high-pressure effort, described in Chapter 1, was Gil Wyland, who, as chief engineer, became a key figure in the success of Sparkman & Stephens.

Perhaps Rod's most famous technological contribution in this early era was the "*Dorade* vent," his ingenious solution for letting fresh air in while keeping salt water out belowdecks. This clever pipe-within-a-box has never been surpassed as a medium for frustrating the spray. By such devices and improvements—as well as by being ever ready to go aloft hand-over-hand or out to the end of a boom while sailing before the wind—Rod Stephens asserted additional S&S principles. Their boats would be given the best rigs, the best chances of surviving a blue-water contest.

As the range of S&S products expanded during and after World War II, Rod continued to focus on each one of the myriad details that might weaken or strengthen a boat—from compasses (he disapproved of corrective magnets, tended to throw them overboard) to engine exhaust systems, which must not be allowed to work like siphons. Another one of his fixations was that the helmsman's wheel must turn easily (no more than 1 foot-pound of pressure needed, otherwise the builder didn't get paid) and that a third reef should not be taken (instead, the mainsail should be dropped, the boom secured, and a storm trysail rigged that's sheeted to the deck, not to the end of the boom). On both ocean racers and one-designs of those years, as well as on his own New York 32, *Mustang*, Rod asserted these principles, gaining worldwide respect for his special kind of applied genius.

Indeed, although Olin and Rod were treated as members of the "after guard" by Harold Vanderbilt and owners of other yachts on which they sailed, the Stephens brothers were called "oceangoing jockeys" by some gentlemen skippers who disdained the unceasing zeal with which the Stephenses campaigned their boats on both sides of the Atlantic. But, as Olin explains, these hard-fought, widely reported contests were an essential part of the firm's rise to prominence, for "racing victories led the way; that's the way it seemed."

Such a string of racing victories continuing across the decades could only have been won by a design firm willing to advance beyond concepts laid down in the long-ago twenties. *Finisterre* had to differ (and differ radically) from *Gimcrack*: for her own reasons and purposes, *Finisterre* had to be chubby and shallow. S&S traditions were all very well, but a 12-meter designed by the firm in the 1970s looked not much like the ancient, beloved *Vim* or *Nyala*.

New materials were coming into play, as well as new challenges—even including mass-production boats and new kinds of owners. There had to be constant evolution; changes upon changes; risks taken, some that paid off, some that disappointed. When it came to changes contemplated in the designs for *Intrepid*, Olin recalled: "then we made a second model more or less according to ideas that had been working around in the back of my head for some time; and this model, I might say, was a complete disaster." Many, however, led to significant breakthroughs—such as the tricky trimtab that had never before been applied to a 12-meter (*Intrepid*, so equipped, sailed on to victory).

A Change of Skippers, Not of Style

Olin Stephens believes that the most dynamic period for S&S (during this century, if not the next) may have been the early seventies, a time when the firm capitalized on past international successes by producing a large number of winners for foreign owners. This was also the time when Sparkman & Stephens, having always been a firm known for working cooperatively with ambitious designers elsewhere (such as Aage Nielsen), solidified its reputation as a training place for young designers (such as Mario Tarabocchia).

In 1979 Olin Stephens, approaching his own seventieth year and recognizing the quality of the talent around him, decided to step down from the chief designer's office. A similar and simultaneous decision was made by chief engineer Gil Wyland. Yet, to the astonishment of the industry, Olin (then and now the dean of American yacht designers) gave his baton not to a recognized giant in the profession but to S&S designer Bill Langan, aged twenty-five—just a bit older than Olin was when he and Rod established the firm. The chief engineer's title was passed to young Alan Gilbert, who had joined S&S's design department in 1971.

A dynastic line of succession and of continually successful yachts can be traced from the 1969 *Running Tide* (one of Olin's favorite designs) through *War Baby* (which, as *Tenacious*, won the Fastnet Race in 1979, when a scandalous number of boats were lost or storm ravaged) to *Ebb Tide* (a luxurious, 83-foot, Dutch wonder-ketch produced in 1984). The same emphasis on exquisite lines, on safe and sensible rigs, and on custom interiors for the particular owner may be noted. "I haven't seen it as my job to leave my imprint on S&S," Bill Langan says. "For me the challenge is to combine what S&S is (what it embodies) with new elements and come up with a solution that has both features."

But there have been obvious changes; first of all in boat size. Alan Gilbert, with typical precision, has charted the growth of average boat lengths over the last dozen years. The size curve swings awesomely upward toward the "mega-yachts" of the 1990s—a curve steep as the bow of a catboat. In the mid-nineties, even while S&S is designing many boats in the 40- to 60-foot range, the average length is something like 115 feet (32 meters).

Then there's the factor of engineering. Even though that has always been a strong suit at S&S—whether for their handsome power yachts or for their intricate sailboats—it has in recent years become a major strength. For each of the stupendous vessels now being brought forth is a miniature floating city, with all systems but food and fuel self-supplied. Engineers peer into computer screens to make sure that those planned systems blink and glow as they should.

"*Dorade* wouldn't happen today," Bill Langan remarks somewhat ruefully. It's not just so much that more is known about fast-moving hulls but that the whole material substance of the craft would be different; everything from titanium rigging to carbon-fiber rudder. He and Olin agree that more knowledge means that advances can now be made more swiftly; perhaps the number of breakthroughs per decade is accelerating at the same curve as the curve of average lengths.

There are many other factors differentiating the work done

today from that of yesterday—including lack of call to design according to the whim of the latest international racing rule. But even more impressive is the continuing S&S emphasis on sea kindliness, on testing, on individuality. To fit their new breed of mega-yachts, the firm's designers must create anew not only the fixed and running rigging (as done for grand racers of the prewar era) but also electronic and hydraulic systems never before witnessed. This total design process means that a new boat requires a number of years rather than a number of months from concept to launch.

Bill Langan and Alan Gilbert recognize that one of the fortunate developments that has facilitated today's operations was the invention of the "stowaway mast," into which the mainsail of a large boat can be rolled up; this permits owners to go for a larger boat without having a large number of beef-eating crew members aboard. Nonetheless, such a recent yacht as the widely heralded, 115-foot *Astral* (definitely not designed as a racer) can move with a swiftness that recalls past S&S winners. In a 30-knot breeze, easily maintaining full canvas, she surges along at upwards of 12 knots.

Astral and the other mega-yachts sail near the parade's end of the 100 and more boats presented in the following pages, all representing important developments in the evolution of S&S designs. Closer toward the front, produced a full decade ago, sails a boat that might be identified as the exemplary, transitional design between Olin and Rod Stephens's time and that of the new hands. She's Design Number 2390, the Stevens 47, and a wonder she is (see Chapter 13).

Though a production boat, the Stevens looks like every sailor's private dream, at 46' 10" and 6 feet of draft. The clue to her transitional status is her artfully shaped underbody: the medium-length keel is clearly a compromise between the full-length keel with vertical rudder at after end of old-fashioned boats and the short, deep fin keel with separated skeg and rudder of new-style racing boats. Also a compromise is the generous beam, which means that, though a notably fast boat, she carries the full range of cruising comforts below.

Olin Stephens continues to believe that sensitive, imaginative compromise is the essence of successful yacht design. A designer could work eternally on a design, after all, making new tests and endless, subtle revisions. "So, in a sense, every boat is a compromise that you're forced into by the calendar and the clock," he avers. The trick is to produce the very best you can within that time, within those demands, within the scope of that owner's dream.

Here are those brilliant compromises—the best of Sparkman & Stephens's best designs.

THE BEST OF THE BEST

1

Six- and Eight-Meters and the Greatest of the J's

On a day when no one in his right mind would have been out sailing, the Stephens brothers did go sailing. And on that day in 1921 they lost their hearts to the 6-meter class of international racing sloops—to the benefit of American yacht design.

It was a gusty, rainy Saturday. The young men, in their late teens, had just finished a grim thrash across Long Island Sound, over to Lloyd's Neck and back to Larchmont. They had sailed in a regrettable boat with a leaky deck which they happened to own at the time. Now what each wanted most of all was a hot shower, a change into dry clothes, and a ride home.

Then into the shower room came Sherman Hoyt, distinguished yachtsman and advocate of the 6-meter class. "Anyone here want to go for a sail in one of our two new boats?" he called. So the brothers put their sopping togs back on and went out to learn the joys of these sleek, glamorous 35-foot racers.

The boats faced up brilliantly to the challenge of the heavy chop, the fine entry of their bows allowing them to slash rather than crash through the waves. Olin and Rod Stephens grasped what was so importantly different here, and how removed it was from American boatbuilding as the art was then practiced. Soon they persuaded their father that to own a 6-meter was an essential step in their advancement as sailors and designers. The 6-meter *Natka* thus became a member of the Stephens household. Though never swift, she provided an opportunity to learn the intimate secrets of this class; now Olin and Rod could design some American sixes that would show the world.

In U.S. yacht design circles before the 1920s (circles which did not regard 6- or 8-meters as sufficiently American to be worthy of serious consideration), there were essentially two traditions of yacht design. The first of these schools looked back to the great days of American fishing schooners and, led by the designer John Alden, turned out deep and beamy seaboats, noted for both sturdiness and speed. The second school, led by Nathanael Herreshoff, looked to England for inspiration, coming up with grand racers with lofty spars and vast quantities of sail, deep fin keels, and valiant names.

But a few amateur and professional designers were beginning to turn out popular American racing classes, like the R's and the Q's. Leader of this innovative fraternity was Starling Burgess, son of the designer Edward Burgess and sometime follower of the Herreshoff tradition; by the 1920s he was daring to apply principles of airplane design to naval architecture.

To ambitious and possibly naive Olin Stephens, the challenge of coming up with a winning design during this period seemed (as he wrote later) "rather simple for someone with some boat sense and a good eye." Of his initial designs, including the instantly famous *Dorade*, several seemed to reflect the principles of the 6- and 8-meters. That is, they were narrow and deep forward, with minimum wetted surface. Everything about them—the rig, the deck layout, the fittings—was calculated to make for greater speed and efficiency.

The Stephens brothers had learned well the lesson that Long Island Sound had to teach them on that blustery day. The finesse apparent in *Thalia*, the first 6-meter which Olin designed (winter, 1928-29), seemed to indicate that along with the promised speed of the boat, there was a new philosophy, more sophisticated than naive. Olin wrote: "[This] design is intended primarily for light weather. In any design the most important factors of speed seem to be long sailing lines and large sail area, with moderate displacement and small wetted surface. Then comes beauty, by which is meant clean, fair, pleasing lines. Though per se beauty is not a factor of speed, the easiest boats to look at seem the easiest to drive."

Then that philosophy was put into action around the buoys. Olin and Rod raced the boat in Long Island Sound that summer and the results were encouraging, though less so in Bermuda the next spring. But *Thalia*'s beauty and record had caught the attention of competitive yachtsmen on both sides of the Atlantic; would-be owners began knocking on S&S's doors.

The results of those meter boats abroad seemed even more impressive than here. In the words of a contemporary journal, the American-designed boats "caused a bit of a rumpus in England this past season." Rod believed it was most significant for future developments that some of the best S&S meter boats won their laurels in foreign waters. He had in mind particularly the Swedish 8-meter *Iskareen* (Design Number 275), which was built by Plym, a shipyard that "always did everything just right."

Facing page: Jill. *See page 20.*

These historic 8- and 6-meter boats, which led directly to the creation of the magnificent J-boat *Ranger* in 1936, remain examples not only of how yacht design can be advanced by selective emphasis but also of how fresh enthusiasm and intelligence can make a difference within an established profession.

Conewago - Design 9

LOA: 48' 8"   DWL: 30' 4"   Beam: 7' 11"   Draft: 6' 6"   Sail area: 890 sq. ft.

Designed in the same year as *Dorade* (1929), this sharp-ended 8-meter did not at first appear to prove the superior skills of the young designers. She had been built by a Rochester syndicate determined to win the Canada's Cup in 1930; instead, she lost rather badly to a fellow American contestant in the elimination races. "She never goes to windward when you want her to!" the owner complained to Rod Stephens.

In the fall of that year, fortunately, *Conewago* was bought by another group of freshwater sailors who campaigned her with great success. Her owner, Wilmot ("Rooney") Castle, not only grabbed the Canada's Cup but also won the championship of Lake Ontario's sizable 8-meter class, American and Canadian. He had no difficulty at all going to windward. In fact, after noting that the boat seemed to be faster in light than strong air, Castle altered the sail plan slightly and added ballast, greatly improving her heavy-weather performance.

Though primarily a day-sailer, this design called for 5 feet of headroom below and simple accommodations for sleeping two aboard. The layout called for two cockpits, as in a bi-plane; this feature was common on 6-meters but rather rare on 8-meters.

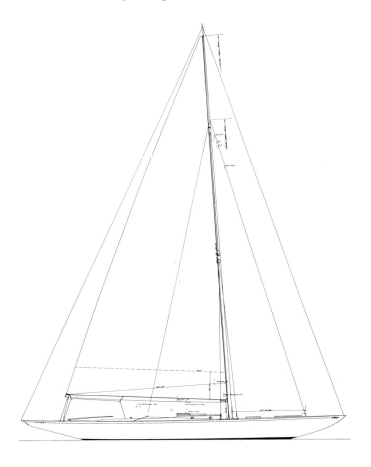

Cherokee and Jill – Designs 10 and 16

Cherokee: LOA: 37' 3"   DWL: 23' 4"   Beam: 10' 7"   Draft: 5' 5"   Sail area: 455 sq. ft.

Jill: LOA: 36' 4"   DWL: 23' 7"   Beam: 6' 7"   Draft: 5' 4"   Sail area: 436 sq. ft.

In the two decades following the founding of Sparkman & Stephens Incorporated, nearly a dozen 6-meters were designed, stimulated by strong interest among yachtsmen in the British/American Cup (raced for by two teams of four boats each). American teams were generally sponsored by the Seawanhaka Yacht Club.

Most of the S&S meter boats designed during this period were so successful that it seems unfair to leave any off the best-of-the-best list. Nonetheless, three of them stand out: *Cherokee* because she was among the first (1930), *Jill* (1931) because her lines and sail plan were drawn by Olin himself, and *Goose* (1938) because she was unarguably the best. Rod Stephens remembered with amusement two owners of S&S-created 6-meters who were angry at him and Olin because the boats both performed so well and so equally that neither of them could prove he was the better sailor.

Rod limited himself to the remark that *Cherokee* was a "very competent competitor." But a 1933 newspaper report by the eminent yacht-racing columnist Everett B. Morris provides some saltier adjectives. In describing how this early 6-meter was not to be outdone by her younger sisters, Morris wrote:

"[Skipper Herman] Whiton had *Cherokee* climbing up wind like something on the end of a towline, and she was not exactly dragging anchor on the leeward legs.... *Cherokee* carries the smallest, flattest mainsail in the fleet. It is hardly large enough to provide a background for her identifying numbers, but she went amazingly well with it to weather."

Morris also pointed out that Olin himself, in a newer boat, was outsailed by the swift *Cherokee*. The keen competition in these events on Long Island Sound was fostered by a committee of the Seawanhaka Corinthian Yacht Club, which did everything possible to elevate the level of U.S. boats and skippers above that of international rivals.

Another notable aspect of these wooden, S&S meter boats is their longevity. *Goose*, which was reconstructed in 1957, is still winning races on the West Coast. *Jill* went on for another couple of decades as a delightful cruiser after her conversion in 1950. Moved easily by a 7½-horsepower outboard in a well, she offers two full berths in the main cabin plus two quarter-berths, with 6 feet of headroom beneath the low-profile trunk cabin. In this form she earned a new reputation as "an ideal, small, fast cruising boat."

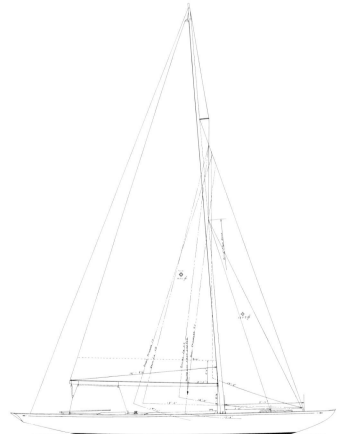

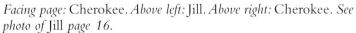

Facing page: Cherokee. *Above left:* Jill. *Above right:* Cherokee. *See photo of* Jill *page 16.*

Ranger – Design 77

LOA: 135' 2"   DWL: 87'   Beam: 21'   Draft: 15'   Sail area: 7,950 sq. ft.

This was indeed "the last and greatest of the J's," those enormous and extravagant yachts which today epitomize heroic glories of bygone sailing eras. Named for John Paul Jones's eighteen-gun warship, *Ranger* succeeded in blasting her British challenger, *Endeavour II*, in all four events of the 1937 America's Cup races. Yet, even with the reputations they were earning in the early 1930s, it does seem rather amazing that the youthful Stephens brothers were invited by owner Harold Vanderbilt to be part of his supreme, gold-plated effort to defend the cup.

The lead designer he selected was the preeminent naval architect Starling Burgess. But, having met Rod when that all-competent seaman had sailed aboard *Rainbow* in the J-boat contest of 1935, and having a suspicion that American yacht design needed new blood, Vanderbilt was eager to bring the brothers onto the team.

While partner Drake Sparkman handled negotiations for the proposed association with Burgess, Olin Stephens in his usual tactful way proceeded to introduce that aging gentleman and

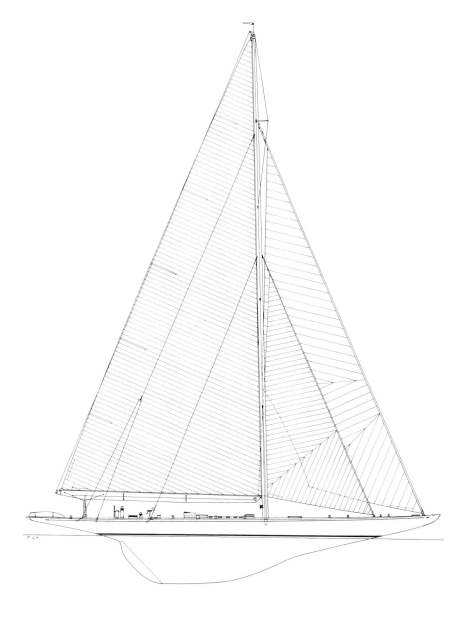

Harold Vanderbilt to the new science of tank-testing small models. As mentioned in this book's introduction, three models were tested. One of them was clearly the best; the full-scale hull would be built lightly yet ruggedly of steel and (in comparison with the British challenger) would be a forward-looking and fully modern vessel.

The depression was not truly over in 1937—even the New York Yacht Club was "under financial strain," its historian noted. And Harold Vanderbilt had difficulty finding the additional investors to fund *Ranger*. Therefore, recognizing the problem, management and workers at the Bath Iron Works (Maine) vowed to trim costs down to $140,000 from the original estimates. After a frenzied winter of work, a gleaming hull was launched in May, the aluminum spar (which had cost $18,000) tied on deck.

Although *Ranger* might appear sleek and well-balanced to professional eyes, the workers could not imagine what this super-yacht would look like when actually rigged. Respecting their curiosity and all they'd done for the cause, Vanderbilt made the gracious decision to step the 165-foot mast, even though this meant that the vessel could not be towed to Newport through the Cape Cod Canal and under its relatively low bridges. Now she would have to be towed around the Cape, risking the perils of open sea in an untested boat.

"I have never seen two men work harder than the Stephens brothers did getting this rig ready," Vanderbilt wrote of Olin's and Rod's efforts to keep *Ranger* on track and on schedule. Rod was to ride in the towboat on the overnight passage down from Maine.

It began well enough, under moderate conditions. But as night was falling, Rod became aware that the bar shrouds which supported the mast seemed loose, flailing about. (No one knew it, but there was a flaw in the locknuts by which the shrouds were tightened to proper tension.) Through the long night, as ocean swells whipped the mast this way and that, the shrouds loosened more. By morning's light, Rod saw the inevitable happen: the aluminum mast (designed by Burgess, with assistance from Gil Wyland) snapped off, 35 feet above the deck, over the side.

Ranger and her crew were instantly in danger and her carefully orchestrated racing schedule in jeopardy. But harbor was safely reached and another mast swiftly made. Tales abound of the intensity of this labor under extreme pressure, including an unforgettable vignette of the small boy who worked inside the mast, lying on his back atop a kind of trolley, riding slowly down the length of the aluminum sheath in order to clinch the rivets. The mast was delivered on time; by the second of June,

Ranger was clobbering the best American J's.

Rod had designed the deck layout. As rover, he was in charge of training members of the deck crew. He decreed, among other things, that practice would not be held on rainy days—he wanted to avoid wetting the enormous sails (including the quadrilateral jibs, which look so strange to us today). Another rule was that at the end of each day's sailing practice or racing, that vast mainsail had to be taken off and stowed away—a task requiring the strenuous labors of two dozen men. The rationale behind this was that, in his selection of the proper sail for the next day, Mr. Vanderbilt didn't want to be influenced by the one that might already be set up.

An unusual thing about sail setting on the *Ranger* was that, for all the mainsail's weight and enormity, no halyard winch seemed necessary. It was manpower all the way, the final few inches assisted by a loop or two around the genoa's pedestal winch. In fact, the headboard of the main, when all the way up, was secured not by the halyard but by a masthead hook; then the luff was stretched down by a winch. To lower the main, it first had to be raised clear of the hook.

It was during the course of these training exercises and preliminary races that Rod earned that "Tarzan" nickname; also "Red Devil of the *Ranger*" from the hue of his shorts. Vanderbilt called him "the most colorful member of our after guard." As for Olin, he was constantly observing, observing, and getting a feel for how and why *Ranger* performed best. He liked the way she seemed to "squat down and go," taking advantage of all the length in her overhangs.

Through Olin's helmsman's hands he could sense, with delight, that there was never a lee helm; also, the long keel made her feel, even after a tack, as if she "really wanted to go" in the new direction. Despite her ponderousness (displacement, 166 tons; ballast, 110 tons) and length, *Ranger* was so delicately balanced that Harold Vanderbilt had the (erroneous) impression that the weight of one man way forward would make her hobby-horse. The only disappointment was that the small centerboard got itself permanently stuck in its box; it was never used.

By all records, *Ranger* was the fastest J-boat ever built. Although the British J-boat *Endeavour II* had earned a reputation as an extremely fast sailer, she was no match for the American defender. After the last America's Cup race on August 5, 1939, there were the New York Yacht Club cruise and some other great contests along the East Coast, lasting into September. But then *Ranger's* career, so brilliantly begun, was suddenly concluded. As war clouds rose in eastern skies, the era of the J's came to an end.

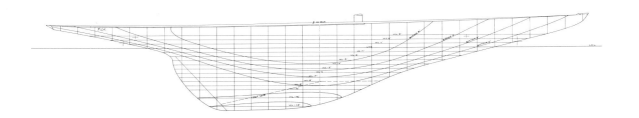

Goose – Design 243

LOA: 37'   DWL: 23' 8"   Beam: 6' 6"   Draft: 5' 6"   Sail area: 474 sq. ft.

Unlike the story told by Rod about the two friends angry because their 6-meters sailed too much alike, Olin tells a story of two family members who had the discomfort of finding that their 6-meters were dramatically different. The two boats had been ordered by George Nichols (father-in-law) and Henry S. Morgan (son-in-law) at virtually the same time. But between Design Number 238 (Morgan's, named *Djinn*) and Design Number 243 (Nichols's, named *Goose*) there existed a vast performance gap.

It resulted from one important design change, caused by Olin's study of figures resulting from tests of models in the Stevens tank. His hunch that a sharper, deeper fore-section allowed the boat to move with less resistance seemed to be supportable. Unfortunately, *Djinn* was built before that improvement could be effected. *Goose*, on the other hand, became an instant triumph; she is said to have lost only one race in her entire, brilliant career.

Rod Stephens used to say that *Goose* always sailed "in a class by herself." Whereas the prevailing wisdom was that, in order to win, a 6-meter had to be the fastest to windward in the fleet, *Goose* picked off most of the opposition while reaching.

But Rod would add that she'd win on any heading, under any conditions: "didn't make a damn bit of difference if the breeze was strong or light." Olin believes that she was indeed good, "but not that good."

Ironically, when it came time to design the hulls of the modern 12-meters, Olin's studies revealed that the dramatic innovation which had made *Goose* a "breakthrough boat" had to be reversed. That is, the fore-section had to be made shallower and more rounded before the junction with the keel. Though this remains something of a mystery, Olin believes the explanation may lie in the fact that the twelves competed in one-against-one match races, the sixes in fleet races. For the former, swift tacks were mandatory, moving the bow immediately from one heading to another in order to cover the opponent; for the latter, a tack could be more leisurely, the more important matter being on-track speed. Perhaps that's the answer.

When it came time to reconstruct *Goose* in 1957, very little was done, as might be suspected, to change the hull or rigging of this nearly perfect boat. Save for an aluminum mast with single spreader, she's still pretty much the same.

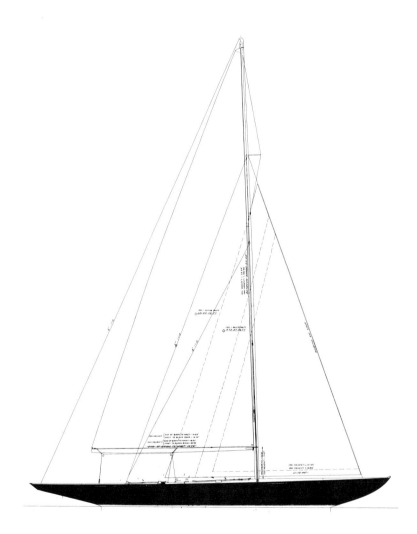

This page: Goose.
Facing page: Iroquois.

Iroquois – Design 1862

LOA: 43' 7"   DWL: 31' 6"   Beam: 8' 4"   Draft: 6' 7"   Sail area: 845 sq. ft.

An interesting contrast to *Conewago* (1929), *Iroquois* represents state-of-the-art 8-meter designing as of 1968. For all of their differences in hull and rig (note *Iroquois*'s resemblance to the 12-meter *Intrepid*, her multiplicity of winches, and her adjustable backstays), what's similar here is the boat's successes on Lake Ontario. Although the 8-meter class had diminished numerically there by the 1970s, *Iroquois* found plenty of stiff competition, winning sufficient silverware to make both designer and owner content. S&S's superiority with meter boats had been demonstrated for yet another generation.

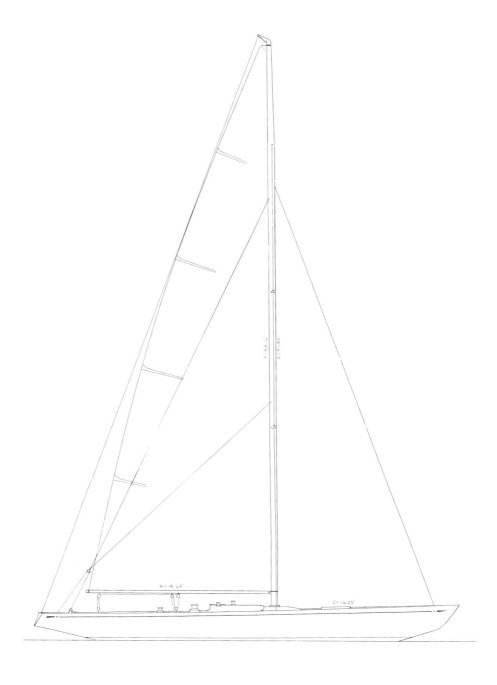

2

One-Designs for Beginners and Fanatics

Even while serious American yachtsmen were contending against European rivals in meter-boat racing at international regattas—where royalty and the privileged caused sailing to be called "the sport of kings"—other less exalted Americans were finding ways to get waterborne. They, too, thanked Sparkman & Stephens for supplying them with some splendid and memorable boats, and for helping to train in those boats the young racers of tomorrow.

Indeed, the very first design issued from the S&S office, drafted in the fall of 1928, was a proposed racing class not for yachtsmen but for youngsters. Called the Junior One-Design (or Sound Juniors), the jaunty little boats featured a very large J inside a circle on the mainsail—J-boats for the little people. (The branch of this class that later flourished at a yacht club in Blue Hill, Maine, went so far as to feature such evocative names as *Endeavour* and *Ranger*.) Later the name of the class was changed to Manhasset One-Design.

In terms of the design philosophy behind such boats, as contrasted to that behind the 6- and 8-meters, this was not a matter of everything for the sake of speed. For the "rating classes" and meter boats, Olin Stephens and his fellow designers would stretch technology as far as possible and try the latest tricks to achieve faster and faster sailing speeds. But here, in the one-designs, other important factors had to be given careful attention. Specifically, low cost, comfort, and ease of maintenance had to be considered in these more democratic creations (whether the skipper was a youngster or a grown-up novice).

But for all those socioeconomic considerations, "The one-designs had to seem to be fast," as Olin expressed it. "Oh yes, they had to be pleasant to sail and good to sit in. But you can't ignore speed."

Nor could you ignore the factor of even-Stephens—these boats had to be exactly alike, testing not design against design but skipper against skipper. In the words of one happy S&S sailor: "Because all boats are identical and because [class] restrictions on variations in sails and running rigging are so stringent, the boat becomes clearly a tactical racing boat rather than a designer's and a gadgeteer's paradise...the winner is either the best skipper with the best crew or the luckiest!"

The business of creating, selling, and delivering these swift but equal day-sailers was also different from S&S's ocean-racer and meter-boat business. The sale had to be made to a yacht club (actually to a committee from one or a number of clubs), among whose members prejudices abounded. They thought they knew exactly what kind of sailboat they wanted for their youngsters; they had formed a committee to arbitrate it. Design by committee, with all those drawbacks? Perhaps.

There was always something delightfully local about these Manhasset One-Designs, these Seawanhaka Seabirds, these Cape Cod Mercuries. Now that racing has become increasingly international, less local, such distinctive character tends to be found less often, and specially created one-designs are seen less frequently.

In those days before and after World War II, the deal was that the purchasing individual or club would deal with the builder, not with the designers. So when a club decided to order a number of boats, the contract was signed with a boatyard—which paid a royalty (often 2 percent of the price) to S&S. For their part, the designers supplied full plans to the builder, and left many details for him to work out in his own most efficient way. This was not at all a matter of Rod Stephens swinging in out of the blue and demanding that the boat be built according to the highest S&S standards.

Yet some absolutely beautiful and wondrously popular boats were created in this manner. Indeed, another feature of one-design boats is how, after a yacht club or two have adopted that class, the owners within the club become fanatically devoted to the design. In the American manner, they organize this fanaticism into class bylaws, a new "Whereas" for every agreed specification, amendments most carefully debated. Technological upgrading is hypothetically encouraged in these protocols (but actually contested all the way, both by traditionalists and by those short of techno-dough).

"These were not gold-platers," Olin Stephens agrees. But he's as proud of some of his one-designs as of the ocean racers. And the practice of producing these adept, comfortable, modest racers, begun at S&S in the 1920s, has continued all across the years. The clever little 1978 sloop Designer's Choice indicates that the practice, though somewhat diminished today, is also an active option at S&S in recent decades.

Facing page: Bermuda dinghy. See page 34.

Sound Junior Class - Design 1

LOA: 21' 6"   DWL: 15'   Beam: 5' 10"   Draft: 3' 6"   Sail area: 230 sq. ft.

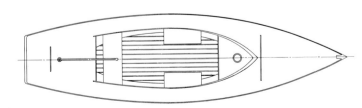

Something like two dozen of these handsome little sloops were built, rebuilt, and variously restored. The passion with which their owners resurrected, renamed, and recannibalized them makes for a certain confusion about precise numbers. The class historian, when pressed to chronicle how the boats came and went from 1929 to the fiftieth anniversary year of 1979, had to admit that the story was fraught with "mystery" and "puzzling aspects."

It's clear, nonetheless, that the original design was a winner. And when the plans were accepted by the Junior Yacht Racing Association of Long Island, beginning designer Olin Stephens was launched on his career. To anyone viewing one of these boats today, she appears to be an obvious classic, with her delicately designed coaming, her subtly raked mast, her gently arched tiller. But perhaps another factor in the instant success was her price—$1,000. "A whole lot of boat for the price," *Yachting* informed its readers.

The price resulted from a deal struck by partner Drake Sparkman with a builder in Poughkeepsie, New York, named Buckout. Fortunately this low-bid builder, unlike some others who would win S&S designs, followed the plans faithfully, producing the designer's dream in three dimensions. Among the innovations that made her so immediately appealing were the "modern, efficient rig," the roomy and well-planned cockpit, and double-planked bulkheads fore and aft. The latter were supposed to make the boat "unsinkable"; yet some, it must be told, did eventually find their way to that dread locker undersea.

After World War II, after the class was renamed the Manhasset One-Designs (the first design is still sailed there), there was considerable discussion of modernizing the rig. Attention was given to Olin's clever device of a slender boom at the foot of the jib which allowed that sail to be self-tending. Some fierce competitors wanted a more racy arrangement, a jib that had to be fine-tuned from either side after tacking. Then came the hot and heavy "spinnaker question." At several fleet meetings, year after year, votes were taken about allowing the use of that powerful sail (for which Olin drafted a plan). But the motion never quite passed.

As the class historian remarked in his fiftieth anniversary windup, "The [prevailing] no-spinnaker rule means that a skipper can invite his next door neighbor out to crew without worrying about his fouling sheets or guys." Although the Sound Junior had by then become something of a precious relic, she was still a delightful boat in which to foster a friendship by sailing together. Proof: new orders are even now being received, and three are presently under construction at the Landing Boat School in Kennebunkport, Maine.

Lightnings – Design 265

LOA: 19'   DWL: 16'   Beam: 6' 6"   Draft: 5" (board up); 4' 11" (board down)   Sail area: 177 sq. ft.

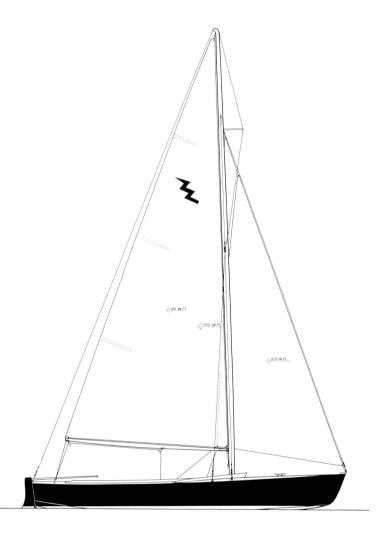

Since the day in 1938 when Rod Stephens flashed the first Lightning down the length of windy Lake Skaneateles in New York, the boat has been an intensely local but remarkably international affair. Today some 15,000 Lightnings have been built, with more than 5,000 still racing and day-sailing on fresh and salt bodies of water all over the world. Particularly active fleets compete in Argentina and Spain. Collectively, Lightnings may be called the most popular S&S design.

In their initial ads for the new boat, the promotional team at Skaneateles Boats stressed that the Lightning would be "distinctly faster than any other boat of her size and sail area." They also spoke (somewhat contradictorily) of her "reassuring stability and docile, yet awe-inspiring power." When one steps aboard, there is indeed a remarkable steadiness about this small boat—perhaps because of her hard chines and heavy centerboard. But the even more astonishing thing is how she takes off when the wind blows. That characteristic undoubtedly results from the dynamics between the relatively light hull and the generous, fractional rig.

While various boatbuilders were promoting the excellence of their construction techniques for producing the Lightning (two layers of planking, for example, the inner running athwartships and the outer fore and aft), home boatbuilders on three continents were merrily building their own. All of this was possible because Sparkman & Stephens—in an uncharacteristic business move which they rue to this day—had sold the plans for the sloop to the Lightning class organization. It was that class, not S&S, which received royalties on each boat built or assembled.

One benefit of an effective, even businesslike class organization has been that modernization of the Lightning has been carefully and steadily managed. The original double-planked wooden hull has been replaced by a self-rescuing fiberglass version. Wooden masts with jumpers have given way to stronger, oval aluminum spars (perform better, cost less). Whereas the original steel centerboards rusted and developed blemishes, the new stainless model seems flawless. As for sails and rig, the new bridle/traveler system and adjustable backstay have dramatically improved heavy-air performance.

Some of the world's best sailors have commenced their careers in Lightnings; many have no intention of "advancing" to a larger or more high-tech boat. For this is where the action is. Olin is delighted to hear the Lightning, for all her dash, referred to as a "family boat"; two generations of the same family are often spotted racing with or against each other. That's training of a special kind.

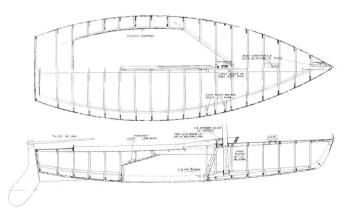

Cape Cod Mercuries and Indian Harbor Arrows
Designs 296 and 739

Cape Cod Mercuries: LOA: 15'   DWL: 13'   Beam: 5' 5"   Draft: 3' 3" (centerboard); 2' 5" (keel)   Sail area: 119 sq. ft.

Indian Harbor Arrows: LOA: 18'   DWL: 16' 7"   Beam: 5' 11"   Draft: 3' 4"   Sail area: 160 sq. ft.

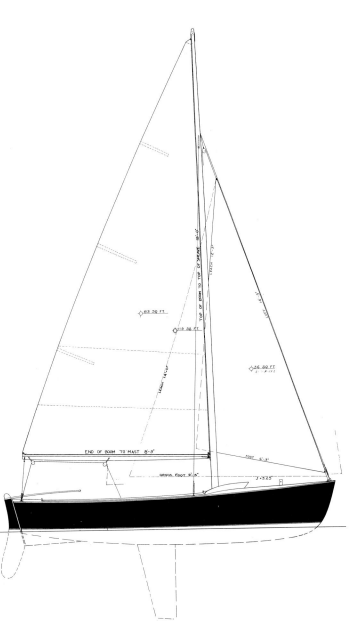

These two one-designs for juniors came along in the wake of the Lightnings. They indicate the evolution of S&S thinking on the subject of smart racers for the kids.

The Mercuries were earlier and 3 feet shorter than the Indian Harbor Arrows. Both of these designs eschewed the hard-chined profile of the Lightnings and the subsequent Blue Jays (see later in this chapter). But while the little and relatively traditional Mercury was given a dagger-like centerboard, the Arrow was equipped with a keel.

A conventional keel had always been desired by the Indian Harbor Yacht Club (Greenwich, Connecticut). But the bulb-fin keel that Olin recommended demonstrated that he was of a mood to challenge the old ideas of other, traditional classes with competitive, up-to-the-minute craft.

His evolutionary one-design program was received well by the public: both of these classes have lived long lives in their respective locations. It's worth noting, however, that the riskier Arrows achieved a wider reputation all along the coast, filling not only the club members' perceived needs but their big dream of universal acceptance.

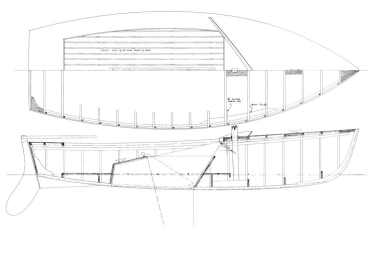

Above: Cape Cod Mercury. Facing page: Indian Harbor Arrow.

Interclub and Bermuda Dinghies – Designs 618E and 2516

Interclub: LOA: 11' 6"   DWL: 11'6"   Beam: 4' 7"   Draft: 5"   Sail area: 72 sq. ft.

Bermuda: LOA: 14' 4"   DWL: 14' 1"   Beam: 5'   Draft: 10"   Sail area: 517 sq. ft.

The rather comical word "dinghy" has distinguished antecedents: it's derived from the days when the queen's navy cruised along the coasts of India; admiring Brits saw the agile little *dingi* passing confidently back and forth between shore and sea-bound vessels. Thereafter many a simple little craft came to be called a dinghy. But in proper yachting circles the word has generally been applied to a species of well-designed rowboats or jibless sailboats with plum bow and stern.

In the United States, dinghies tended to be raced by either callow collegiates or fanatical frostbiters. In Bermuda, however, dinghies are quite a different kind of sporting craft, descended from the overcanvased boats that were sailed by the wild Victorians around Hamilton Harbor.

The contrast between these two S&S dinghies—the trim little Interclub of 1945 and the extravagant Bermuda of 1986—is therefore understandable. Furthermore, although the molded plywood Interclub is in all respects a one-design (promoted by sailors at the Larchmont and other Long Island yacht clubs), the Bermuda dinghy is a custom affair. Designed by S&S for Eldon H. Trimingham, her hull was West system-constructed, with outer fiberglass skin.

Despite their generic differences, both of these handsome dinghies have succeeded splendidly at their different functions. And they both prove the point that sailing in wee boats can, given the right craft, be as challenging and joyous as in ocean racers.

Facing page: Interclub dinghy. This page: Bermuda dinghies. See also photo of Bermuda dinghy page 28.

Blue Jays – Design 805

LOA: 13' 6"   DWL: 11' 3"   Beam: 5' 2"   Draft: 6" (board up); 3' 8" (board down)   Sail area: 90 sq. ft.

Smaller than the Cape Cod Mercury, the Blue Jay was designed for very young skippers, ten to fifteen years old. S&S partner Drake Sparkman had realized that, for many families and clubs, the successful Lightning was way too big—even though that kind of glamorous racing sloop, with spinnaker flying, was the image that these eager, younger sailors had in their mind's eye.

The so-called baby boomers were very different from their parents and from kids in staider times; they demanded to experience for themselves the grown-up thrills of racing. Therefore one of the criteria for the Blue Jay besides stability was that it must carry a spinnaker, must train youngsters how to set up and bring down this excitable piece of nylon. And thus came into being the "Baby Lightning," a nickname instantly won by the tremendously appealing Blue Jay.

Part of the appeal, again, was the ease with which parents and kids could build or assemble these boats themselves. This time, however, S&S retained ownership of the plans; individuals or builders could buy them for $50 a set. By the early 1950s, thousands of the plans and kits had been sold, with fleets springing up on both American coasts and all the waterspots in between. The initial fleet of Blue Jays in the San Francisco Bay area, it must be admitted, consisted exclusively of adults—why should they let their kids have all the fun?

A very successful builder of Blue Jays in Connecticut also recalls that the individual who put in an order for the Pequot Yacht Club was no pressurized father of an eager son or daughter; it was Briggs Cunningham, who had just defended the America's Cup in his 12-meter. He obviously agreed that this little boat was perfect, from whatever age perspective one looked at it.

Designer's Choice – Design 2349

LOA: 14' 8"   DWL: 12' 9"   Beam: 6' 1"   Draft: 5"   Sail area: 120 sq. ft.

This high-performance boat indicates that there may be something new in the wind for one-designs. She was designed not only as a trainer for youngsters but also as a sporty racer that would appeal to the experienced small-boat sailor. After experiencing her thrills, these sailors might well ask: Why do you need a 12-meter or maxi yacht to get the excitement of flying over the waves?

Like boardboats and windsurfers, the "DC" gets up onto a plane with astonishing rapidity. And it accomplishes this even while hauling a skipper and two large-sized crew members through the water. Yet for all that, she is remarkably stable,

allowing one to walk around her mast forward.

The S&S design team accomplished this by providing a new hull shape, with fine entry forward, but not too fine, and good planing surfaces astern. Furthermore, she is meticulously detailed; her self-bailers work at any heading, providing a dry boat at all times.

Because of her excellence and new approach, Designer's Choice was instantly popular, with some 700 boats sold in four years. Today her builder continues to sell them by the dozens to young and old, vets and novices alike.

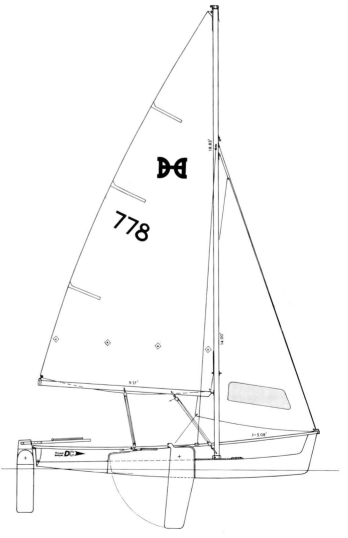

3

Prewar Winners

It all began at sea, seemingly a gift of the sea. The Stephens brothers' devotion to and understanding of splendid and swift ocean racers go back to a salty passage on the high seas in 1927, shortly before the founding of Sparkman & Stephens. It's a story rather parallel to the boys' discovery of the joys of 6-meters.

In this case, a syndicate of Long Island Sound yachtsmen had ordered fourteen identical 10-meters to be designed by Starling Burgess, built in Germany (at Abeking & Rasmussen, where work was both expert and inexpensive), and shipped over to Halifax. Because of the Canadian landing site—made advisable by a law which freed from duty any boat which arrived in the United States not on a freighter but "on her own bottom"—crews were needed to help bring the 10-meters down from the North, a voyage of some 500 miles. Olin Stephens jumped to accept the Roosevelt family's invitation to come along and help.

Initially, it seemed a rather easy assignment. The cruise up to Halifax on board a steamer was delightful; by day and night (sun and stars) Phil Roosevelt introduced Olin to the use of a sextant for celestial navigation. Then at Halifax a convoy was formed, with a large, diesel-powered schooner serving as tow vessel for the cluster of "tens." These sloops, it should be added, were fully equipped as cruising boats below (with five or more berths and galley and head), even though their destiny was to be day-sailers around the racing marks. The young men would hardly be roughing it on the voyage home.

But soon the convoy ran into high seas and dubious weather. Towing became unfeasible. The tow lines were cut and each of the tens was on its own. Soon separated from the others, Olin's boat began the rugged business of driving through ocean swells south and west across the Gulf of Maine. Although the 10-meter had a tendency to sail on its ear in a strong breeze, the performance under these relatively easy conditions was impressive. By the time Olin reached Long Island, he had formed a lifelong devotion to this type of wet but ocean-capable vessel.

As mentioned in Chapter 1, Olin had focused as soon as possible on perfecting the design of 6- and 8-meter sloops. His memories of the 10-meter yacht also influenced his early cruising-boat designs. But it must be recognized that naval architecture has never been known for its rapid innovations; advances are made slowly and tenderly. Whether for commercial vessels or pleasure yachts, the idea in the 1930s was still that if a certain type of clunky hull and old-fashioned rig had brought ship and crew home safely a number of times in the past century, that type should be re-created in this century—until experience dictated otherwise. It's no surprise that a writer in *Yachting* had reviewed Olin's work on 6-meters as "interesting...to predict [their performance] is a dangerous undertaking."

Despite Olin's visionary ideas, the initial plan drafted for the first S&S ocean racer—the first design (not built) for the famous *Dorade*—called for a hull and rig that look today amazingly antique. A long and crew-threatening bowsprit juts out from a bluff bow; the cutter rig makes her look more like a North Sea pilot ship of the last century than like a daring portent of change for the future. But a *Yachting* writer, in commenting on this design, ruminated about the moderately risky business of abandoning the traditional gaff rig: "A jib-headed mainsail [has been] adopted for speed and ease of handling, and because there is no gaff to slat and bang around in a calm." He sounded not quite convinced about even that small innovation.

But by the time of the final design (Design Number 7), two elements that would become mainstays of S&S design had asserted themselves: *Dorade*'s hull had taken on a meter-boat look, deep and narrow; and her rig was no longer cutter but yawl. Although certain conservative elements remained (such as a short bowsprit, soon removed) to remind one of the slow pace of advance from the last century, she was now essentially a new and therefore chancy creation. She was distinctly an S&S product.

In *Dorade* and other successful ocean-racing yachts, the Stephens brothers proved themselves not only innovative designers of hull and rig but also remarkable, talented, pragmatic men of the sea. They were conscious not only of what would make a boat go faster but of what would make her easier and safer to handle under all conditions. To owners and yardmen alike, in Europe and on America's East Coast, Olin and Rod became recognized, almost familiar figures. They revolutionized the way seaboats looked and performed, forcing naval architecture

Right: Stormy Weather. *See page 48.*

into new times, new patterns.

Rod—who was still employed at the Nevins yard on City Island during *Dorade's* construction there, with permission to monitor closely the work being done on her—now developed his characteristic, boatyard style. He would be everywhere about a new vessel, tools on a belt around his waist, tinkering and checking. With all the salty language of the sea, it seems far too prosaic that his title after joining S&S was merely "field engineer."

Olin, often the helmsman and perpetually the observer, found it as instructive to sail aboard a new boat as it was to monitor the tank test of a model. He wrote in later years that,

when on board, he was "constantly trying to relate anything observed in performance to the [innovative design] characteristics of the boat."

In this highly personal way, the boats designed and perfected by the Stephens brothers triumphed in their contests at sea. And in that critical era of the 1930s, before the world war which ended with an atomic thunderstorm, S&S yawls and sloops were among the most memorable creations of our threatened civilization. Created for peaceful, competitive pleasure, they were nonetheless indications that, in at least one sector of international life, art and science could work harmoniously together.

Dorade - Design 7

LOA: 52'   DWL: 37' 3"   Beam: 10' 3"   Draft: 7' 7"   Sail area: 1,079 sq. ft.

She's been called "unquestionably one of the outstanding yachts of all time." Originally regarded as something of a freak because of her narrow proportions and sharp ends, she astonished the yachting world by her ability to stand up to any amount of hard driving in rough seas on all points of sailing. Her string of victories has never been equaled, it's said, by any racing yacht in deep water.

Built at the Nevins yard in 1930, she cost Olin and Rod's father $28,000 in depression-era dollars. But, if this was a gamble to promote the excellence of the boys' new business, it was a shrewd one: at Sparkman & Stephens, "racers led the way" to success. It was a risk taken, but the gain was great.

When launched, the hull floated 3 inches deeper than planned, possibly because of added heaviness resulting from close spacing of her steam-bent white oak frames. With a designed displacement of 38,720 pounds, she actually weighed 4,000 more than that as built. Strong and deep, she had no engine but depended on her lofty mainsail and total sail area of 1,079 square feet to get her where she was going. The spars

were of hollow spruce, supported by shrouds that were spliced around the tops of the masts (tangs were then used mostly on day-sailers). To steer *Dorade*, there was a limblike tiller 5½ feet long.

The immediate objective, the test of whether Mr. Stephens's gamble might pay off, was the Bermuda Race of 1930. And *Dorade*'s placement—second in Class B—demonstrated that here indeed was a boat worth watching. As Rod told the story, they might have won their class if a bumped and beat-up sextant had not caused a few navigational errors.

Her record the next year was all the more noteworthy. Having entered the Trans-Atlantic race from Newport to Plymouth, England, Olin and Rod were not at all worried that *Dorade*, at 52 feet, was the tiniest, allegedly most tender of the ten premier yachts in the race. She beat all of them by two whole days, boat for boat (a four-day victory on corrected time), completing the 3,000-mile course in seventeen days plus an hour and fourteen minutes. One reason for this astonishing victory was Olin's daring decision to follow the great-circle

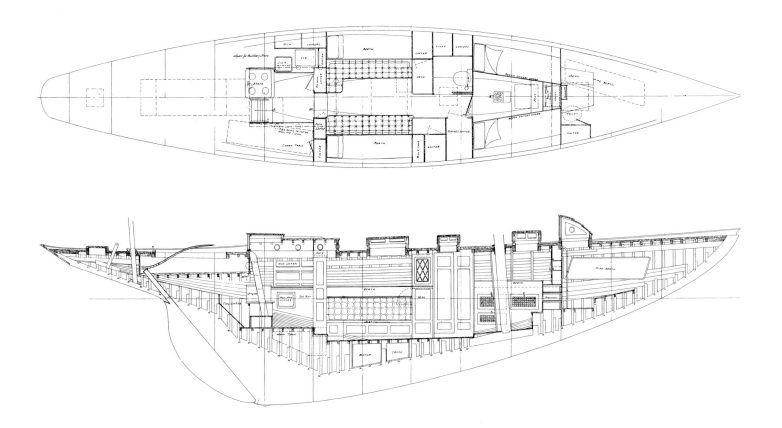

course, which cut some 100 miles from their route and brought them northward into the dangerous zone of icebergs. But the biggest reason for their success was the quality of the boat they sailed and the way they sailed her.

On this race, there were no navigational mistakes. Twice the spinnaker halyard snapped, with the sail collapsing over the side; twice Rod shinnied aloft to replace those halyards while the mast whiplashed its way across the sky. Olin, helmsman for much of the race, could only stand and grin when they got the message: "You are first!" Rod and the young friends brought along as crew were seen to yell and dance. Mr. Stephens, who had chosen not to be left behind, must have been one very proud father.

Dorade capped the Trans-Atlantic triumph by scoring a decisive win in the Fastnet Race of the same year (1931). Then the Stephenses returned home with *Dorade* on board the liner with them. When they arrived in New York, they were given an unprecedented ticker-tape parade down Broadway. For this one moment, the depression seemed to New Yorkers not quite so grim. Not until the America's Cup races of the seventies and eighties would there be such a strong identification of sailing firsts and national pride.

For *Dorade* there followed many more years of racing victo-

ries and delightful cruises, including one through the Hebrides to Norway. Back in this country, *Dorade* was sold in the mid-thirties to James Flood of the St. Francis Yacht Club in San Francisco. After scoring an immediate win in the fabled Honolulu Race to Diamond Head, she went on to score multiple victories on the West Coast. Summing up, one writer reported that *Dorade* had earned "the unique distinction of having won every major ocean race in the world today."

Mr. Stephens had certainly made his point: S&S was recognized, despite (or perhaps because of) the youth of its partners, as one of America's leading design firms—not for meter boats or for little one-designs only, but also for quality, blue-water yachts. Now a whole new generation of well-regarded racing and cruising boats could roll forth, as shown in the selections that follow.

It's a foolish mistake, however, to consider that all of these successive, wooden creations were but copies or adaptations of the successful *Dorade*. On the contrary, many of them were expansions, exceptions, even contradictions. Sparkman & Stephens would show that in a wide variety of modes, its designers could produce the best. For the worldwide racing and cruising scene of the 1930s, a new standard of imagination and seamanship had been set.

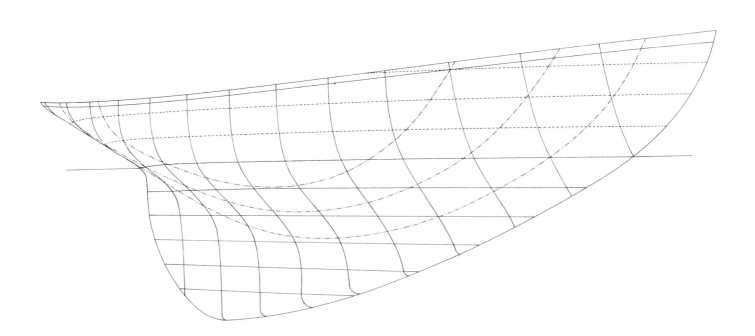

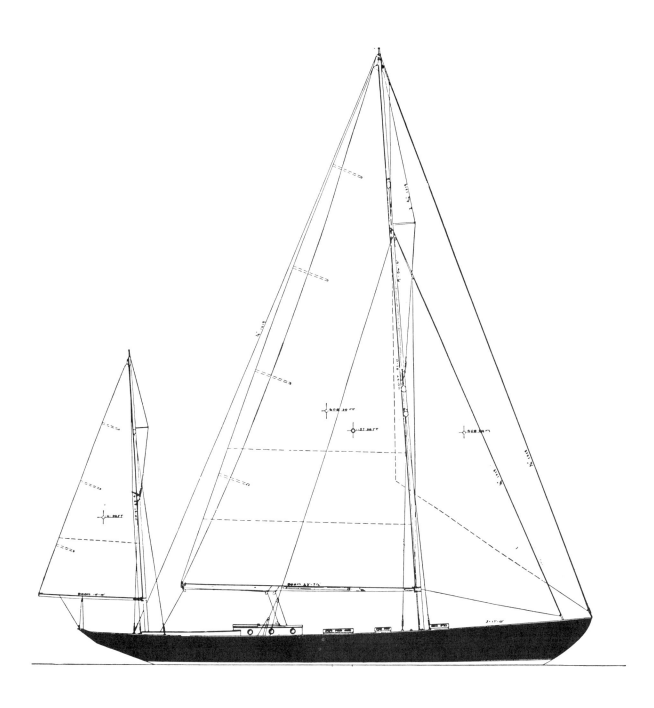

Alsumar – Design 11

LOA: 44'   DWL: 30'   Beam: 9'   Draft: 6' 3"   Sail area: 900 sq. ft.

Designed but one year after *Dorade*, this delightful cruising sloop does seem to be a transference to smaller scale of the best qualities of her big sister. That is, with her trim fore and aft sections, she confirmed Olin's theory that a long, narrow, easily driven hull with small wetted surface would not only move well but also prove herself a competent seaboat.

In keeping with the cruising practices of that era, the layout placed the galley fairly far forward. For it was assumed that the hired hand (whose berth was all the way forward) would do the cooking—and that that entire operation could therefore be excluded from the main cabin. Some criticized the narrowness of S&S-designed bunks, but Olin and Rod found this width to be more secure during a sea passage.

Unlike *Dorade*, long-lived *Alsumar* was equipped with auxiliary power, with access via a panel beneath the companionway. Note that the propeller is on the port side of the rudder (rather than in a cutout niche). Thus the drive shaft and the engine had to be on a slant.

Of *Alsumar*, it might have been said (as it was of *Dorade*), "When you go aboard, the one thing that strikes you is the usefulness of everything on board, and the total elimination of everything else. Wherever experience has shown a cleat, a snatchblock, a fair lead, or a handhold would be useful, right there is one to be found, and not a half-inch from where it should be. Every cleat is turned at the proper angle, every block and lead runs exactly true... She is a sailor's delight."

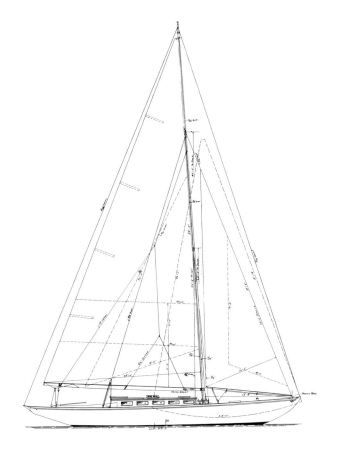

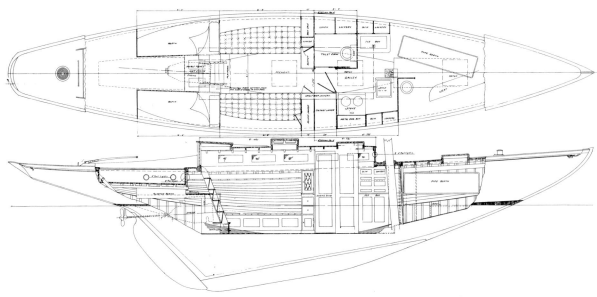

Gimcrack – Design 19

LOA: 34' 4"   DWL: 23'   Beam: 7'   Draft: 4' 7"   Sail area: 434 sq. ft.

This is the famous sloop which served as subject for studies made by Olin and Ken Davidson of the Stevens Institute of Technology. Because S&S had an ownership interest in her, *Gimcrack* was available for the time-consuming tests. In some of them, the sloop was towed by a launch from the Nevins yard where she was built; in others, Olin sailed her "with simple but accurate instrumentation for windward performance." The results of these tests were compared with Davidson's tests of models in the Stevens tank—invaluable for the understanding of resistance and the furthering of optimal hull design.

Quite apart from that distinction, *Gimcrack* was both a handsome day-sailer and a strong entry in a competition as the model for a large and popular East Coast racing class. Sparkman & Stephens made every effort in detailing her construction specifications to keep things as simple as possible, for the reduction of costs.

In contrast with many competing one-design class boats old and new, *Gimcrack*'s freeboard was not racing-style low. This was because Olin imagined that some owners of this proposed class might enjoy a bit of cruising and might prefer a dry ride. For the same reason, he allowed room enough in the cabin for two berths and other cruising facilities, in addition to the large cockpit—well designed for a working crew.

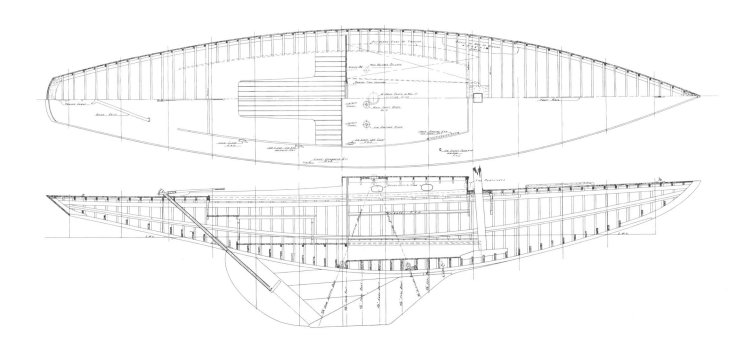

Stormy Weather – Design 27

LOA: 53' 11"   DWL: 39' 9"   Beam: 12' 6"   Draft: 7' 10"   Sail area: 1,332 sq. ft.

As well known as *Dorade* in international racing circles, this nearly same-sized yawl is very different in one important respect: she is beamier by more than 2 feet. This results from a decision by the Cruising Club of America to penalize in their rating rule any boats that were as slim (and damnably swift) as the early S&S designs. But, while bowing to that decision, Olin still managed to keep *Stormy Weather* fairly slim—as well as deep.

He reached the conclusion that these proportions would work after many comparative tests of a *Dorade* model and a *Stormy Weather* model in the Stevens Institute pool. Yet, after *Stormy*'s first big race (to Bermuda in 1934, in which she finished unimpressively), that conclusion seemed faulty. It was only when she won the Trans-Atlantic race to Norway the next year, immediately followed by victory in the Fastnet, that the yachting fraternity got a hint of her true potential. For that successful overseas campaign, Rod Stephens was *Stormy*'s skipper.

Although Rod removed the engine from *Stormy Weather* for the races abroad (which step, taken to make room for additional gear, may have improved her performance), power was soon reinstalled—with no slowdown in the number of victories. *Stormy* also proved herself to be a wonderfully comfortable ocean cruiser, more so than *Dorade* because of the added beam. The installation of the navigator's compartment at the foot of the companionway was but one idea that made her such a convenient and pleasant boat to sail on.

Several yachtsmen were fortunate enough to become owners of *Stormy Weather* down the years. One of them, James J. O'Neil, campaigned her strenuously (with slightly enlarged rig) in Southern Ocean Racing Circuit events, winning Class A in the Miami-Nassau Race six times. Says O'Neil: "I don't

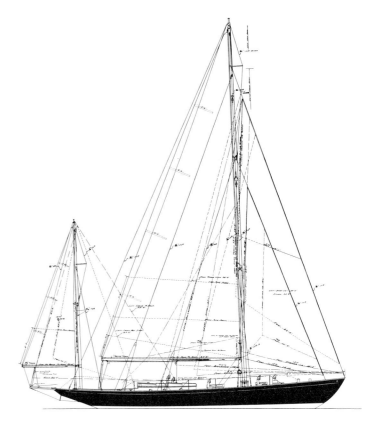

think her layout has been improved upon since building.... She has the substance of a great racehorse."

Rival naval architect John Alden, on contemplating *Stormy*'s beautiful form, said, "In my opinion, a better design would be impossible to achieve."

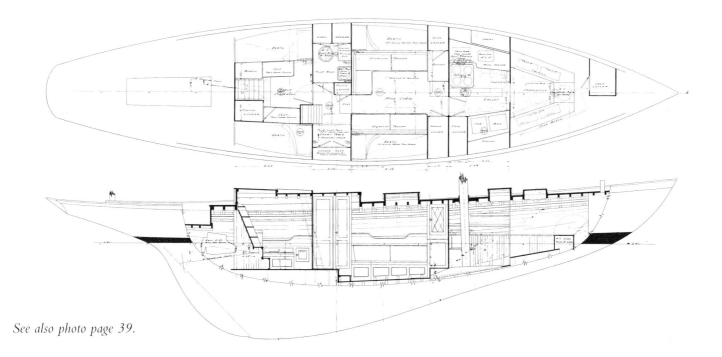

See also photo page 39.

Roon II – Design 28

LOA: 38' 6"   DWL: 32' 3"   Beam: 11' 4"   Draft: 5' 4"   Sail area: 815 sq. ft.

Like *Stormy Weather*, *Roon II* was launched in 1934. But unlike *Stormy* and other high-recognition S&S yawls and sloops, this solid, sturdy ketch has nothing of the racer about her. In the words of Rod Stephens, "she's an out-and-out cruiser."

Although *Roon II* was designed to ramble from one coastal harbor to another and not to charge across the seas, she has many hallmarks of the Sparkman & Stephens ocean racers. Well ventilated and roomy below, she is steered by a seaman's tiller; she's the model of efficiency on deck. To no one's surprise, she proved herself to be a powerful and successful sailing vessel—despite her beam of more than 11 feet.

Even under heavy weather conditions, *Roon II* was an easy boat for two people to handle. The "triple head-rig"—with three overlapping headsails hung from respective stays—may seem aerodynamically inefficient, but ensures that no sail would be too bulky to manage. Furthermore, the innermost of the headsails, the boom-footed forestaysail, is self-tending.

Also contributing to that ease of handling was the layout below. Recognizing that there would most likely be no paid hand on this vessel, Olin completely revised his usual cabin plan. First, he located the galley aft, so the skipper or his wife when cooking could be a part of either the cockpit activities or the cabin conversation. Then he devised a wraparound settee that embraced the dining table. A double berth is forward.

In many respects, this humble 1934 cruiser anticipates the far-ranging yachts that would be produced by Sparkman & Stephens and other naval architects in the decades following World War II. Her capability, her comfort, and above all her sea kindliness distinguish her. She conformed 100 percent to what

her initial owners had desired. In Rod's words, "Olin certainly had the ability to make a boat do what the owner wanted."

A decade ago, on August 7, 1984, her new owners staged a dress dinner at the Seawanhaka Yacht Club to celebrate the fiftieth anniversary of *Roon II*'s launching. She looked just as ready to go as ever.

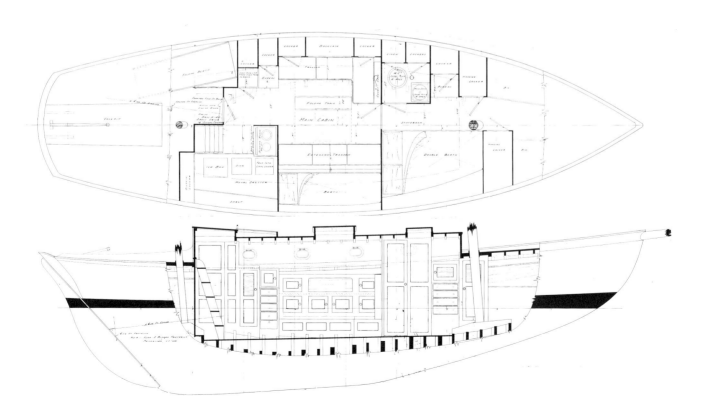

Landfall – Design 54

LOA: 44'   DWL: 32'   Beam: 9' 9"   Draft: 6' 6"   Sail area: 859 sq. ft.

The first request to design a speedy yawl for a foreign client came not from expectable contacts in England or the European continent but from Tasmania—such was the spread of S&S's reputation. And although *Yachting* headlined its story about the design "A *Dorade*-Type Yawl for Tasmania," a study of *Landfall's* plans shows that she's really quite different, an imaginative adaptation based on the client's needs.

First of all, the beam is far more generous than a mere copy of *Dorade* would have allowed. Even more important is the pronounced in-curve of the hull at the bilges forward—what naval architects call "lack of deadrise." This carving away of hull mass demonstrated Olin Stephens's endorsement of the concept that

the less wetted surface to be dragged through the water the better. And the faster.

Landfall, with her powerful rig (including a large-sized jib topsail), did prove herself to be an enormously effective performer, winning both the Wass Island Race and the Sydney-Hobart Race. Furthermore, she gave a wonderful ride. The accommodations below were even more convenient and comfortable than on other early S&S yachts: note the full forward stateroom and the roomy galley extending across the breadth of the vessel.

It's no wonder that *Landfall*, forerunner of *Starlight* and the New York 32s, was called "an unusually sweet creation."

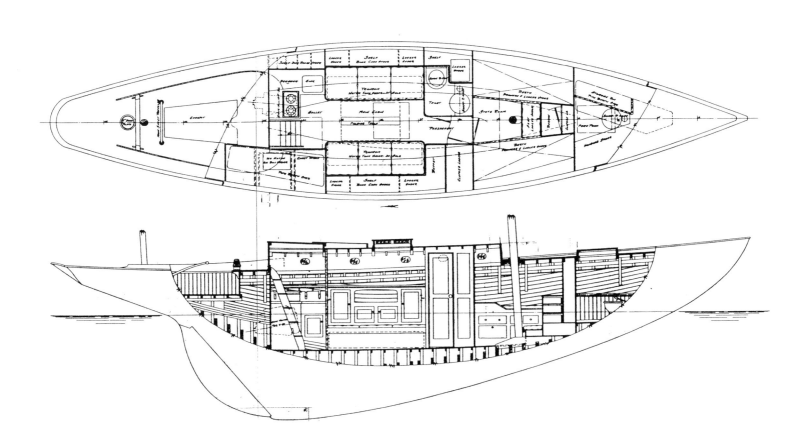

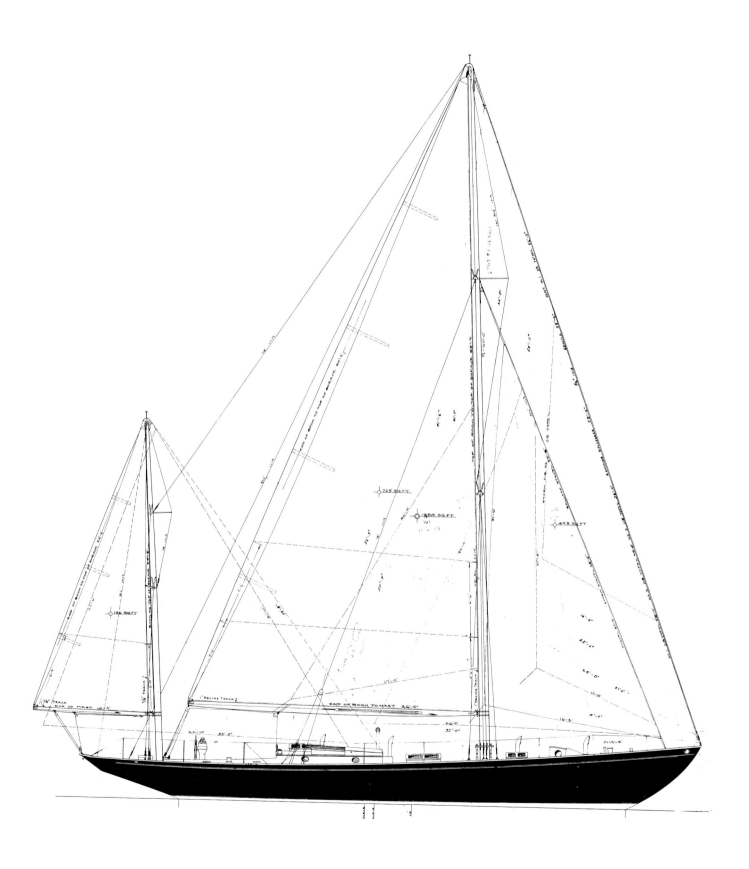

Avanti - Design 85

LOA: 55' 8"   DWL: 40'   Beam: 12' 5"   Draft: 7' 9"   Sail area: 1,354 sq. ft.

In the all-conquering way of the best S&S yachts, those designed primarily for cruising also brought home more than their share of silver trophies. Perhaps the best example of this was the gorgeous, light gray yawl crafted for Walter Rothschild in 1935. Her name, *Avanti*, means "Forward!" in Italian—and that's exactly how she went.

Although Mr. Rothschild had requested that the sail plan be slightly smaller than might be expected for a yawl of this size, and although she was built somewhat heavier than expected in order to ensure easy motion at sea, she could not be slowed down. She won the highly competitive Gibson Island Race as easily as if she'd been designed to do nothing but win.

Of particular interest in her cabin layout is the vast after stateroom and the galley forward, with oil-burning shipmate range. Above the table in the conveniently located navigator's station (where today one would find electronic gear) were cleverly designed chart stowage and signal flag lockers. Sad to say, all this careful planning and beautifully polished execution came to a sad, crashing end during the New England hurricane of 1938.

One of this book's authors remembers *Avanti* lying on her beam ends, high above the tideline of Padanaram Harbor (Massachusetts), smashed but somehow still beautiful. Despite this tragic destiny, *Avanti* lives on in another sense, for she served as a guideline boat or "parent form" (in Olin's terminology) for many subsequent yachts, notably *Blitzen*.

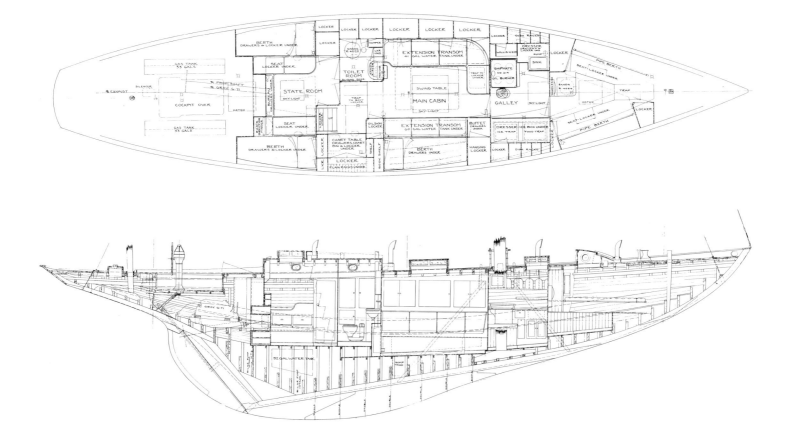

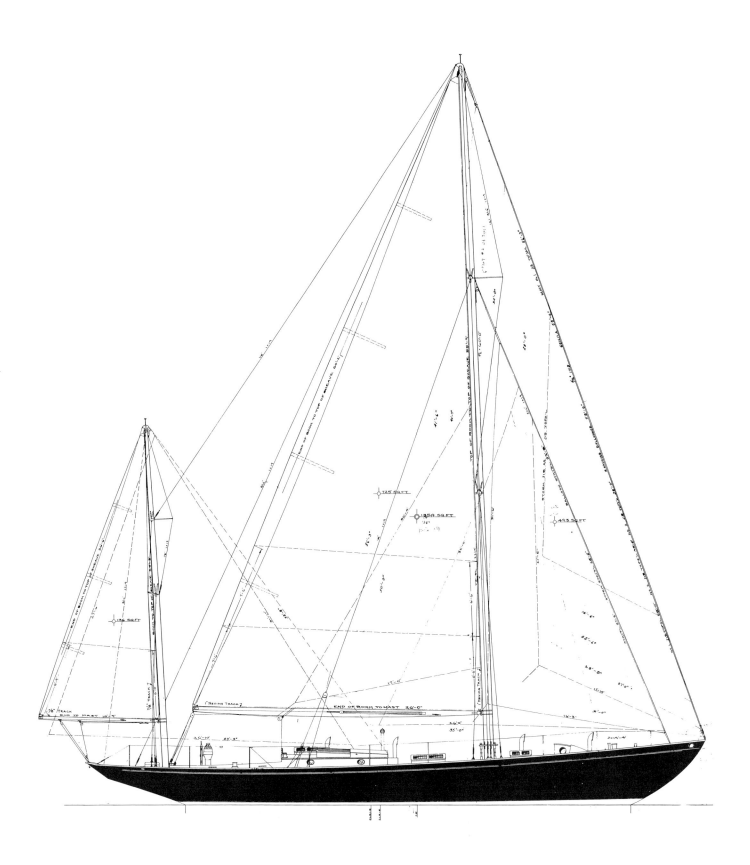

Babe – Design 97

LOA: 30' 6"   DWL: 26' 1"   Beam: 7' 10"   Draft: 5' 4"   Sail area: 543 sq. ft.

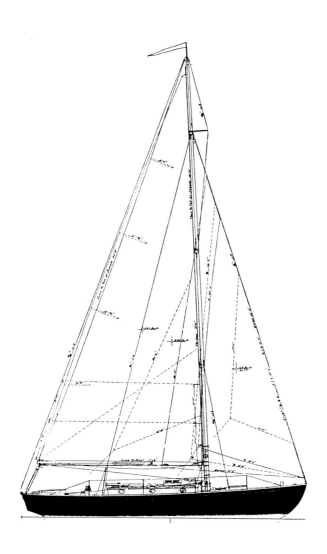

Another notable departure from the parade of *Dorade* direct descendants was the small, agile S&S sloop *Babe*. In many ways she represented a big step in the direction of the tall-rigged, light-displacement racers of the future. *Babe* displaced a mere 11,200 pounds, barely more than what was required by the then-operative Universal Rule.

Her impressively lofty sail plan was designed to "get the greatest driving power out of a moderate area." Indeed the whole idea of the boat was to move swiftly and win races—hence the "cutoff stern" (Rod Stephens's characterization) which sacrifices the usual beauty of an S&S hull for the benefit of the measurement rule of the day. Her relatively long waterline length was also an advantage.

Rod went on to say that she was a "very interesting little boat, fast for anyone who sailed her" with her racing record bearing out that assessment.

With accommodations a secondary matter, *Babe*'s belowdecks plan is spare but practical, ice chest under a large chart table to starboard. The toilet is concealed beneath a seat between the two berths in the main cabin. Forward is a narrow pipe berth—but lots of room for sail bags.

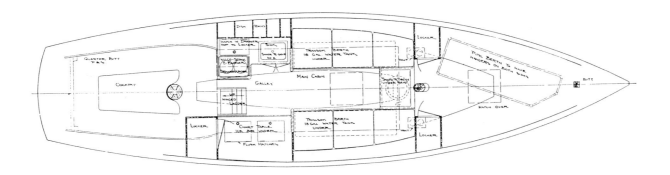

Zeearend – Design 126

LOA: 54' 7"   DWL: 40'   Beam: 12'   Draft: 8' 4"   Sail area: 1,311 sq. ft.

This powerful yawl, so reminiscent of *Dorade*, has the distinction of being Sparkman & Stephens's first European winner. She was designed in 1936 for Claes Bruynzeel of Zaandam, Holland, a friendly and generous patron of European and American naval architects.

The beginning of that friendship remains part of S&S lore. It dates back to the time when Rod was sailing the engine-less *Stormy Weather* about Europe, following the victory in the 1935 Fastnet. Mr. Bruynzeel, who then owned a large, well-powered ketch, had noticed that *Stormy*'s route from Amsterdam south could only be accomplished via the North Sea Canal—down which a headwind was certain to blow the next day. So he kindly offered to tow *Stormy*, a proposal which Rod gratefully accepted.

But when the Bruynzeel ketch got under way, Rod had already begun the passage along the canal, tacking arduously back and forth to make forward progress. Because *Stormy* completed all those tacks (150 of them, Rod estimated) so successfully, the would-be towboat never caught up to her. What was caught instead was a client; over a meal the next day, Mr. Bruynzeel put in his order for an S&S yawl.

Built at the DeVries yard in Amsterdam, *Zeearend* (meaning "Sea Eagle") was launched in the spring of 1936. Immediately her string of victories began in European waters. When she sailed to North America to compete in the Bermuda Race and scored as the highest European finisher that year, all could see that the spirit of *Dorade* was flourishing.

Blitzen and Gesture – Designs 221 and 381

Blitzen: *LOA: 55' 3"*   *DWL: 40'*   *Beam: 12' 5"*   *Draft: 7' 9"*   *Sail area: 1,303 sq. ft.*

Gesture: *LOA: 57' 4"*   *DWL: 40'*   *Beam: 12' 7"*   *Draft: 8' 2"*   *Sail area: 1,452 sq. ft.*

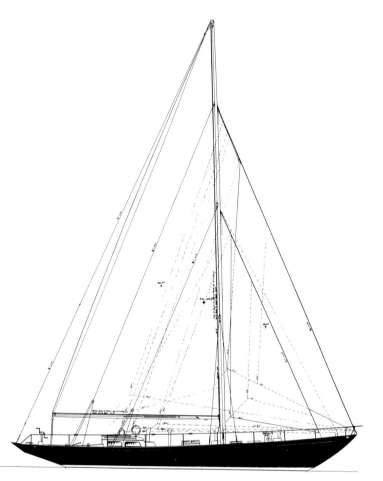 

Two other boats built in the final years of the 1930s merit special attention: the cutter *Blitzen* and the sloop *Gesture*. Take away the streamlined doghouse from *Blitzen*, and there's your famous *Dorade* shape; take away the modern, grinder winch and the radar from *Gesture*, and you might say ditto. Both of these large vessels were tiller-steered, as of yore; both were narrow and deep.

But appearances are not quite the same as reality. Look more closely and you find such interesting differences as *Blitzen's* huge main cabin, a predecessor of the grand spaces that would come in the mega-yachts of the future. Also consider her trimming centerboard; it was because of this sensitive

device that she balanced so beautifully (allowing for victories that would take place in the 1950s).

Gesture, a somewhat larger boat, was equipped with electronics that bespoke a far different kind of sailing and navigation than had obtained on *Dorade's* ocean crossings. Illustrations show the direction-finder loop, the Kenyon speedometer, the telemagnetic compass (to tell the helmsman if he's steering off-course). She was indeed a new age about to happen.

Nonetheless, one report of her arrival announced ominously that "*Gesture* was the only ocean racer launched on the Atlantic coast this year [1940]." Yachting was about to close down; but it had the seedlike power to be reborn.

Above left: Gesture. Above right and facing page: Blitzen.

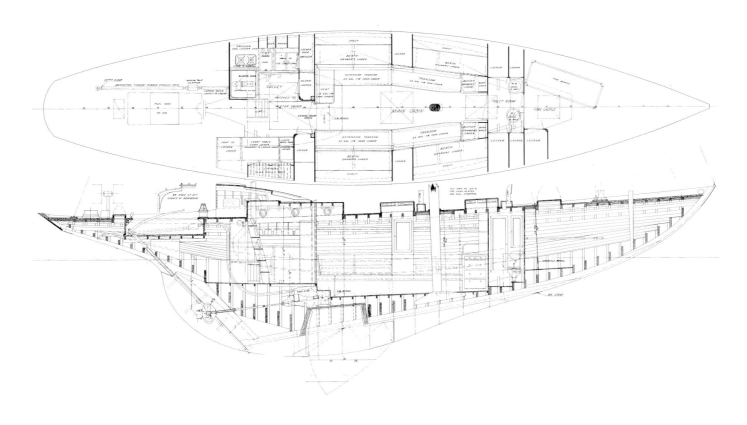

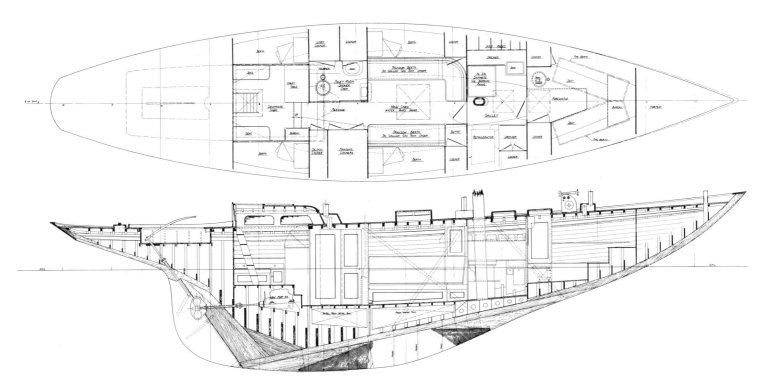

Facing page: Gesture. *Top:* Blitzen. *Bottom:* Gesture.

Baruna – Design 222

LOA: 72'   DWL: 50'   Beam: 14' 10"   Draft: 9' 6" (board up)   Sail area: 2,342 sq. ft.

From one perspective, Henry C. Taylor's splendid yacht *Baruna* was the grandest extension of the *Dorade* hypothesis. At 72 feet (about the size of a modern 12-meter), she had the same narrow proportions and deep forefoot, supplemented by a centerboard. Launched in 1937 (at a cost of $55,000), she went on to win the Bermuda Race the next year, breaking the record in the process.

But from another viewpoint, *Baruna* was a creation unto herself. Her beauty had a special majesty; she stood forth as a waterborne national treasure. Even the staid *History of the New York Yacht Club* broke conventional rules of objectivity to single *Baruna* out for her "sleek, black beauty." Consider but one detail: her generous, midship deckhouse was designed not as an upright box, but (given a certain amount of tumblehome) as a shape to conform to the totality of the hull.

In her heyday—which lasted for many a year, before and after the war—she was maintained by a Norwegian paid hand. One of this book's authors recalls how, in her home port of Cold Spring Harbor on Long Island, her brightwork could be seen sparkling across the waters, the black topsides set off by the gold-leaf cove line. Her Port Orford cedar deck was always scrubbed and gleaming; not a blemish could be detected in her varnished, hollow spruce spars.

In her majesty she represented not the end of an era (though World War II was about to break forth in Europe), not the end of the glamorous twenties and thirties. No, she represented the good life—as well as certain truths of design and technology—that deserved to be continued when peace reigned once more.

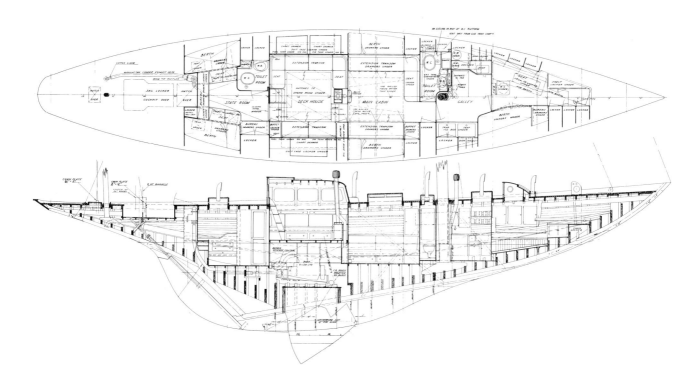

4

Great Seaboats for the Seven Seas

Although Sparkman & Stephens romped to the head of the fleet in American naval architecture primarily because of the swiftness of its designs, a constant theme at S&S had always been seaworthiness. Therefore, certain boats must be included in the chronicle of S&S "greats" which might, at first glance, seem rather brutish—more like a draft horse than a jumper. But what these great seaboats lack in fashionable sleekness, they more than make up for in utilitarian handsomeness. And in some cases (for example, *Brilliant* and *Bolero*) they are masterpieces.

Designed in 1930, *Brilliant* was patently the paradigm for this type of boat and this maritime theme at S&S. A very special creation she was. *Yachting* publisher and writer William H. Taylor wrote of *Brilliant* that she "just exuded the power of an able vessel, even lying at anchor." Her owner, Walter Barnum of New York, had wanted a boat that was virtually "unbreakable," for he had lots of blue-water sailing in mind. Oh, yes, he wanted her to move well, but most of all he demanded a boat that would provide comfortable and safe and even enjoyable ocean crossings—within a reasonable length.

Olin Stephens responded to Mr. Barnum's request for an offshore cruiser with a solidly built hull and a rugged, old-fashioned schooner rig. *Brilliant* displaced a formidable 38 tons. She looked, at first glance, of a piece with the rugged, fishing-schooner-type yachts of John Alden and the chunky coasters of William Hand. But on more careful inspection, *Brilliant* shows a fine entrance forward, with a little hollow at the waterline that suggests speed. And although she's roomy enough below, she could by no means be called beamy. In fact, for all her heavy scantlings and heavy, teak planking (1 ¾ inches thick), she seems no great contradiction to *Dorade*.

But the essential difference between those boats was brought out in the Bermuda Race of 1932, which was the last great contest between American schooner yachts. *Brilliant* clearly could not keep up with the racing boats and was even whipped by Alden's latest design, *Malabar X*. The next year, when *Dorade* and *Brilliant* were both entered in the Fastnet, *Dorade* scored her second win, while *Brilliant* did not distinguish herself (the air having been notoriously light).

Nonetheless, *Brilliant*'s 1932 crossing to England lives on in the annals of cruising as one of the most remarkable passages of all time. It was indicative of the kind of splendid seaboat that she—and her successors—could be when challenged.

On board with Mr. Barnum for the crossing were a number of seasoned yachtsmen who had responded to the invitation in order to see what a truly comfortable trip across the Atlantic on a 60-foot sailboat might be like. They did some experimenting with the squaresail hung from a yard arm, and discovered that that was only truly effective when the wind was about one point abaft the beam, so the sail did not blanket the headsails. They also discovered that although light westerly winds had been forecast, a strenuous southerly was pushing them along at a great rate—an astonishing rate, in fact.

For two straight days the breeze blew that way, with *Brilliant* heeled well over on the starboard tack. It was not the easy, upright pleasure cruise that the gentlemen had subscribed for. On the contrary, it was tremendous sailing: the navigator announced to everyone's amazement that in each of those two days they had spun off more than 200 miles. At once, the passengers realized that they were enjoying a possibly record-breaking run. As one of them tells the tale, when Mr. Barnum realized what was about to transpire he turned to his passenger-crewmen and commanded: "Boys, set the genoa jib and be damned quick about it!" Then, from the depths of the sail bin, he added, "All right... we'll put a couple of topsails on her too."

On toward Europe they drove *Brilliant* under mainsail, foresail, forestaysail, genoa jib, main topsail, and fisherman staysail—a glorious spread of canvas. Although the initial plan had been to shorten sail when night came, no one felt inclined to admit that the sun had fallen; they surged through the dusk-to-dawn hours under full sail. As a result, for the five days while the southerly held, *Brilliant* continued to average 200 miles a day. Best day's run: 231 miles (a speed of nearly 10 knots).

Brilliant made the entire 1,077-mile run from City Island, New York, to Plymouth, England, in seventeen days, eighteen hours. Though no record, this time of passage stands up well against that of both the tall-sailed clippers in previous decades and the racing machines of later decades. And everyone on board had a splendid time.

Facing page: Brilliant *as she appears today with her Marconi mainsail.* See text page 68.

Brilliant - Design 12

LOA: 61' 6"   DWL: 49'   Beam: 14' 2"   Draft: 8' 10"   Sail area: 2,082 sq. ft.

When Olin Stephens was designing this heavy, flush-decked schooner for Walter Barnum, he urged that she be built at the Henry Nevins yard at City Island, where Rod was then working. The yard, they thought, turned out work consistently superior to that of others in this country. Recently Olin was informed that the bent oak frames that he'd specified for her construction were the largest ever bent at Nevins; they still look solid as bronze.

As additional strengtheners, Olin called for Everdur bronze straps that not only prevent the planks from working against each other edge-to-edge but also provide a solid way of tying in the chainplates to the rest of the construction. Such straps hark back, Olin believes, beyond the era of Herreshoff yachts to clipper ships of the preceding century.

Today *Brilliant* may be seen in real and solid life at Mystic Seaport (to which facility she was given, along with a generous endowment, by the eminent American yachtsman Briggs Cunningham). At Mystic, as one phase of the Historical Association's training programs, she offers cruises to a variety of groups. And although her rig has been somewhat modernized (the gaff-headed mainsail was converted to Marconi more than fifty years ago), she still provides the essential experience of manning a classic seaboat.

One of the original *Brilliant* concepts that may be seen is the engine room completely encased in metal (against explosions and leakage of gasoline fuel or vapors), located well forward between the masts. Although this is perhaps the best place for the engine room, freeing engineers from the usual stooping and crawling, it demands that the engine be equipped with an extra-long shaft. The large galley wraps conveniently around the engine room.

Olin is well pleased with the way Mystic has maintained *Brilliant*, even as the wood suffers inevitably from the effects of age (deterioration is observable right next to the bronze straps, probably because of electrolic action). And he is all the more pleased with the role *Brilliant* continues to play in getting new generations of Americans ready for seagoing.

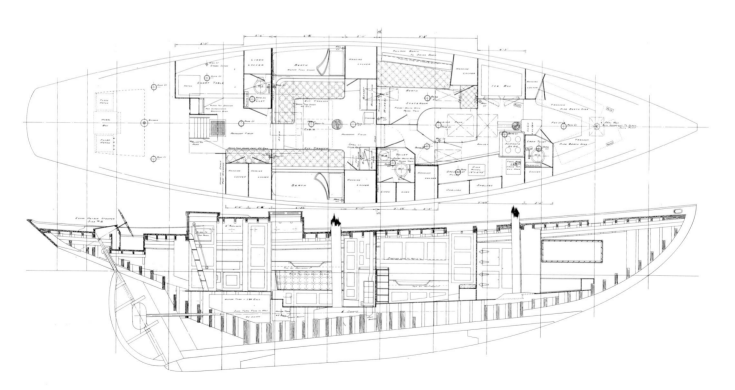

See photo page 66.

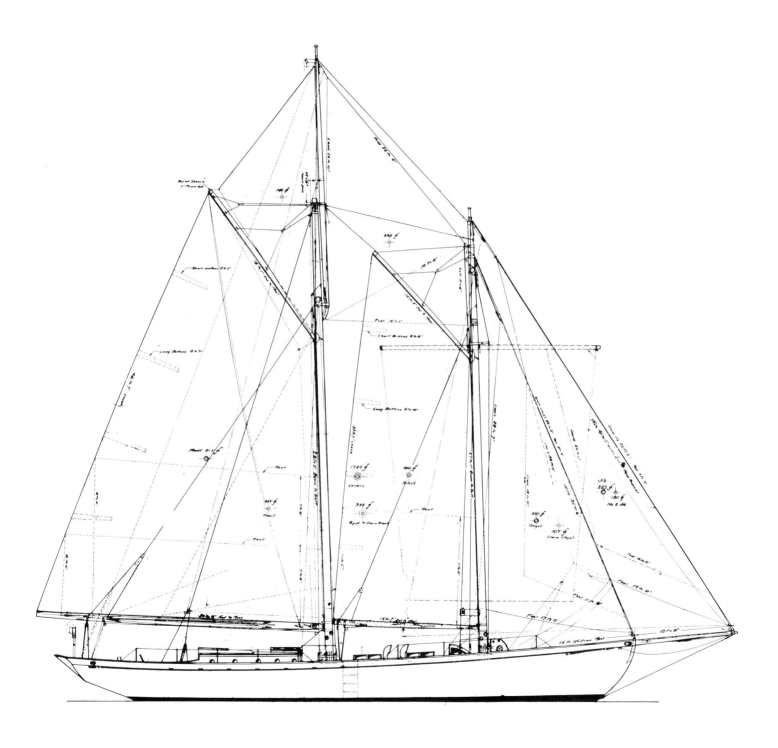

Aweigh – Design 24

LOA: 41' 1"   DWL: 35' 8"   Beam: 11' 9"   Draft: 6'   Sail area: 929 sq. ft.

An early seaboat of which Olin Stephens is especially fond (as was Rod), *Aweigh* appears to some other observers as merely a high-sided cutter, not at all the S&S kind of thing. Part of the reason for the brothers' fondness was her performance: though essentially a cruising boat, designed to be safe and dry, she surprised everyone by winning the Miami-Nassau Race soon after her launch. Rod credited her relatively long keel for her excellence to windward and her steadiness at sea.

Yet another reason for the brothers' affection for *Aweigh* was the satisfying process of planning and building her. Olin recalls the "unusual list of requirements with which the owner wanted us to deal." She had to be modest of draft because he wanted to sail her in the Bahamas (a desire more common among yachtsmen of the next generation), yet she had to be roomy—a difficulty solved by means of high topsides and flush deck.

Having produced that unusual design, Olin today has the pleasure of looking back on a boat that might be considered the grandmother of later, non-centerboard, shoal-draft sailers (see next chapter).

Rod once happily recalled that the builder—M. M. Davis at Solomon's Island, Maryland—"would do anything we asked him to." He also recalled sadly that the foreman had a heart attack when working on the job; Rod carried him up from the pier to a sofa in his house. Despite such stresses, the work was accomplished flawlessly.

The double-head rig in *Aweigh*'s large foretriangle delivered a hefty amount of pull-power. The after stateroom and main cabin (equipped with cabin heater) both seem wondrously capacious. A splendid boat for going anywhere.

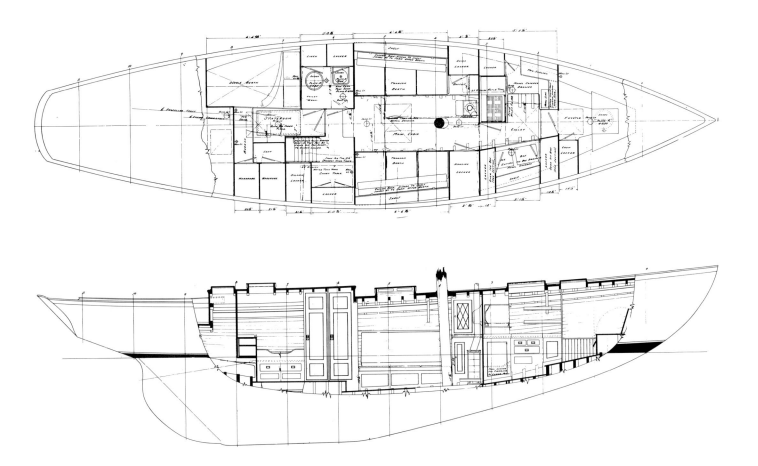

Edlu I and Good News – Designs 35 and 291

Edlu I: LOA: 56' 2"   DWL: 40'   Beam: 13'   Draft: 7' 10"   Sail area: 1,143 sq. ft.

Good News: LOA: 64' 6"   DWL: 45'   Beam: 13' 5"   Draft: 8' 10"   Sail area: 1,841 sq. ft.

These beauties may be viewed as two successive stages in the development of S&S seaboats, possessing quite different rigs and profiles but a family similarity. The smaller of them, the early cutter *Edlu*, has a cabin house. But it's so low-lying that she looks almost as flush-decked as her larger, later sister, *Good News*. Both stand as elegant denials that seaboats must be brutish and awkward.

One of *Edlu*'s well-remembered escapades was the trouncing of S&S's much-proclaimed international winner *Stormy Weather* in the Fire Island Race of 1936. *Stormy* and *Edlu* had been built but two years apart, with the latter imagined to be far less dashing than the former. But by 1936 she had been re-rigged as a yawl and her owner, Rudolph Schaefer, had acquired considerable confidence in her speed (on the strength of a Bermuda victory). Although *Stormy* got the jump on the

fleet early in the race, *Edlu* went right through her in the tide-swept waters of Plum Gut and could not be caught thereafter.

Among the many modern features of *Good News* was her duraluminum mast, the first to be stepped in an ocean racer. Much as Rod Stephens favored this rig, he was appalled, as a traditionalist and a seaman, at owner Robert Johnson's intention to put the halyards inside the mast to save windage. This struck Rod as a typically unsafe idea, the kind of shortcut you'd expect from someone who was more interested in going fast than in staying safe at sea. He recounted to Johnson many a tale of wild nights on the Atlantic when, unless they'd been able to grab hold of the halyards... But Johnson, "not an easy guy to work with," would not be dissuaded. And, in retrospect, Rod concluded he was probably right. *Good News* sailed around the world and was never in serious jeopardy.

Above left: Edlu. *Above right and facing page:* Good News.

An idea of Rod's that Johnson did subscribe to but that has never caught on among other ocean cruisers was that of inboard lifelines. A man going forward in heavy weather without a harness would not have to reach *out* to the lifelines in order to prevent himself from being tossed overboard by the waves; he could reach *in*, with far greater safety.

In later years and under subsequent owners, *Good News* endured several revisions, including the lopping off of her stern so that the transom sloped inward. This was done to save weight aft and to diminish hobby-horsing. She was also converted to ketch, then cutter rig. But by her many admirers the original yawl will not be forgotten, for beauty in composure and grace in action.

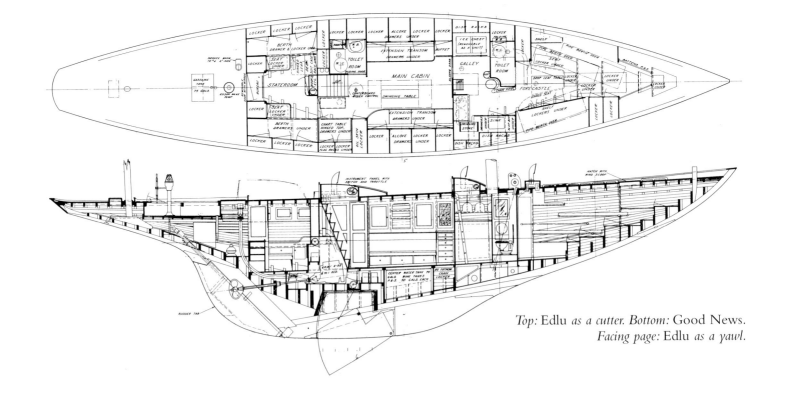

Top: Edlu *as a cutter. Bottom:* Good News.
Facing page: Edlu *as a yawl.*

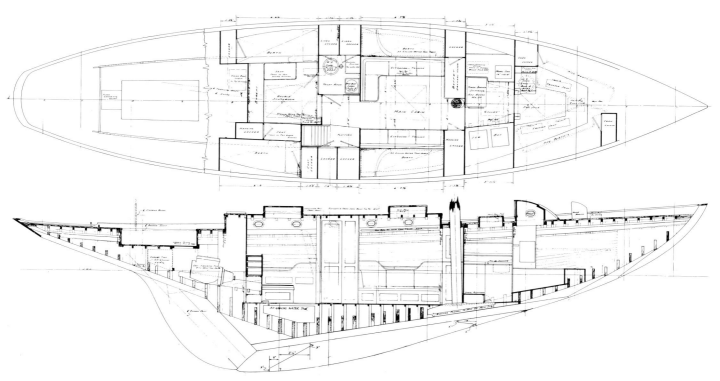

Loki - Design 619

LOA: 38'   DWL: 26'   Beam: 9' 7"   Draft: 5' 8"   Sail area: 701 sq. ft.

Designed for the veteran cruising yachtsman Dr. Gifford Pinchot, the name *Loki* soon came to signify distant voyages for a less-than-40-footer, made under the most rugged sea conditions.

A history of the Cruising Club of America—entitled *Nowhere Is Too Far*—tells of many of the little yawl's adventures. These include one epic passage from Norwalk, Connecticut (her home port), to Bergen, Norway, via St. John's, Newfoundland, a passage accomplished in thirty days. Encountering an extraordinarily heavy gale in mid-Atlantic, *Loki* was reduced to minimal canvas; the history describes how she "fore-reached about two knots on course under a trysail." Another memorable passage was a thrash to windward of one whole week from Bergen, Norway, to Cowes, England.

But she was also capable of showing her heels to the fleet. She won her class in the Bermuda Race of 1950; her sister ship *Chance* was a spectacular winner on Lake Ontario.

Loki's inboard yawl rig was designed to be handled easily by a small crew; running backstays for the mainmast are necessary only under the roughest weather circumstances. She proved herself a steady sailer under jib and jigger (a great convenience on a single-handed passage).

Both *Edlu*'s owner R. J. Schaefer and Dr. Pinchot (like most Sparkman & Stephens clients) were happy to cooperate with S&S policy that copies and near-copies of their boats could be built for other yachtsmen. (Indeed, the plans remain S&S prop-erty.) This was, in fact, *Loki*'s ultimate destiny: more than a half-dozen sister ships were produced in emulation, for the great benefit of America's cruising fraternity.

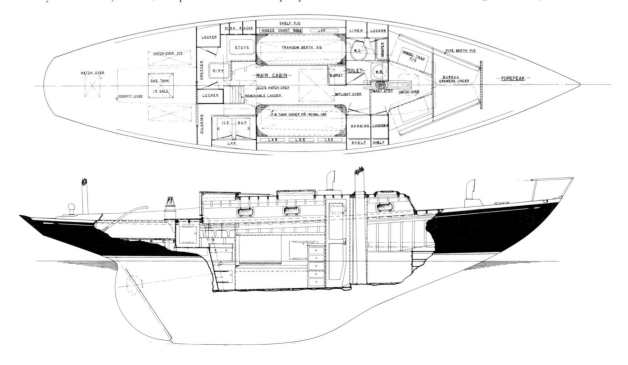

Bolero – Design 711

LOA: 73' 6"   DWL: 51'   Beam: 15' 1"   Draft: 9' 6"   Sail area: 2,480 sq. ft.

Billed as "the largest modern Ocean Racer," *Bolero* splashed down the ways at the Nevins yard in 1949, so she (and *Loki*) represented the new era of postwar technology. Her distinctive beauty and her matching relationship with *Baruna* are described in the next chapter. Her racing triumphs (such as her many wins on the New York Yacht Club Cruise, on which she often sailed in the 1950s as "Queen of the Fleet") were particularly impressive as *Bolero* rated as almost a limit boat by the maximum-size regulations then in effect for major ocean races.

For this book's purposes, however, it's best to look at her not as an exception but as a grand seaboat within the S&S tradi-

tion. Interesting features that contributed to her success under extreme strain conditions at sea were a Monel web frame mast step which distributed the stress over a wide area of the forward structure, a balancing centerboard, a removable forestay, and two pedestal winches amidships.

The accommodations were similarly grand. As specified by her owner, Commodore John Nicholas Brown, she was laid out for an owner's party of eight and a crew of four. They rode the ocean wave in style.

Bolero is undergoing an extensive and complete restoration, with a scheduled completion date of June 1995.

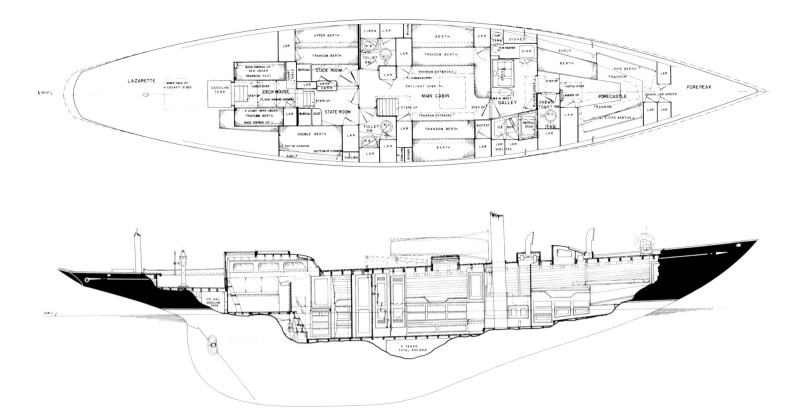

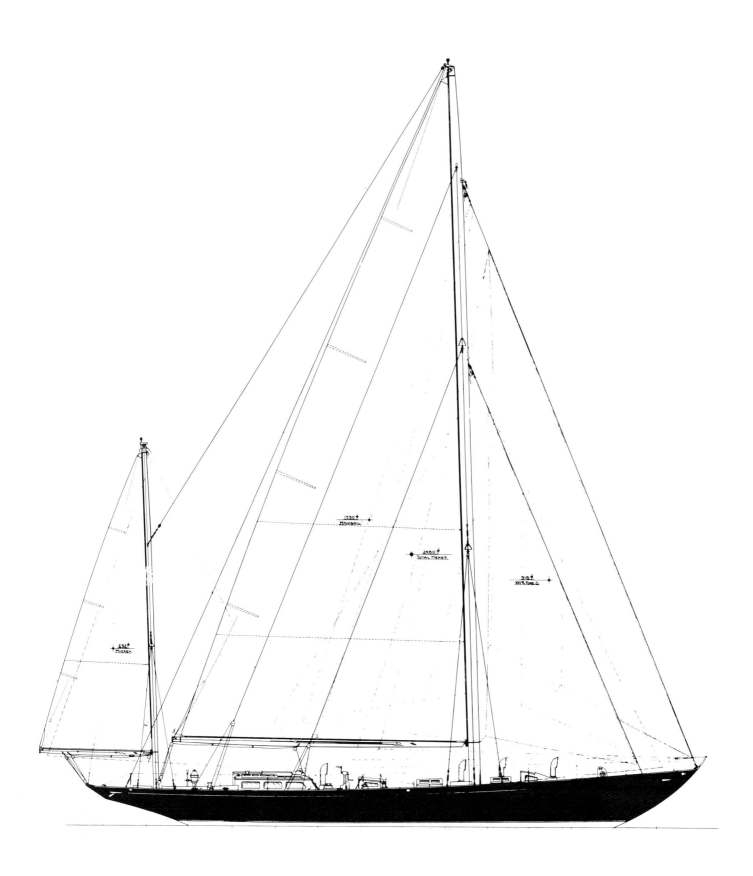

Kay – Design 1110

LOA: 52' 6"   DWL: 36'   Beam: 12' 1"   Draft: 7' 5"   Sail area: 1,325 sq. ft.

Designed for a Swedish owner, *Kay* gave postwar Europeans a new understanding of how swift and beautiful a seaboat could be, swift as well as sturdy. Soon after launching, she scored an impressive win in the race from England to La Coruña, Spain—first on corrected time by a margin of fifteen hours.

With *Kay*, the S&S principle of keeping things simple at sea was extended even further. Her mast requires no running backstays (note the wide spacing of the lower shrouds—that arrangement balances the forestay). To give the mast extra stiffness, its fore-and-aft dimension is greater than its breadth.

Equally impressive and serviceable is her seaworthy layout abovedecks and below. Her wide side decks make for easy passage forward; the dinghy fits precisely between the low doghouse and the mast. The owner's stateroom is forward, making for an unusually spacious saloon, even with all the space devoted to lockers.

In the S&S manner, all engineering and spatial factors have been integrated in a coherent design. It must be added by one of this book's authors (R.B.) that *Kay*, in her beauty and integrity, shows off the architectural design skills of the other author (F.K.).

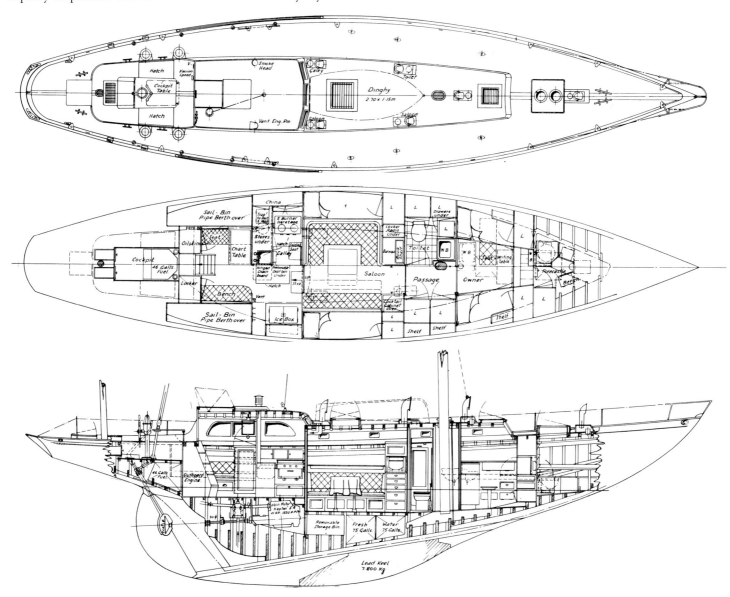

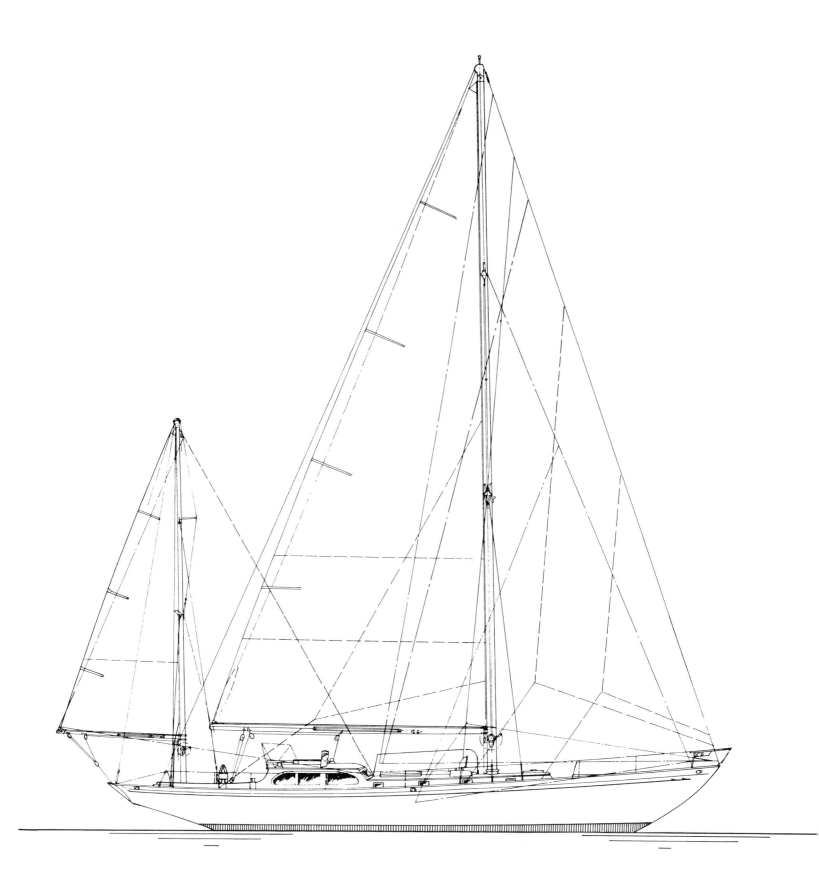

5

Racing and Cruising Stars of the Fifties

After World War II American yacht designers had a number of advantages over foreign competitors. As well as being located in a country not laid waste by warfare, they addressed a friendly, believing audience at home and in foreign lands. They based their new productions on the technological advances that had been made, many of them by Americans, during the war. The tumultuous era of the 1950s—when *Bolero* and *Finisterre* and some of Sparkman & Stephens's most memorable winners were created—can therefore be viewed as the era when American naval architects, flying overseas with a freedom never before possible, took charge of the business at home and abroad. Sparkman & Stephens led the way.

Although Olin stresses that there was nothing revolutionary, in terms of design, about the development of the racing stars of the fifties—reiterating the similarity between prewar *Baruna* and postwar *Bolero*—he recognizes that the broad-beamed, centerboard yawls of the new era were indeed something new. Also that the use of aluminum, for hulls as well as for spars, represented a technological advance.

Although designers and engineers at S&S kept their ears cocked for reports on how America's new fiberglass industry was progressing, nothing very encouraging developed. The process seemed to be too expensive for boatbuilding (and would remain that way until the advent of room-temperature polyester resins). So they concentrated on perfecting their creations in wood and aluminum. Actually, there was one fiberglass boat turned out by S&S at this time, prophetically called *New Horizons*.

Another factor nudging S&S designers away from concepts of yore and toward something new was a clientele with slightly different objectives. First there were the international clients. Then there were the postwar American skippers, veterans of a four-year war. This typical vet was certainly just as eager for oceanic victories as his prewar predecessor, but now he also wanted to take his ease, with wife and friends, amid the shallow waters of the southern islands. The cruel and comfortless thrash across the Atlantic—blue water in the face and beneath the keel—had a decreased appeal for him. He yearned for silver beaches and green lagoons.

Harvey Conover epitomized this new spirit. His passion for

racing and cruising led to a treasure trove of trophies and to his election as commodore of the Cruising Club of America. Strong friend of and fierce competitor with Rod Stephens, he sold his New York 32 to Rod—who changed the boat's name from *Revonoc* (Conover spelled backwards) to *Mustang*. The boat is detailed in Chapter 7; two subsequent S&S-designed *Revonoc*s, both stars of the fifties, are profiled in this chapter.

By profession, Conover was the aggressive chief of the powerful Conover-Mast Publishing Company, producer of seven industrial magazines. At sea he was just as aggressive, a big and hearty man, happily joined by his wife and willing crew members on legendary voyages in both northern and southern waters (not to mention his participation in more than half a dozen Bermuda races).

Conover, as Everett Morris wrote, was "the sort of deep sea sailorman with whom you would want to be in any kind of going: strong, courageous, clear-thinking and knowing in emergencies." Tragically, his life ended as he struggled to cope with just such an emergency at sea, en route from Key West to Miami. On January 2, 1958, this great and leading skipper of the fifties encountered a freak, 70-mile-an-hour gale that struck the Florida coast from the northeast without warning.

The gale reached full force "within a matter of seconds," the Coast Guard later reported; the assumption is that Conover turned to run before it under bare poles, trailing drogues, charging through the high and steep breaking seas of the Gulf Stream. *Revonoc* disappeared; only a dinghy, ripped from the cabin top, was found. Skipper and all hands were presumed lost—including Mrs. Conover, their twenty-six-year-old son Lawrence, and a friend of Lawrence's. Rod Stephens was one of many who flew in to help broaden the search all across the waters south of Florida, the Bahama Banks, the hundreds of spits and islands. In vain.

The story of the tragedy is worth repeating for a number of reasons; but mostly, here, because it demonstrates the approach of an experienced seaman like Conover. He makes a maximum investment of thought and skill and money in his boat, finding the best possible, most trustworthy designer. And then he sets forth, trusting; taking but not necessarily succeeding in the test.

Carleton Mitchell is, similarly, a man of the sea. Back in the

Facing page: Dyna. *See page 92.*

1950s, he, too, liked the idea of not playing submariner across the North Atlantic with a bunch of grizzled die-hards but, instead, of sailing through the Bahamas with wife and friends. A hull for him could not be a cramped, narrow-beam racer with deep keel but must be wide enough for comfort and shoal enough for shallow harbors. Another great advantage of such a design would be that, in the eyes of the CCA racing rule architects, it should be favored in the ratings.

Another similarity between Conover and Mitchell was that they had both been around boats all their lives. In contrast with some of the jazzy racing skippers of the future, who came into sailing from other fields of aggression and display, these gentlemanly yachtsmen of the Old Guard could talk knowledgeably and soulfully about the qualities they wanted to have built into their boats. Far more important things were on Mitchell's mind than a quick victory or a shortcut of the rules. "I give you my word," he was once quoted as saying, "that not once in my discussions with Sparkman & Stephens when we were building and planning *Finisterre* did we mention the ratings, or any way we could beat the rule."

In this way, with the ardent encouragement of America's Old Guard yachtsmen (joined by distinguished yachtsmen in Europe), Olin and Rod Stephens developed what might be called a gentler kind of ocean racer in the 1950s. Both professional accomplishments and creations of great joy and pleasure, these lovely yawls remain attainments for other ages to envy.

Revonoc and Revonoc III – Designs 602 and 1252

Revonoc: *LOA: 45' 4"   DWL: 32'   Beam: 12' 1"   Draft: 4' 5"   Sail area: 1,014 sq. ft.*

Revonoc III: *LOA: 42' 7"   DWL: 29' 6"   Beam: 11' 9"   Draft: 4' 5"   Sail area: 889 sq. ft.*

The first of these two good-looking yawls was somewhat larger than the second—the one which was lost at sea. Built right after the war, in 1946, she filled the gap left when Harvey Conover sold the original *Revonoc* to Rod. And a family relationship can certainly be seen between the offshore cruiser and the earlier racing sloop—they're both 40-plus feet long. But the important difference is the centerboard versus the keel, as well as the generous, live-aboard plan. There's enough room for a full forward stateroom and pipe berth ahead of that, with galley and chart table at either side of the companionway aft.

Even more interesting is the evolutionary contrast between the two yawls, the second of which was built in 1957. Here the most important difference is the forestay on the newer *Revonoc*; it gave her a far wider choice of headsail combinations. She was equipped (all thought) to face every possible circumstance at sea; shortening sail would be far easier. Below, she had less room than her older sister. But, with the centerboard housed completely below the cabin sole, the main cabin was still roomy.

An S&S write-up of the new boat noted that among her distinctive features were the aluminum mast plus the location of her binnacle and steering wheel in the forward end of her cockpit "where the canvas hood will afford protection to the helmsman. An unusually commodious and convenient galley as well as artificial refrigeration has been provided—as a continuing encouragement to her attractive chef, who is almost as much a fixture [on board] as the Skipper, himself."

Conover made sure that this *Revonoc* was built solidly. The Derecktor yard at Mamaroneck, New York, gave her laminated oak stem, keel, deadwood, and frames; she was double-planked with mahogany over cedar, and Everdur fastenings. Tinned copper tanks for 70 gallons of fuel and 140 gallons of water plus a hefty diesel power plant allowed her to cruise for extended periods between ports.

It's also of great interest to discover that, for all the thought given to *Revonoc III*'s cruising qualities, her planners must have also kept an eye on her relative rating: whereas her sister rated 35.2, she came in at an enviable 29.3. The dinghy that was discovered soon after her disappearance may be noted in the drawing, atop the deckhouse.

Facing page: Revonoc III.

Above: Revonoc. *Facing page top:* Revonoc III; *bottom:* Revonoc.

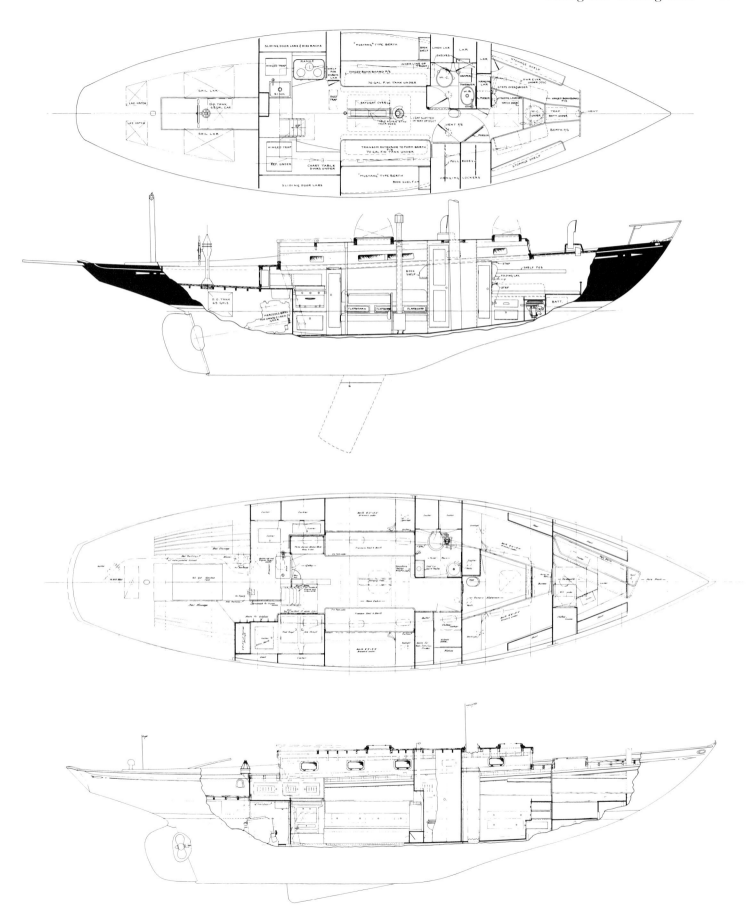

Finisterre – Design 1054

LOA: 38' 6"   DWL: 27' 6"   Beam: 11' 3"   Draft: 3' 11"   Sail area: 713 sq. ft.

This S&S design was "immortalized," a yachting writer proclaimed, when *Finisterre* won the Bermuda Race three times in a row. But when she was launched in 1954, *Finisterre* struck many of the racing fraternity as too round and fat to be believable. "People said she was a clunker," owner Carleton Mitchell recalls. "It's just as though you entered a sports car race in a big boxy sedan."

"My idea in *Finisterre* was to build a floating home for two people," he confesses. And at only 38 feet, that was quite a trick in itself. Nonetheless, he wanted this mini-cruiser to be capable of sleeping a full racing crew of seven. "Nothing was left out of her that could contribute to the good life afloat [for all hands]."

He did not, however, mean seven ordinary crew members. He always managed to have with him a team of ocean racers who were themselves superstars. One opposing Bermuda racer said of *Finisterre*'s team, "We'd be sort of nervous to have some of them aboard!" Another explained Mitchell's extraordinary racing record not by the money put into the machine (more than $60,000), not by her deliciously low rating, not by all of her go-fast equipment, but by this trick: "He sails the hell out of her."

A subtle but key differential between *Finisterre* and the previous generation of S&S boats is the existence of a wheel. The more sensitive tiller—macho indicator that the seaman-skipper of a given boat was going to sail her with muscle and constant attention—has been sacrificed for this more convenient device,

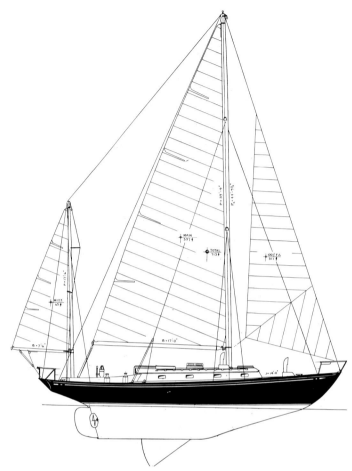

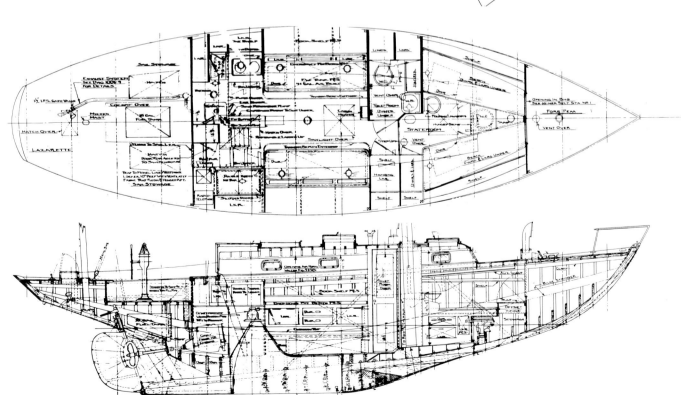

in part because the mechanism for a wheel could be adapted to take an automatic pilot. Yes, an automatic pilot.

The analogy of driving a sedan rather than a racing car also extends to *Finisterre*'s construction, which is as heavy as it is sophisticated. Mitchell picked the lumber with exquisite care. For the frames, Connecticut white oak ("Better than Maine oak"), winter-cut to be free of sap. For the interior, African mahogany and teak. For the topsides, double planking, with ¾-inch Honduras mahogany over ⅜-inch Port Orford cedar.

Total displacement (including the mechanical shower, icebox, etc.): 22,330 pounds.

Mitchell had a complete plywood mock-up of the cabin made. Sportswriter Ezra Bowen reported that the owner/planner "crawled all over the mockup to find out what the paper plans had not told him." For example, the cabin seemed to be too narrow, so he widened it. The result: a superbly comfortable as well as a winning boat; a model vessel in which to risk the pursuit of happiness.

Refanut – Design 1104

LOA: 62' 10"   DWL: 43' 9"   Beam: 12' 9"   Draft: 8' 11"   Sail area: 1,903 sq. ft.

Designed to be the fastest yacht in Sweden, *Refanut* performed well enough to claim a more global title. Built at the famous Bengt Plym yard in 1955, she immediately started winning races in northern Europe (including several victories in the Round Gotland Race); then, after a major refit in 1978, she sailed south to the Mediterranean and the Caribbean where she won a worldwide reputation as a fast cruising yacht. During the 1980s, after winning her class in the 1981 Newport Classic Yacht Regatta, she sailed back to Scandinavia for another refit, then on to the Mediterranean and Caribbean again. She remains one of the most remarkable S&S designs—and a superb example of what foreign clients believed they could get from Sparkman & Stephens.

Although very much a creation of the up-and-coming fifties, with aluminum mizzenmast and air conditioning, *Refanut* also recalls the previous generation of deep-keeled ocean racers. She draws a full 9 feet and has the long, lean look of *Dorade* (or, more accurately, *Stormy Weather*). During the 1978 refit, the galley was moved from forward of the mast to starboard midships (where a single cabin had been located); the space forward was then converted into a stateroom for four. As a result, she now sleeps nine in three cabins, including the saloon.

To Rod Stephens, *Refanut* had always been a special creation, "a one-off; like a 12-meter, but with heavier scantlings." That's the tradition.

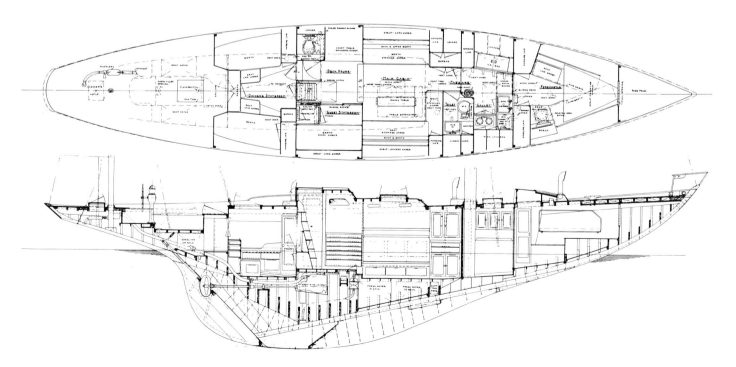

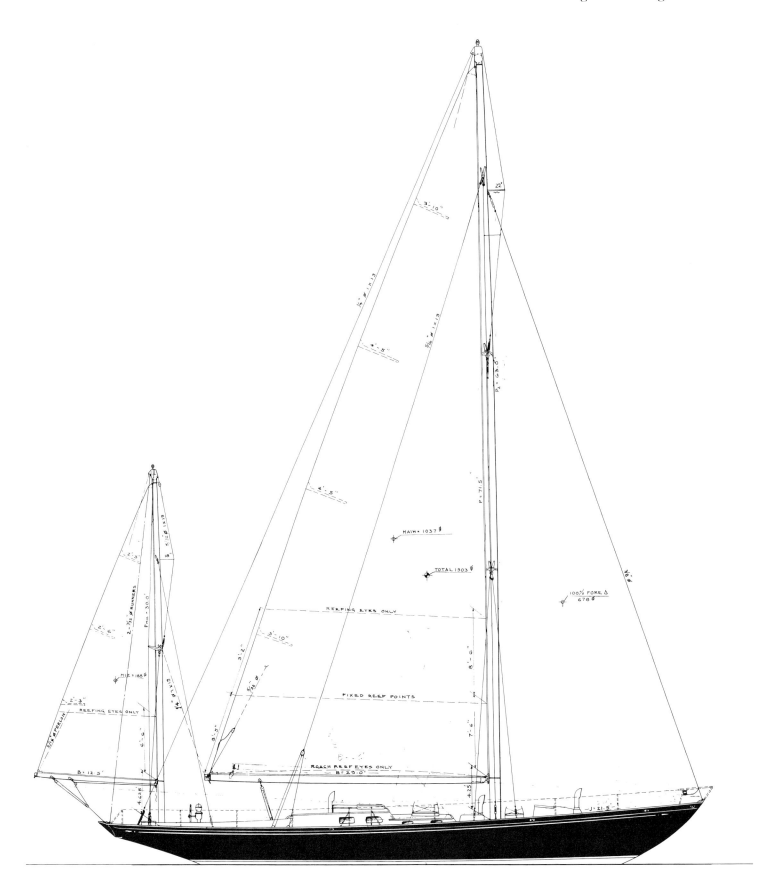

Dyna – Design 1177

LOA: 57' 11"   DWL: 40'   Beam: 13' 6"   Draft: 5' 6"   Sail area: 1,604 sq. ft.

By all appearances, Clayton Ewing's famous yawl *Dyna* seems to be one of those very radical, very shoal and centerboard yawls of the 1950s. But Olin Stephens points out with his reserved smile that, actually, in the many tank tests that were conducted, it was an old, prewar hull model (for a fairly good performer named *Onkayha*) that finally prevailed as *Dyna's* selected hull form. This choice was made over many more modern shapes. To be sure, the full-scale *Dyna* was built of welded aluminum—that was a first for S&S. And, also, she was given every possible modern wrinkle (such as an extra-tall rig). But, even with her innovations and all her successes, she was no "breakthrough."

For fear that a bow-on collision might puncture the risky aluminum skin and sink the boat, a watertight bulkhead was built in between the crew's quarters and the forward stateroom. With her considerable beam, there's room enough belowdecks to fit both an icebox and a huge refrigerator into the galley at the foot of the companionway. The enlarged ports of a low doghouse provide extra light in the galley area. Abovedecks,

Dyna's rig has the same flexibility (removable forestay) as *Revonoc*.

Although *Dyna* was designed to be raced on the Great Lakes (where she won both the Chicago-Mackinac and the Port Huron-Mackinac twice), she also won her class in the Bermuda Race and won the Annapolis-Newport Race twice. But undoubtedly the height of her fame was achieved in 1963 when, on one of her three crossings of the Atlantic, she lost her rudder in mid-ocean and still finished. Steering by sails alone, Ewing (another one of those Old Guard yachtsmen) navigated the last 1,000 miles without assistance, finishing the race in fourth place on elapsed and corrected time.

After three decades and more, what remains is a much-belaureled boat and a thoroughly delighted owner. Ewing said not long ago: "There have been almost no changes in her....We have tried to keep abreast of refinements and improvements in details of rigging, etc. But fundamentally she is the same boat that was launched in May of 1957, and she is still thoroughly competitive."

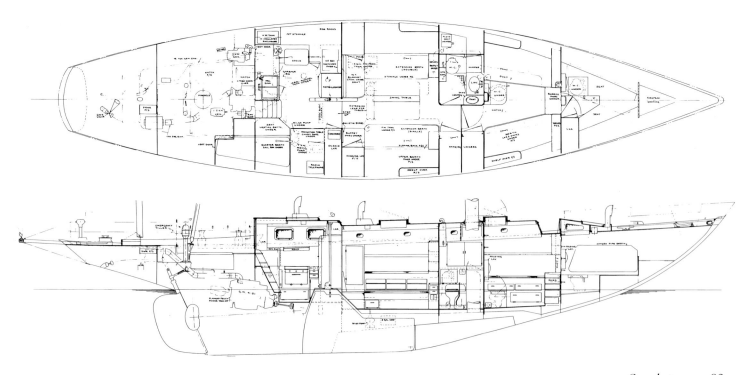

See photo page 82.

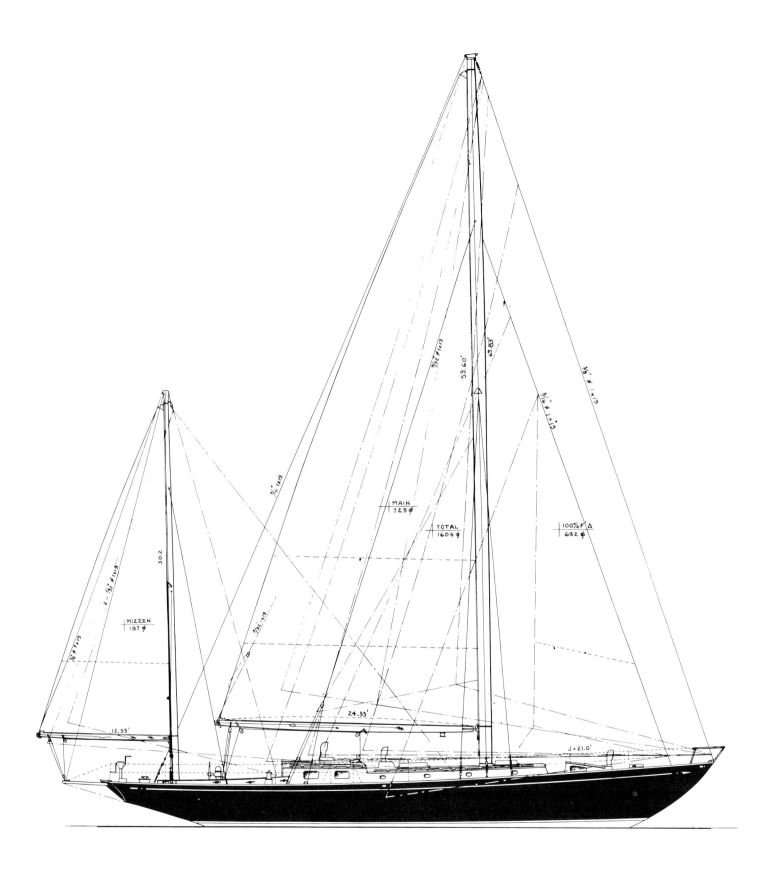

Windborne II and Northern Light - Designs 1197 and 1226

Windborne II: LOA: 40' 2"   DWL: 27' 10"   Beam: 10' 10"   Draft: 5' 9"   Sail area: 752 sq. ft.

Northern Light: LOA: 42' 9"   DWL: 29' 6"   Beam: 11' 9"   Draft: 4' 3"   Sail area: 847 sq. ft.

These two little S&S vessels of about 40 feet—one a yawl, the other a sloop—demonstrate the diverse and attractive alternatives that could be worked up from the basic *Finisterre-Dyna* theme. They were both notably successful, and seem to have always had a certain dash about them.

The yawl was created for veteran yachtsman A. Lee Loomis and carries a centerboard. But the sloop has a keel of less than 6 feet. A British writer pointed out that, in the judgment of his fellow countrymen, the keel was the greatly preferred version—a beamy boat with a keel. He went on to make light of "yachtsmen in the top flight of the sport" who had been so intimidated by the success of the new American racers that they were "suggesting that the only way to win races was to adopt extreme amounts of beam, hardly any draft, and centreboards!"

To counter that opinion, he quoted Olin Stephens himself as saying, "I am naturally very pleased by the success of the larger centreboarders.... Nevertheless, I don't think that the centreboard should be, or is, essential to success in long-distance racing, although I think the American rule encourages considerable beam, which so many people find desirable because of the accommodation it provides. At any rate, *Windborne* is an example of a beamy keel boat, and one which I hope will hold her own with centreboarders in long-distance racing. The principal disadvantage of the centreboard is its high cost, and this is a point that should not be overlooked."

Above left: Windborne II. *Above right and facing page:* Northern Light.

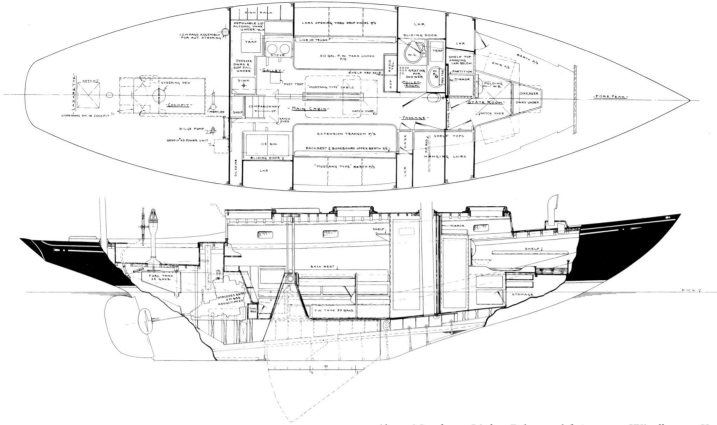

Above: Northern Light. *Below and facing page:* Windborne II.

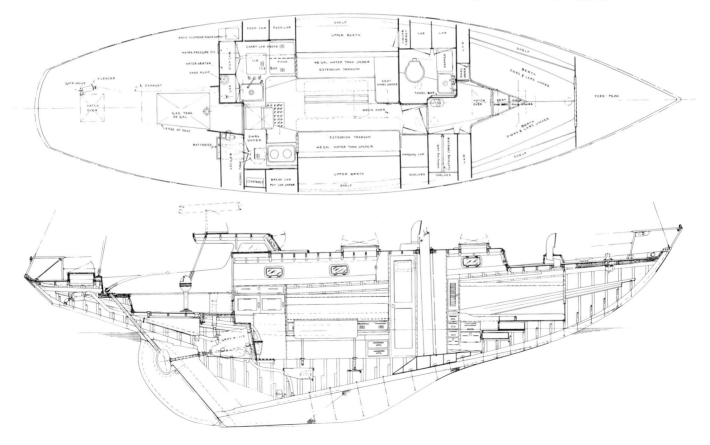

Antilles – Design 1221

LOA: 45' 11"   DWL: 32' 6"   Beam: 12' 10"   Draft: 4' 8"   Sail area: 1,042 sq. ft.

One of the most successful, larger versions of the *Finisterre*-type yawls was *Antilles*, designed in 1957. But she is actually a ketch, with mizzenmast forward of the rudder post. To those who might believe that a ketch, with smaller mainsail, could never rival a yawl for speed, one writer responded by mentioning two of *Antilles'* extraordinary passages in the Caribbean: the first of 920 miles in five days (184 miles per day); the second of 960 miles in five days. Hard to beat.

Here again a part of the answer may lie with her skipper, another member of the Old Guard, named Percy Chubb II. Mr. Chubb went on to own a number of S&S yachts, all of them designed to favor a certain personal inclination at that time in his racing-cruising career.

One unusual feature of this handsome yacht is the tiny cabin house in the very stern. Caboose-like, it has just barely room for the paid hand's berth. By clever juggling, Olin was also able to squeeze in the W.C. and a tiny tot heater. This is a far more pleasant location for a hand than in the eyes of the boat, where the motion can be extreme when anchored in a seaway. And somehow, when viewed under way, *Antilles'* caboose hardly makes an impression on the eye, so lovely is the sheer.

A British yachting magazine, in reviewing *Antilles'* plans, remarked somewhat prolixly, "It is probably true to say that nobody understands more than Olin Stephens about shaping this class of hull, and he apparently achieves the best results by adopting the radically unbalanced shape of the boat in which quarters of exceptional fullness are combined with long, lean

bows having a narrow angle of entrance at the waterline. It is, as it happens, a traditionally American form adapted to modern usage." But, in fact, this was not just a matter of "as it happens"; this was S&S consistency.

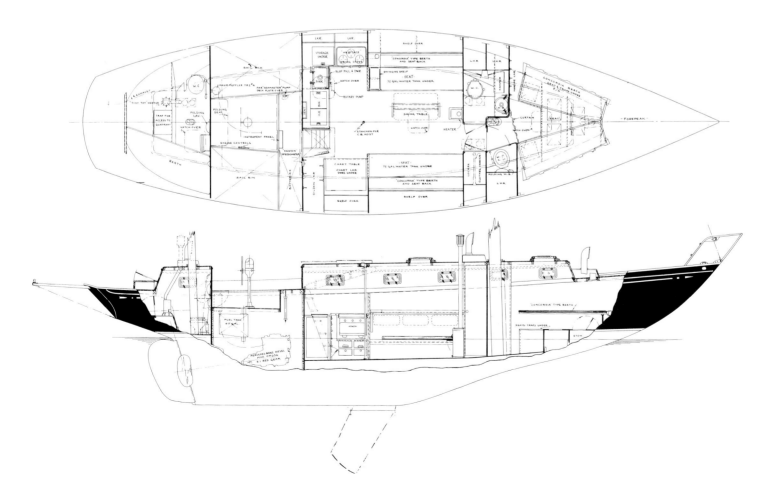

Jubilee – Design 1474

LOA: 60' 5"   DWL: 42' 6"   Beam: 14' 5"   Draft: 6'   Sail area: 1,757 sq. ft.

Designed in the last year of the 1950s, *Jubilee* represents one of the largest extensions of the centerboard-yawl concept. Indeed, it was regarded as somewhat weird that so big an ocean racer, heavily built and ready for the most severe type of blue-water racing, should have a board—usually the mark of a coastal sailer. But she was true to her lineage: a line of American boats that brilliantly succeeded in combining racing with cruising.

Given a lower rating than her smaller sister *Dyna* (because she'd been built of heavy timbers, not light aluminum), *Jubilee* was seen as a formidable competitor. One yachting writer called her "The Ocean Racing Debutante of 1960." And her

record bore out that promise.

Driven by a powerful masthead rig that resembles that of *Dyna* and *Revonoc*, *Jubilee* had the additional advantage of a pedestal winch in the very stern that allowed swift adjustment of the large headsails. Another advantage—of special value when cruising or day-sailing in close waters—was a pull-down chart table in the doghouse: the navigator would not have to keep running up and down the companionway.

To all who watched her perform, *Jubilee* with her modern features seemed a splendid continuation of the tradition set by those classic S&S yachts *Baruna* and *Bolero*.

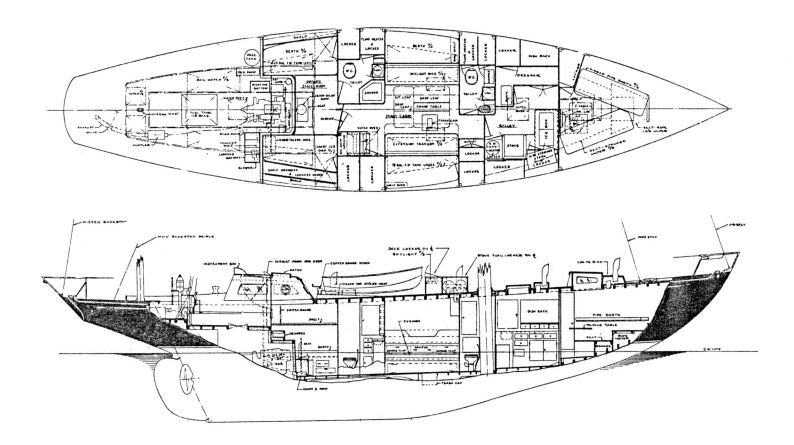

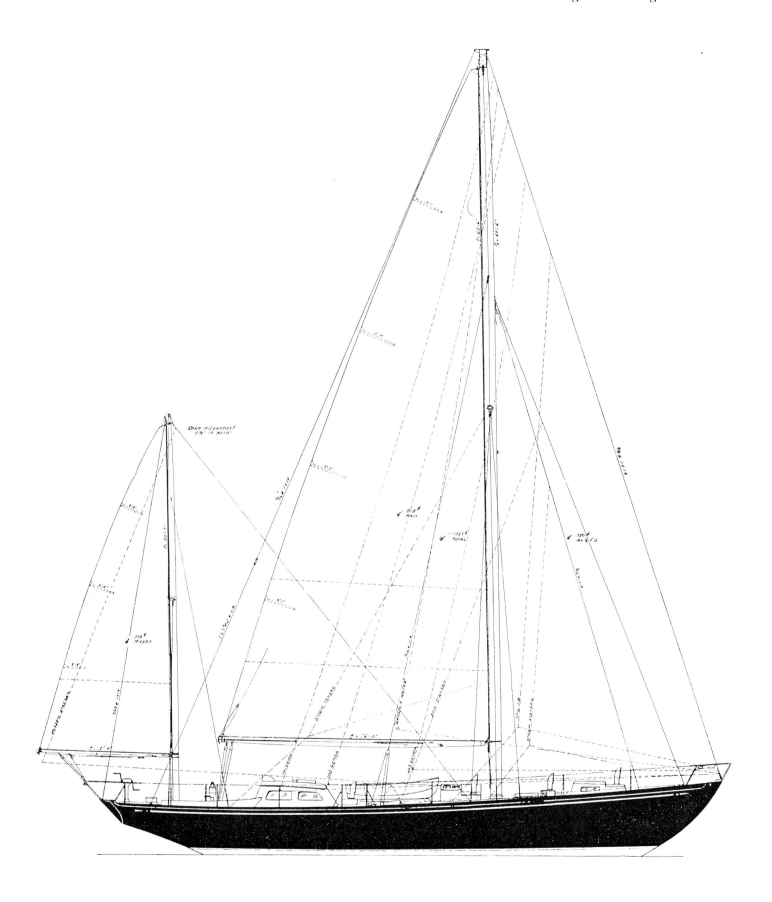

Corsaro II - Design 1505

LOA: 69' 4"   DWL: 50'   Beam: 16' 1"   Draft: 9' 6"   Sail area: 2,231 sq. ft.

Nor were the Italians to be left out of the new mode of sucessful ocean racing. The Italian Naval Academy ordered this keel yawl from Sparkman & Stephens in 1959 and launched her in November 1960. Speaking of the planning phase, Rod recalled that the Italian naval officers involved were terribly worried about how much the boat would tip, that is, how she would rate on an incline test (a matter of greater concern on powerboats than on sailboats): "Never have I seen so much lead put down so low!"

The objective was to have a vigorous contender in the TransPac Race which was to start from Los Angeles on July 4th of the next year. It was a well-executed plan: *Corsaro* finished first overall, giving the midshipmen crew the ride of their lives. *Corsaro* went on to triumph in subsequent European and oceanic races.

Hardly the conventional racing-cruising yacht, she had a full complement of fifteen, officers and midshipmen. Her deckhouse is especially large, allowing for conferences and instruction while at sea.

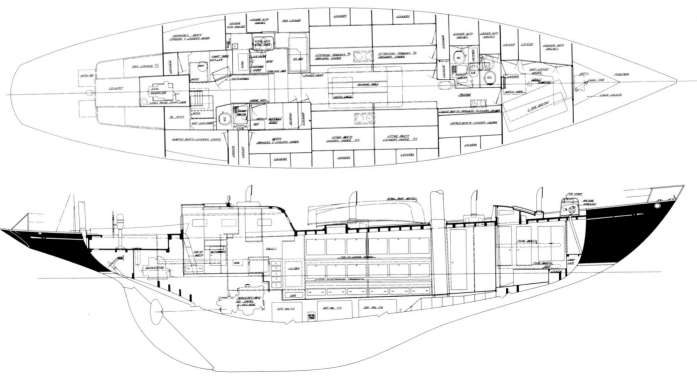

Saraband and Sapphire – Designs 1519 and 1540

Saraband: LOA: 35'   DWL: 29'   Beam: 8' 6"   Draft: 5' 3"   Sail area: 572 sq. ft.

Sapphire: LOA: 41' 1"   DWL: 27' 6"   Beam: 8' 10"   Draft: 5' 10"   Sail area: 775 sq. ft.

These two wooden sloops, both built in 1959, show how, at the end of that era, the S&S design team was by no means turning out mere copies of the centerboard yawls. Instead, they were designing ingenious and forward-looking creations.

The smaller of the two, *Saraband*, is a delightful double-ended cruiser with double cabins. The curve down from bow to keel has a distinctive S&S shape to it, making for gentle entry and steady sailing; it is a lovely and dependable boat for modest mariners. By contrast, the keel profile of the larger sloop, *Sapphire*, seems precipitous and racy.

Sapphire was indeed conceived as an all-out racer, for a client in New Zealand. Her very tall stick can be adjusted fore and aft by runner backstays controlled by block and tackle, led to a winch. The New Zealanders, observing her immediate string of victories, wrote that that "is to be expected from Sparkman & Stephens who must be the world's most experienced at successful interpretations of rating rules, as well as being the world's leading designers of racing keelers." Plus a few centerboarders.

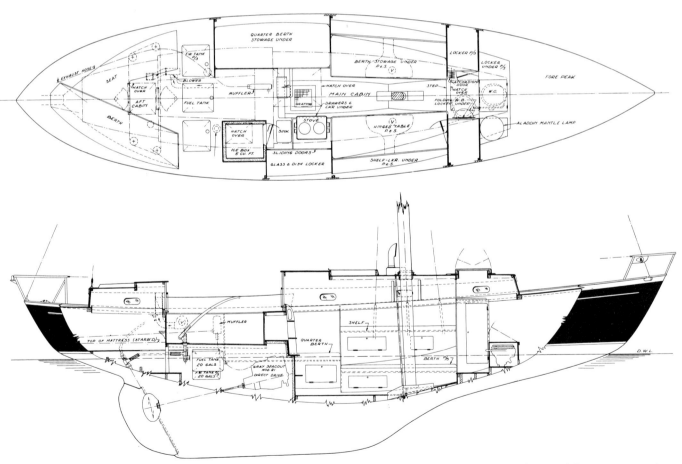

Above and facing page: Saraband.

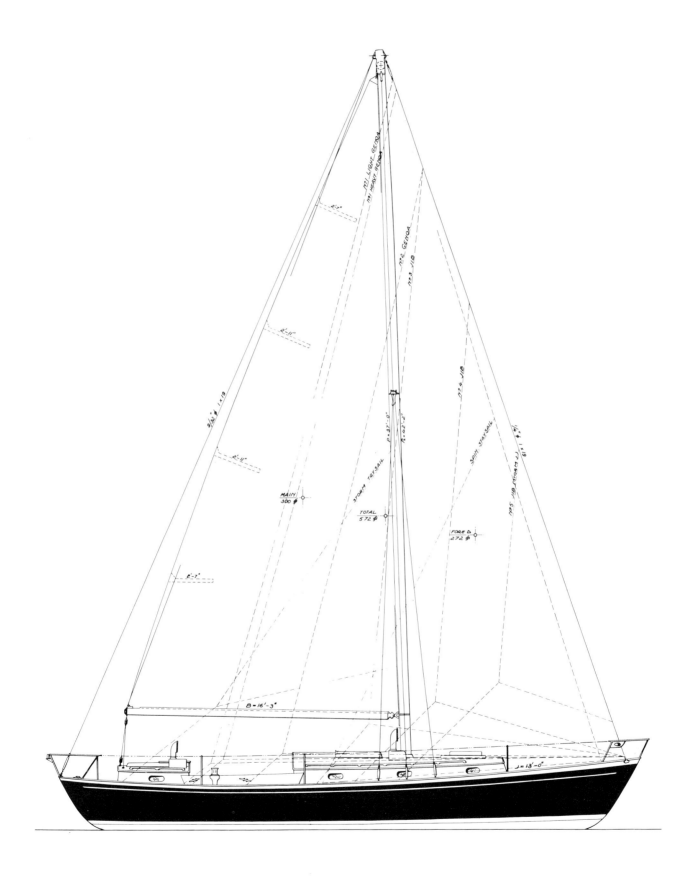

An interesting note on *Sapphire* is that she was originally designed with an ultra-modern, 12-meter-like transom, sloping forward. But when the decision was made to use the maximum sail area allowed, the designers had to put in a conventional transom in order to get the backstay clear of the sail. Thus, for all her advanced features, she still looked like a creation of the fifties—and all the more beautiful for it.

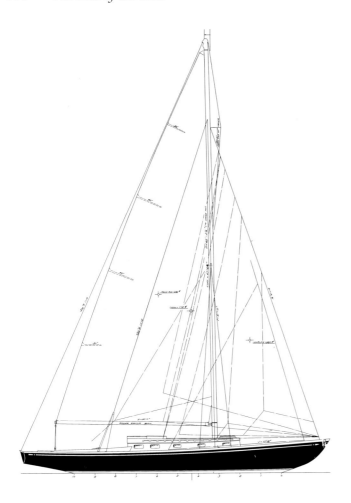

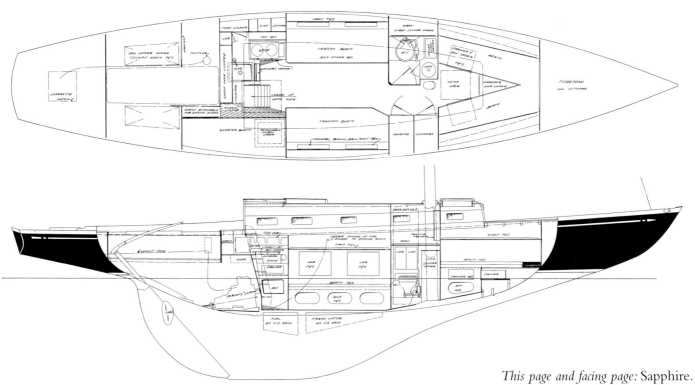

This page and facing page: Sapphire.

6

Victories Overseas

During the 1960s, most every summer Monday morning at the S&S office on Madison Avenue, a cable from overseas would arrive. Rod remembered this warm-weather liturgy fondly: the cable would be opened, read, and another victory for the great English racer *Clarion of Wight* recorded by her designers.

While the American yachting press was focusing on the performance of S&S winners in regattas on both coasts and the Great Lakes (plus certain blue-water events like the Bermuda Race), the international press had another story to tell—the astonishing story of how well S&S boats did overseas. *Clarion of Wight*'s victories were in keeping with a strong tradition that Olin and Rod had worked hard to bring about: the fierce, successful competitiveness of their designs for foreign clients.

Indeed, Olin considers that in those years immediately after World War II, English and European sailors were more win-oriented than Americans. Whereas American yachtsmen were interested in leisurely cruises with their wives in the Bahamas and a few exciting races in between, the Europeans wanted to try every trick for victory, banish all other considerations but victory.

Since barrages of letters back and forth were not really the best way to keep in touch with European clients and builders, Olin and Rod found themselves in Europe frequently. There they augmented their prewar reputations as seamen and designers who could produce winners. Yachtsmen who had marveled at *Dorade* and *Stormy Weather* now wanted the Stephens brothers to produce unique winners for them, winners shaped to their European inclinations as well as to the international measurement regulations (that is, the Royal Ocean Racing Club rules).

One typically eager European was W. N. H. Van Der Vorm of Rotterdam. During the war he had managed to conceal his large, S&S-designed yacht from the occupying Germans; now he was pleased to be sailing in peaceful waters again. But he wanted a new and swift cutter that he and his son could race—and he wanted Olin and Rod to create her for him. Named *Zwerver* (Design Number 1142), she was to be built at the de Vlitj yard in Holland, with the son supervising the construction. At first Rod was moderately annoyed at the young man's insistence on this and that detail. But he admitted, "the guy knew just what he wanted—and he was right. They were great people."

Olin believes that a look at *Zwerver* and two other designs of the fifties—*Hestia* and *Mait II*—gives a good idea of how these European boats differed from their American contemporaries. They all have very fine (one might even say "pinched") ends, for this style was encouraged by the RORC measurement regulations. They also displace more tons, as heavy scantlings were favored. One international client went so far as to have a steel deck made, really pushing the boat down into the water. Initially Olin thought that less freeboard was also favored, then he realized that that dimension was actually neutral.

Whatever the racing-rule rationale for these wooden boats, they do have a distinctive style...as well as an awe-inspiring string of victories. *Hestia*'s owner would visit Olin in England every October to present his harvest of seasonal triumphs to the designer, to report any problems, and to ask questions about possible improvements. Though the leader of a distinguished Dutch family, he loved nothing more than racing his 34-foot S&S sloop with his two sons in the stellar European regattas. Now a new generation of the family is scoring additional victories, including second place in the 1991 Fastnet.

As the sixties became the seventies, however, the rules of the game were changed. And the look and the spirit of overseas S&S winners changed with them. When the RORC measurement rules were replaced by those of the International Offshore Rule, many of the old rule's peculiarities were ironed out. Olin played a major role in preparing the new standards, agreeing that the revision was overdue. Yet, while he saw the new rule as "far better balanced," he recognized inherent dangers in the advantages given to very light and beamy boats. With customary diffidence, he suggested further, significant revisions during the 1970s, revisions which were not made.

So it happened that certain other designers, urged on by their eager European clients, sought to take advantage of the wide-open new possibilities (including new high-tech materials that were becoming available). Extreme designs, extra light of hull and extra tall of rig, were then seen crashing around the international courses. The climax of this mania was the disastrous, gale-lashed Fastnet Race of 1979. It speaks volumes that S&S's *Tenacious* (formerly *Dora*), a totally modern yet conservatively designed sloop, not only survived the race but won it hands down.

Facing page: Dora IV. *See page 126.*

Zwerver II – Design 1142

LOA: 56' 9"   DWL: 39'   Beam: 11' 2"   Draft: 8'   Sail area: 1,347 sq. ft.

Remarkable for her fine ends and deep keel, this Dutch racer was launched in 1956. Immediately she began demonstrating her winning ways, taking first place in that year's Fastnet. Although Rod Stephens contributed to the design and rigging, he was not immediately convinced of *Zwerver's* superstar qualities. Of the owning family's Fastnet victory, he said in admiration, "They never should have done it."

The cutter rig, with huge genoa or masthead jib topsail overlapping the forestaysail, gave *Zwerver* tremendous power. Although the tiller marks her as a boat for a serious helmsman, the low doghouse and the commodious layout below demonstrate that she was also a boat for pleasure and family fun.

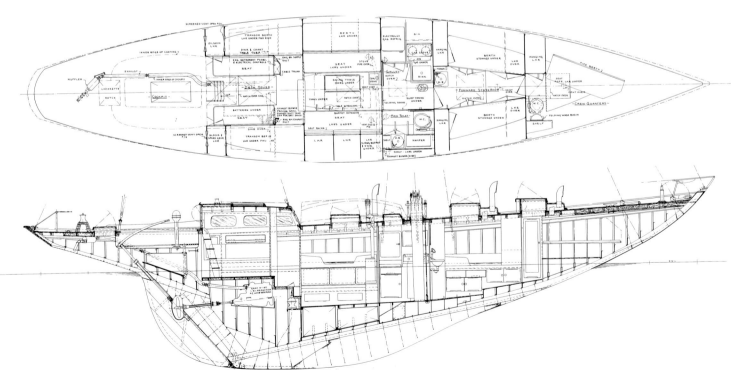

Mait II – Design 1215

LOA: 61' 8"   DWL: 43' 9"   Beam: 13' 6"   Draft: 8' 10"   Sail area: 1,816 sq. ft.

Designed for a zealous yachtsman/hotel owner in Milan, *Mait II* soon earned respect for both her beautiful lines and her racing abilities. Built with exceptional care at the Italian yard of Cantiere Baglietto in 1958 (at a cost of $50,000), her wooden hull had a number of notable features. One of these was that keel and deadwood were so carefully conformed as to be almost sculpted, created of laminated mahogany.

She was indeed an extraordinary boat, exemplifying Olin's European, fine-ended concepts. She became one of the most successful campaigners under the RORC rules in the 1960s and 1970s. In the words of the justly proud Italian press, she proved herself "the boat to beat" (*la barca da battere*) in any contest she entered.

After those many years of success, the owner (Commodore Italo Monzino) made the gracious gesture of giving *Mait II* to the Italian Yacht Club so that she could serve as a training vessel for the youth of that country.

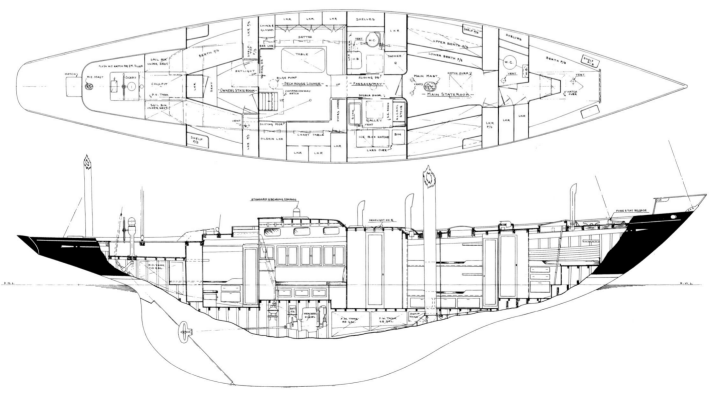

Anitra – Design 1358

LOA: 48' 2"   DWL: 33' 6"   Beam: 12' 4"   Draft: 6' 11"   Sail area: 1,062 sq. ft.

By contrast with her other European sisters, *Anitra* seems more typical of the contemporary American S&S yawls. That is, she's relatively beamy and looks at first glance like a typical centerboarder. In fact, *Anitra* was that anomalous creation, a deep and beamy boat—along the lines of *Windborne*, of which *Anitra* was a further development. In keeping with the tradition established by her swift S&S predecessors, she won the Fastnet Race and then went on to claim a multiplicity of other honors.

With gleaming, varnished hull and glowing stainless-steel fittings, *Anitra* was always a delight to behold, even by her opponents (one of whom rued the fact that she was so "miraculously fast"). She was also, according to Olin, a great pleasure to steer, even though equipped with a wheel.

One theory put forth to explain her European-American look was that her owner, Swedish shipping magnate Sven Hansen, spent more time in his New York office than in Stockholm. She was built at Europe's premier yard, Neglinge Varvet, by Bengt Plym in 1959.

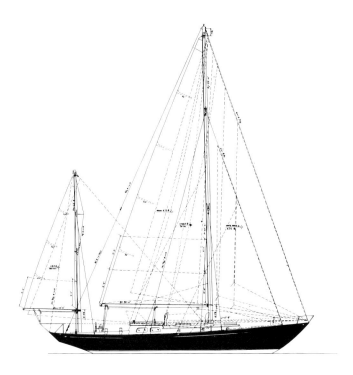

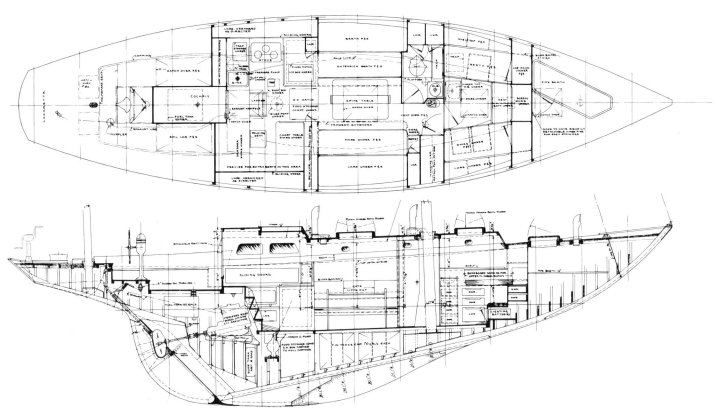

Hestia - Design 1478

LOA: 34' 5"   DWL: 25' 6"   Beam: 9' 8"   Draft: 6'   Sail area: 579 sq. ft.

A consistent winner at England's venerable Cowes Race Week, little *Hestia* was an important statement for Sparkman & Stephens to make on the European racing scene. As well as prestigious victors in Class A, they could create winning boats for Class C—whether they were raced in heavy weather at open sea or in gentle, coastal waters.

Olin and Rod remembered, however, that owner H. A. Van Beuningen drove them to distraction in the early days of planning *Hestia* by insisting that she be "lighter, lighter, even lighter!" (This was a tendency that contributed to the complex, calamitous Fastnet of 1979.) Nonetheless, Olin delivered a design that, while being rather heavy relative to her length, gave the owner the racer he wanted. There were spare accommodations below (full headway only in the companionway area), everything arranged for racing abovedecks.

It's interesting to observe that this distinctly European design—note the slightly pinched-in look of the deckline forward—is an adaptation of S&S's Pilot class (see Chapter 7). Adapted, yes—adapted to win in Europe.

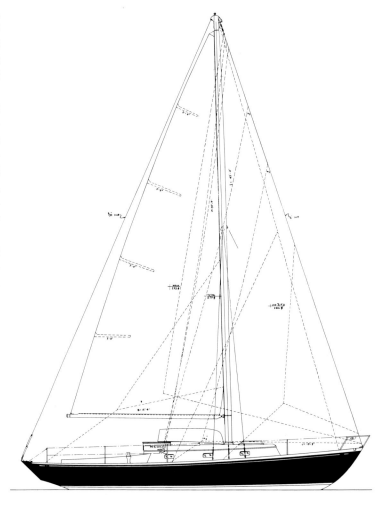

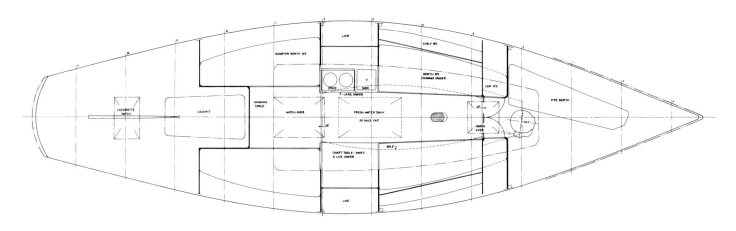

Tiziana – Design 1663

LOA: 116' 9"   DWL: 80'   Beam: 24' 1"   Draft: 10' 4"   Sail area: 5,346 sq. ft.

This large, impressive auxiliary yacht, designed in 1963 for Giovanni Nasi of Turin, stands as something of a contrast to her smaller European contemporaries. Her size (116 feet) and construction (steel) seem to move her out of the category of the wooden race winners. Nonetheless, she's included here because of her sixties-era beauty and her surprising speed.

Rod played a decisive role in building that speed into *Tiziana*, for it was he who insisted that she be equipped with a single rather than a double screw. Her owner, who wanted a fast yacht but believed that two propeller shafts were necessary for safety and control, took some persuading. Finally taking Rod's advice, he never regretted the decision.

Another design factor that made *Tiziana* a handy sailer was the provision of two centerboards in addition to her fairly deep keel. The larger board amidships gave her additional thrust to windward; the smaller one aft ensured good balance. To counter her tall rig and expansive sail area, she was ballasted with 52,000 pounds of boiler punchings in concrete plus 2,000 pounds of lead pigs for inside trimming.

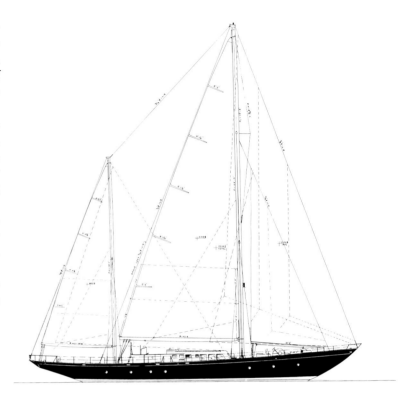

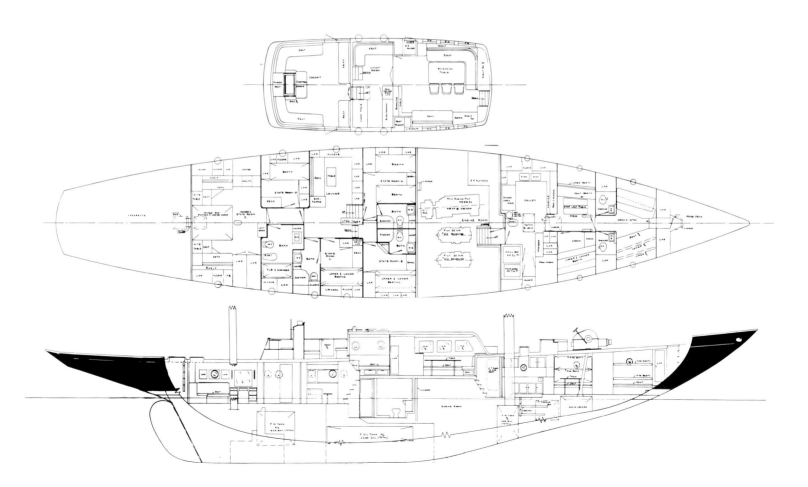

Palynodie – Design 1673

LOA: 39' 10"   DWL: 28' 9"   Beam: 10' 1"   Draft: 6' 6"   Sail area: 690 sq. ft.

The mayor of Marseilles, M. Gaston Deferre, requested that S&S design a swift, short-keeled sloop for him in line with the RORC rules. And the result was the lovely but not particularly adept *Palynodie*, built in England in 1962. Note the forward-slanting transom—a sign of the new age.

Reports at the end of each racing season revealed that this rather light boat was somewhat awkward, difficult to control. Subsequent experimenting and planning by Olin resulted in the addition to the hull of a trim tab way aft. This extra stabilizer—developed as a concept during the tank-testing of models for the 12-meter *Intrepid*—gave *Palynodie* much greater ease on downwind legs. And the S&S team demonstrated once again their willingness to continue working with a client on his boat until the desired results were achieved.

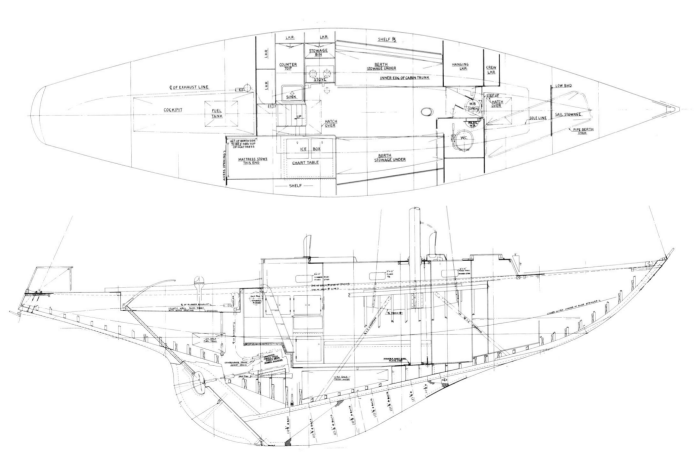

Clarion of Wight – Design 1698

LOA: 43' 6"   DWL: 30'   Beam: 10' 11"   Draft: 6' 8"   Sail area: 725 sq. ft.

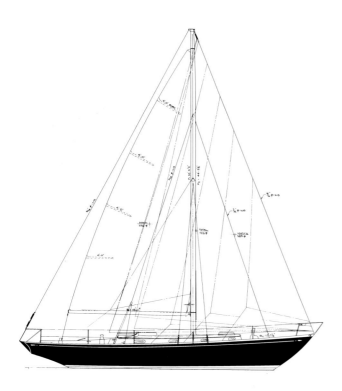

Somewhat larger than *Palynodie*, this rather short-rigged sloop proved to be one of England's most dazzling successes on the racing circuits, starting off with an overall win in the 1963 Fastnet Race.

This was the triumphant boat about whose victories Rod would receive the Monday-morning cables. In his opinion, *Clarion*, as well as being a splendid seaboat, was "very well sailed" by her owners. Speculating on why she and others of her medium size fared so well in the high seas and heavy weather that characterized the Fastnet, a British writer concluded that whereas smaller boats might not be rugged enough for the challenge, very large boats faced the problem of crew members being exhausted by the task of tacking and changing large, heavy, Dacron sails. To manage a boat of *Clarion*'s size, and to race her just as hard as possible, was not only feasible; it was fun.

Olin regards *Clarion* as "the last and perhaps the best" of the foreign, RORC-regulated racers. Her fine ends forward certainly confirm her membership in that group of S&S winners.

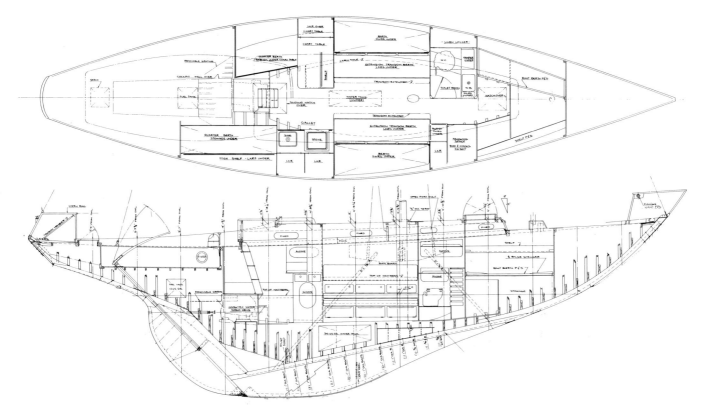

Roundabout and Clarionet – Designs 1856 and 1857

Roundabout: *LOA: 36' 5"*   *DWL: 26' 7"*   *Beam: 9' 11"*   *Draft: 6' 3"*   *Sail area: 494 sq. ft.*

Clarionet: *LOA: 36' 10"*   *DWL: 26' 8"*   *Beam: 9' 11"*   *Draft: 6' 3"*   *Sail area: 512 sq. ft.*

This page: Roundabout.

These two famous English sloops represent, in their design, the fresh thinking that turned traditional yacht design around at the end of the sixties. *Roundabout* was designed for Sir Max Aitken, *Clarionet* for Derek Boyer—both gentlemen being keen defenders of Britain's reputation at sea.

The boats were designed to meet specific requirements for the international "One-Ton" competition and to rate well within the RORC regulations. The most obvious sign that something new was going on is the dolphin-like shaping and the separation of keel and rudder. The separation seemed (again according to 12-meter test tank results) to improve steering control in strong winds. It also seemed to increase speed in light air, as well as maneuverability.

Roundabout has less displacement and spreads slightly less sail area than *Clarionet*. The latter's forefoot has been cut away to gain the longest possible leading edge on the keel. By contrast, *Roundabout*'s forefoot was intended to be as sharp as possible. Both boats performed admirably (though they were occasionally difficult to control), driving one writer to complain that the pair constituted a "pincer attack" by the American S&S against British naval architects. But it was less of a military attack, really, and more of a demonstration of science and art.

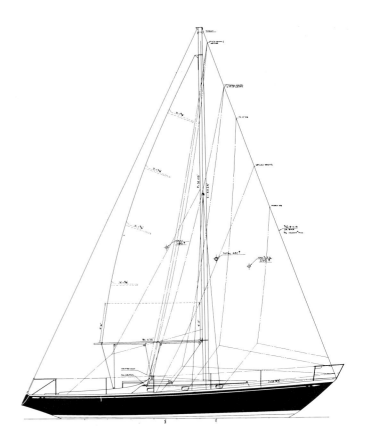

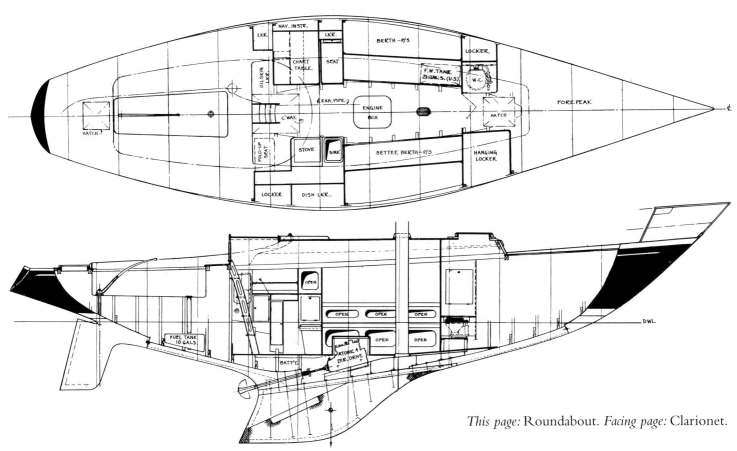

This page: Roundabout. *Facing page:* Clarionet.

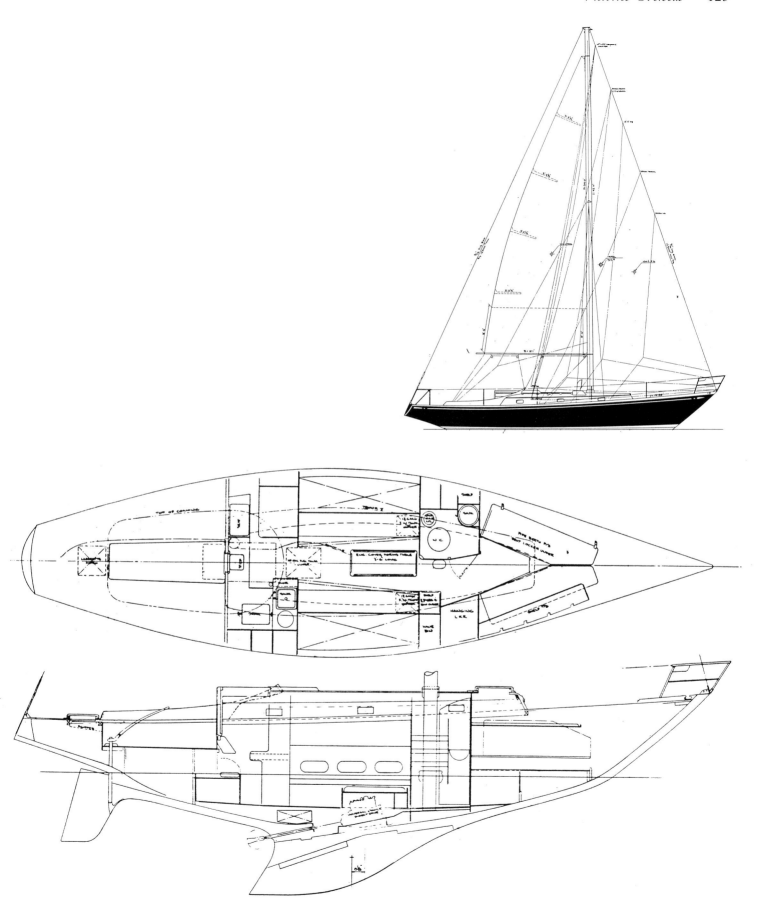

Ragamuffin and Saga – Designs 1949 and 2082

Ragamuffin: LOA: 48' 7"   DWL: 36'   Beam: 12' 6"   Draft: 7' 9"   Sail area: 1,060 sq. ft.

Saga: LOA: 57' 8"   DWL: 42' 9"   Beam: 14' 10"   Draft: 8' 10"   Sail area: 1,440 sq. ft.

Larger than the preceding pair, *Ragamuffin* and *Saga* represented further advances into the new age of yacht design. They also represented the spread of the new S&S concepts to other lands, for the former was designed for an Australian client, the latter for a Norwegian (whose business interests were in Brazil).

As a result of outstanding performance in trial races in Australia, *Ragamuffin* was selected to lead the nation's One-Ton cup team in 1969. A winner in that race, she went on to place in nearly every race she entered. Both she and *Saga* (which was built of fiberglass rather than wood) proved themselves to be superior ocean racers in an era of exciting shifts in design and technology. Because *Saga* came forth after the replacement of RORC by IOR regulations, her hull is relatively light and cut away; in profile, it seems to differ as much from *Zwerver*'s as from *Dorade*'s.

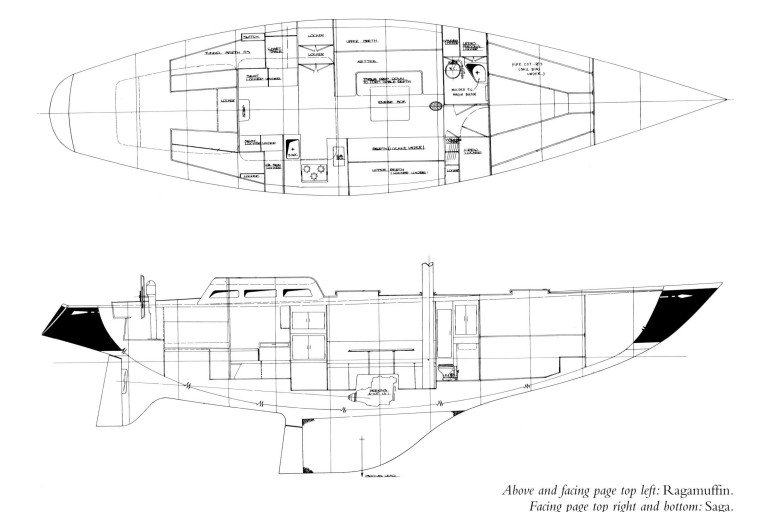

Above and facing page top left: Ragamuffin.
Facing page top right and bottom: Saga.

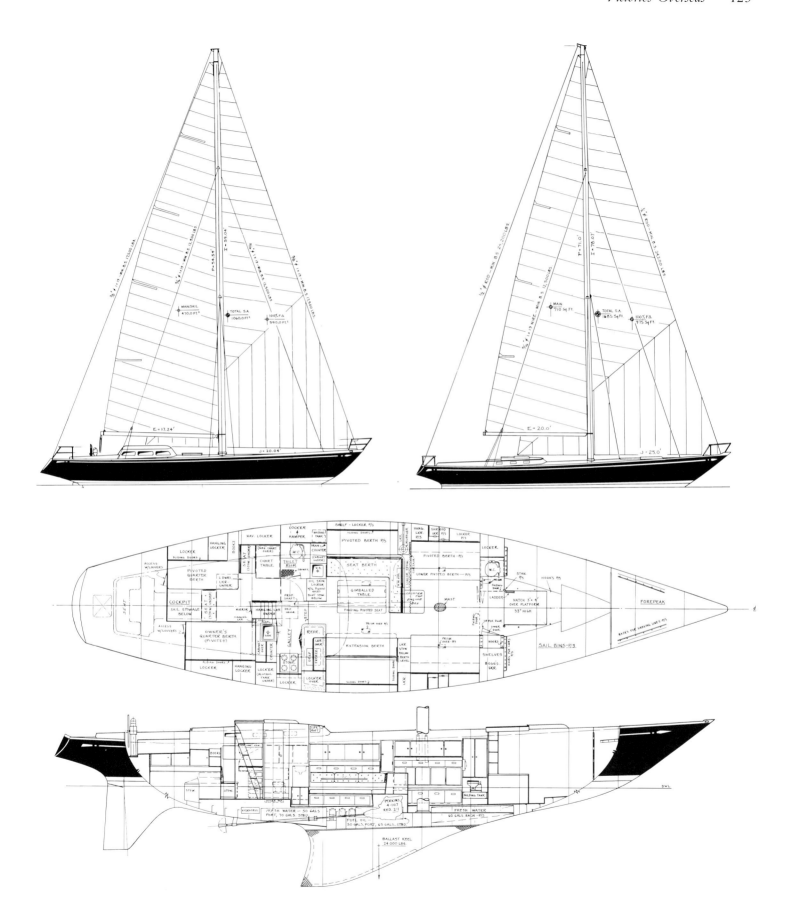

Dora IV - Design 2089

LOA: 61'5"   DWL: 46'   Beam: 15' 8"   Draft: 8' 11"   Sail area: 1,685 sq. ft.

Under her original name, this IOR racer cleaned up in her first season (1973) on the Great Lakes. But under the name *Tenacious*, she won fame abroad by her victory in the tragic Fastnet Race of 1979. Later, under the name *War Baby*, she would go on to enjoy a remarkable career as a fast ocean cruiser (including a voyage to Spitzbergen and Jan Mayan Land). Olin and Rod received a letter from her first owner declaring, "The winning record belongs to your design; we made many mistakes and were bailed out by sheer speed."

But the main reason for including this speedy, American-built (Palmer Johnson) boat in this international section is the beneficial effect she had on out-of-control developments in naval architecture overseas, developments allowed or encouraged by the IOR. Whereas many designers were producing

ultra-light and ultra-lofty contenders, Sparkman & Stephens believed that *Tenacious* was as far as one should go in the direction of a maximum-performance ocean racer. A journalist headlined his story on her with the phrase, "S&S Stick with Proven Ocean Racing Formula." This was the formula that enabled her to survive the Fastnet Race, the formula that other designers ignored at their peril.

Also, in the configuration of her fine-ended hull, who cannot see a resemblance to the S&S overseas winners of the 1950s and 1960s? She appears to be a triumphantly transitional design, between the traditions of mid-century and the evolutions that would be granted to yachtsmen at the end of the century.

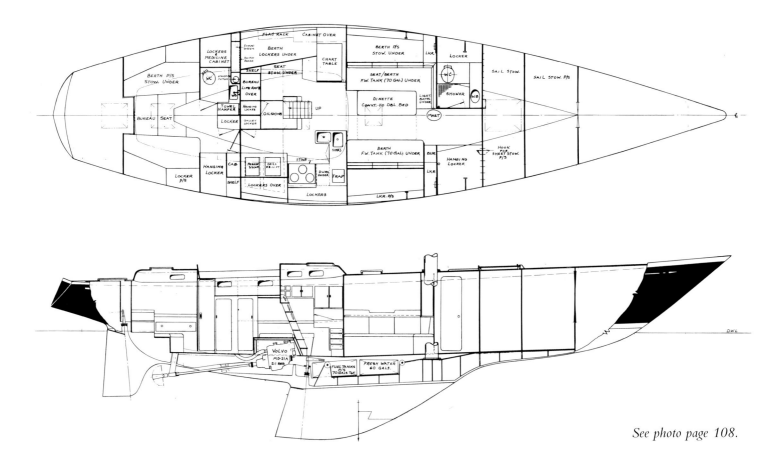

See photo page 108.

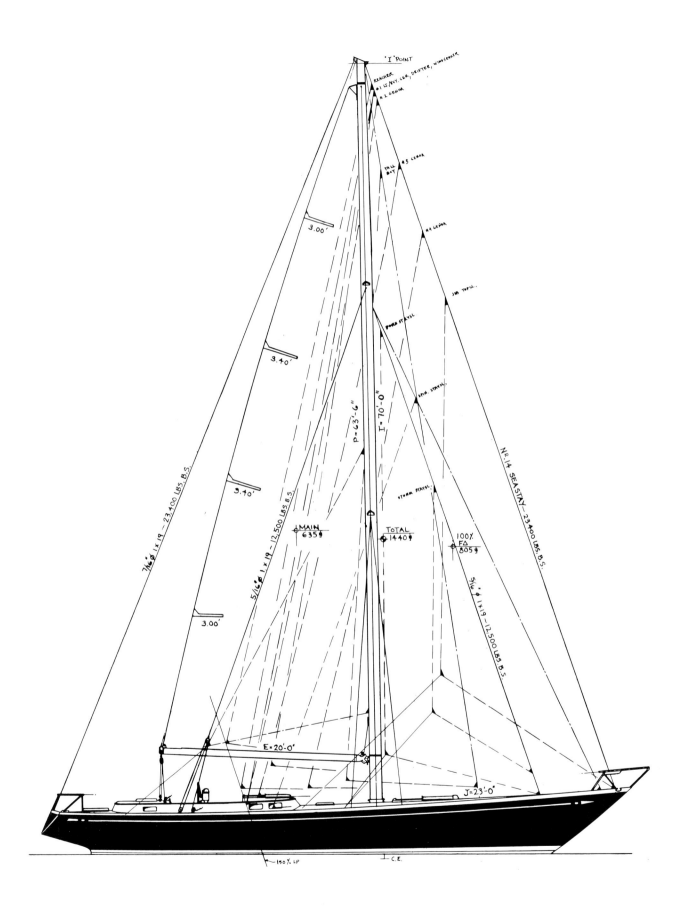

7
The Beauties of Production

Early in 1936 a yachtsman named Donald B. Abbott came into the Sparkman & Stephens office to discuss with Olin and Rod a concept that was entirely different. Mr. Abbott, a racing skipper with twenty years of onshore and offshore experience, was interested in helping to create the ideal family boat, to be designed without reference to racing measurement rules.

For nine years Abbott had been working to collect opinions on prerequisites for a racer/cruiser that would answer the needs of Mr. and Mrs. Everysailor. The opinions were so numerous and varied and even contradictory that a hideous scramble of compromises seemed, at first, the only way to bring them together. But Olin Stephens was intrigued by the challenge and brought forth one of America's most popular production boats: the Week-Ender.

A "production boat" is a design that can be produced by a given builder in great quantities, for substantial savings. As with one-design class boats, these boats do not deviate from each other in hull or rig design (though owners of non-racing production boats may and do revise them at will). But whereas one-designs are usually day-sailers ordered by yacht clubs (whose members yearn to race against each other), production boats, usually cruising boats, are ordered by individuals not from S&S but from the builder. Then the owners may find ways to race against each other in their respective regions.

Nonetheless, it may be said that the first S&S production boat was the New York 32 class. Although these yacht-club-commissioned sloops were thought to be one-designs, the mass-production form of construction employed by the builder seems to identify them as production boats. There were only twenty New York 32s allowed to be built; all were constructed in the mid-thirties at the Nevins yard according to a new principle, upside down upon the same mold. Also, because they were racer/cruisers, emphasizing seaworthiness rather than the around-the-mark agility of one-designs, they do seem to belong in the production-boat category.

Rod Stephens came to be called the "Godfather" of New York 32s. Having bought one of the original group of twenty boats from his friend Harvey Conover in the mid-1940s, he campaigned her with such zeal that all looked to him for advice and leadership. There's the story, for example, of another purchaser of a secondhand NY 32 who leaned on Rod for help and advice—which was, of course, freely given. Gratefully he then asked Rod, "If you could do one thing to your boat, something more, what would it be?" And when Rod answered that he had always hoped one day he might afford a special bronze maststep installed with stirrups leading to the chainplates, the man nodded, ordered one of those expensive retrofits for his boat, and secretly had one installed on Rod's *Mustang*. Such special improvements would not, it should be noted, be allowed on strict one-designs.

Furthermore, it was the way that Rod kept *Mustang* that not only inspired owners of other NY 32s but also convinced owners of other production craft that, if they attained similar standards of seamanship, they too could be renowned victors and eminent yachtsmen. These activities were taking place, it should be remembered, in the troubled years of the 1930s and 1940s, when it was a point of pride to keep things simple and low-cost as well as yare and salty. So it seemed not comical at all that Rod should choose to replace his mainsheet every night with a messenger line; that way he kept the same mainsheet for twenty of the twenty-five years he owned the boat.

Rod babied his beloved *Mustang* in a way few would think of today. For two reasons, he never overpowered her with too much sail: first because he believed that "when a boat is overpowered, she doesn't handle very well"; second because he believed that an overstressed wooden boat would soon leak and fall apart. Rod thought absolutely unforgivable the modern practice of making the boat go faster by tightening up the rigging till it rings to the touch like a tuning fork. "I think it's just dreadful what they do with hydraulics on backstays today," he remarked in a *WoodenBoat* interview. "Obviously, that's done by people who don't have any feelings for their boats."

When Rod sold *Mustang* in 1969, he told her new purchaser that she didn't leak at all. The man listened to that boast much as he would to a car salesman's pitch, and gave it a similar amount of credit. But at the end of the season he called on the phone. "Gee!" he exclaimed to Rod, "you said that *Mustang* didn't leak, and she hasn't—not a drop!"

Since the prewar days of the NY 32s and the Week-Enders, there have been many types of S&S production boats—keel

Facing page: Mustang. *See page 130.*

and centerboard, fiberglass and aluminum—and they have grown in size from the 30-footers of the early days to the 70-footers and more of recent times. They have also advanced, many of them, from justifiable dismissal as mass-produced plastic "Chlorox bottles" to adulation for sophisticated exterior and wood-rich interior designs.

And another important factor has changed: while these boats (specifically the Week-Enders) were conceived in their own times to be "compromises," sacrificing much for that democratic ideal, the best of them are now regarded (by Walter Cronkite, for example) as "uncompromising." That is, they have such excellence designed and built into them at the behest of their individual owners that no one can fault their custom-style quality.

A production boat may still lack something of individuality. But perhaps that characteristic is part of an American myth which, at sea as well as on land, deserves reevaluation.

Mustang - Design 125

LOA: 48' 4"   DWL: 32'   Beam: 10' 7"   Draft: 6' 6"   Sail area: 990 sq. ft.

The New York 32s were designed not many months after *Dorade*. And they obviously belong more to that emerging tradition than to the old pattern established by the famous New York Yacht Club "Thirties"—which the 32s were designed to replace. The old boats, created by Nathanael Herreshoff, had been magnificent, overcanvased, gaff-rigged racers with scant cruising accommodations. By 1935, however, NYYC members wanted boats that they could race to Bermuda, or across the Atlantic, as well as around the buoys of Long Island Sound.

Olin Stephens and the Nevins yard therefore came up with hulls heavily planked with Philippine mahogany, frames of white oak (1⅝ inches on 8-inch centers), and bronze strapping. All for $11,000 each.

The rig was simple and all-inboard; the seven-eighths jib was relatively small and loose-footed. Whereas the old 30s had had light cabin houses, equipped with plate glass—a frail defense against a wild wave that might come smashing aboard at sea—the cabin houses of the 32s were low-lying and structurally solid. Despite their ruggedness and weight (displacement of 24,550 pounds), the 32s immediately proved themselves to be brilliant winners. A yachting writer in 1937 called them "well-nigh unbeatable."

They also proved to be well-nigh unsinkable, with about two-thirds of the original fleet still sailing more than fifty years later. There was, of course, a tremendous need to work at keeping the boats in shape, including the caulking of the seams. Rod always regretted that he had, tactfully, stayed with *Mustang*'s original dark blue color, yielding to compliments of friends who told him how beautiful she was. But the sun treats seams of light-colored hulls more kindly, and dark colors show the seams more clearly than do light colors. "You could always see her seams," Rod later said. "I love boats that don't show seams at all."

With his determination never to overpower *Mustang*, Rod developed a quick reefing system that allowed him to reduce the large-sized mainsail with amazing rapidity when the wind piped up. He liked to tell the story of a practice sail before one Bermuda Race. The breeze increased suddenly as *Mustang* tacked out of Newport Harbor; by the time she cleared the headland, there were two reefs in the main. To puzzled observers who swore they had seen him leave harbor with full sail, Rod explained that he and his crew had schooled themselves to tie in a reef in less than fifty seconds: the two reefs were completed one each on the two brief tacks out.

None of this interest in reefs should be interpreted as timidity from Rod Stephens or fragility for *Mustang*. In fact, what Rod said he liked most about his NY 32 was how she "could punch through the seas," in the *Dorade* tradition.

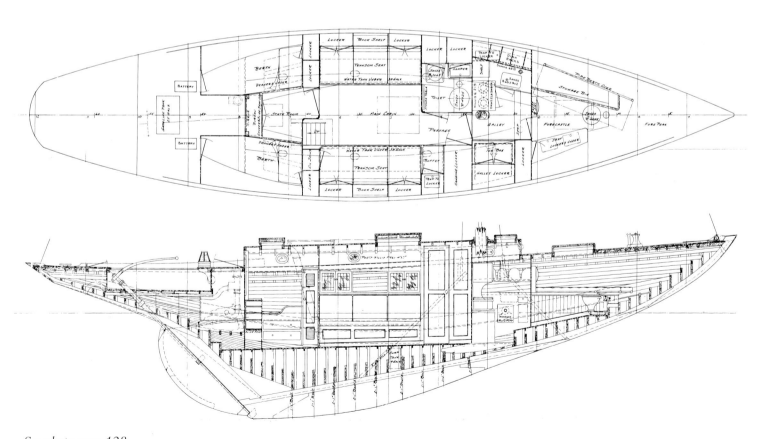

See photo page 128.

Week-Ender – Design 208

LOA: 35'   DWL: 27'   Beam: 9' 6"   Draft: 5' 7"   Sail area: 562 sq. ft.

The name was picked as an appeal to hardworking Americans who could not afford the wealthy yachtsmen's leisurely full weeks at sea. And those Americans responded in great numbers: in the first two seasons for this design—1937 and 1938—some thirty-seven boats were built.

What the workaday Americans discovered to their great joy was that they had picked a winner: Week-Enders won trophies from the Mackinac Race to the American Yacht Club Cruise. Wrote one happy owner to S&S, "In light airs with genoa jib she will outsail many of the so-called racing classes; and at the same time, she is stiff and able in a breeze."

On corrected time, Week-Enders challenged even *Baruna* and the NY 32s. Yet with 6' 2" of headroom below and broad dry decks, they came through as first-class cruising boats, just as promised. Cockpit seats were 6' 6" long and bunks were 6' 3".

In 1940, the design was somewhat modernized—but with careful attention paid to equality for the older boats. The head was enlarged; the starboard main cabin bunk was converted into an extension double berth; bronze winches were added for mainsheet and main halyard. They couldn't think of much else that needed doing.

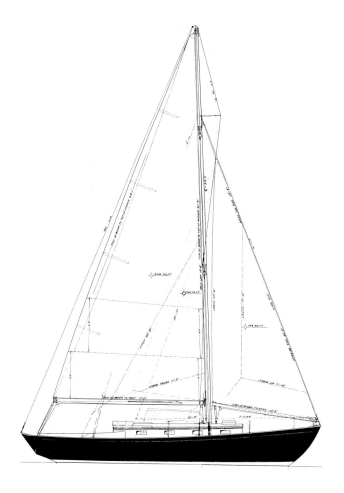

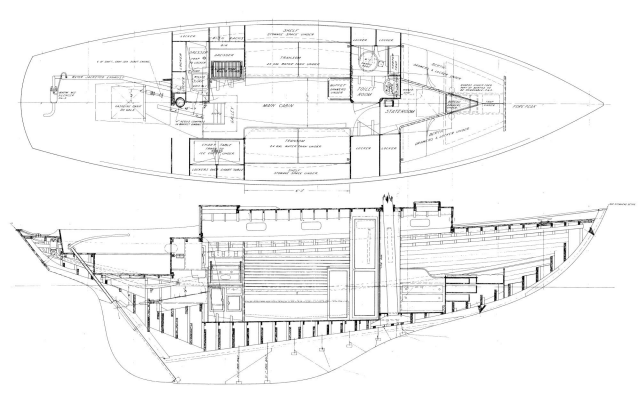

Pilot – Design 1219

LOA: 35' 1"   DWL: 24'   Beam: 9' 7"   Draft: 4' 9"   Sail area: 528 sq. ft. (sloops); 552 sq. ft. (yawls)

Some of these sloops (and a few yawls) were built by the Henry R. Hinckley yard in Southwest Harbor, Maine, in 1956 and 1957, others by various builders elsewhere. From all sources and in all settings they looked extraordinarily handsome, with their conventional transoms and their masts placed fairly far aft for generous headsails.

This is the design that fathered the famous Dutch racer *Hestia*. Given the beauty and effectiveness of the design, it's no wonder that insiders at S&S report that some twenty-eight individual plans, plus five type plans, were drafted as the Pilot developed on the boards. And a proto-version of the boat—an American yachtsman's sloop named *Puffin*— had required thirteen plans before that.

As a result of that intensive pencil-scratching, a boat emerged for all ages. Pilots in wood and fiberglass are still selling and sailing briskly today, with major fleets on both the Great Lakes and Long Island Sound.

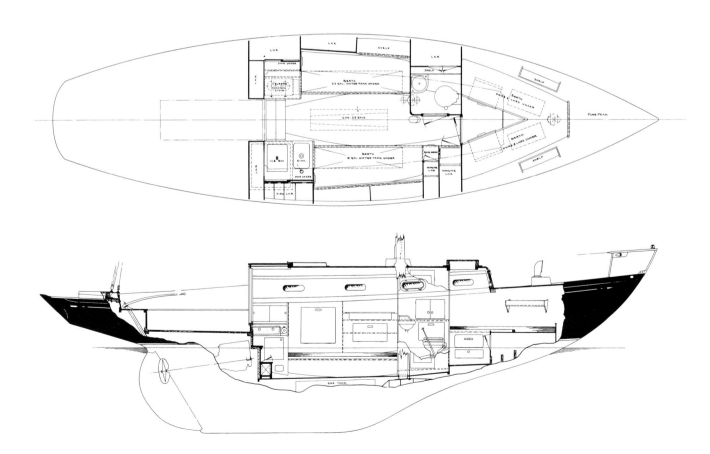

Dolphin – Design 1497

LOA: 24'   DWL: 19'   Beam: 7' 8"   Draft: 2' 10"   Sail area: 296 sq. ft.

Hailed as "midget ocean racers" in the 1960s, these fiberglass, keel-centerboard sloops were designed in 1959. The first builder (O'Day) was succeeded by Yankee Yachts, which made some improvements of underbody—decreasing displacement from 4,544 pounds to 4,250 pounds—and of cabin arrangements. The inboard auxiliary engine was replaced by a 9-horsepower outboard, housed in a well.

Unusual in such a tiny boat is the large galley and enclosed head. With production booming well into the 1970s, builders were able to keep the price down in the neighborhood of $5,000. That was surely a modest investment to yield Storm Trysail and CCA victories to Dolphin skippers.

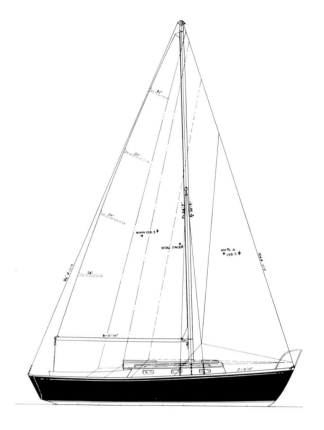

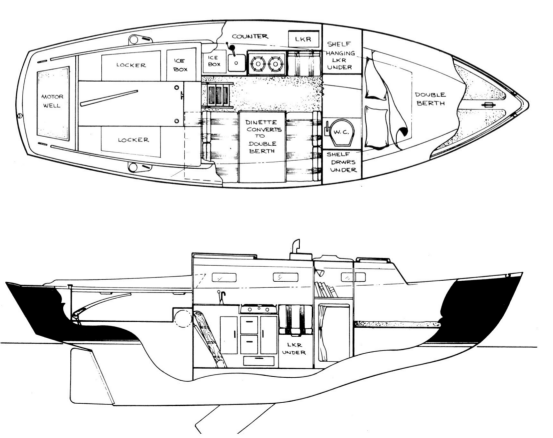

Tartan 27 and Capri 30 – Designs 1617 and 1760

Tartan 27:   LOA: 27'   DWL: 21' 6"   Beam: 8' 7"   Draft: 3' 2" (board up)   Sail area: 376 sq. ft. (sloops); 394 sq. ft. (yawls)

Capri 30:   LOA: 30'   DWL: 25'   Beam: 9' 8"   Draft: 3' 9"   Sail area: 476 sq. ft.

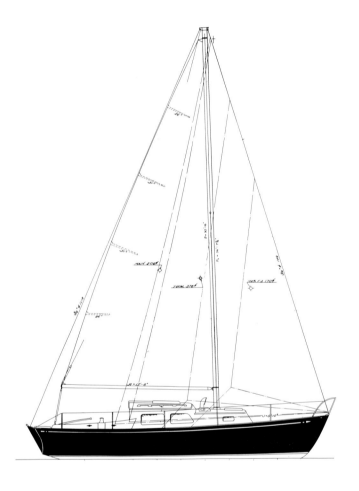

These two production boats, both keel-centerboarders, may be viewed as acmes of small cruising-boat design and manufacturing in the 1960s. The Tartan 27, first introduced in 1960, appears to have been the most popular of all American production boats, with a total of 712 built. The Capri 30, launched three years later, was also tremendously popular and gained more than her share of racing records.

The original Tartan, one has to admit, had a boxy, automobilish look—with an awkward doghouse and short ends. But by the time of the building of the last sixty boats in 1977, the sheerline was raised 4 inches and the doghouse done away with, making her look like a small yacht of traditional proportions. Belowdecks, the cramped dinette was scrapped and a more conventional layout installed, making this rather narrow boat seem a bit roomier.

Yet the real story of the superiority of the Tartan is in her construction. Although she was built in the early days of American fiberglassing, great care was taken to produce hulls that, with proper attention, would last for decades. Thus, the relatively high price of the Tartan—$25,000 toward the end of the production run—was regarded as a wise investment. The price of used boats remained high; some shrewd sellers got more than they'd paid for their boats in the first place. In the words of *Practical Sailer*, the Tartan 27 "has had a successful sales record that has been the envy of the industry."

The association of Sparkman & Stephens and Tartan Yachts was so successful that thirteen larger designs were commissioned in the years 1960-84. And, even more astonishingly, a total of 3,472 S&S-Tartans were built.

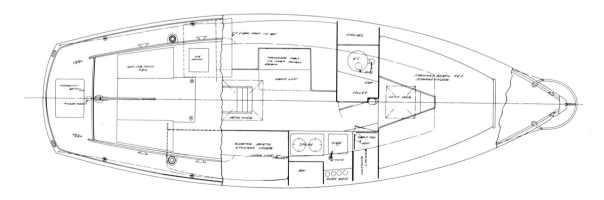

This page and facing page: Tartan 27.

In terms of looks, Chris Craft's Capri 30 does bear a close resemblance to the improved Tartan 27 (though with larger lights in the aft section of her cabin house). The Capri's hull shape also recalls the smaller Dolphin. "Space engineers" at Chris Craft were somehow able to provide 6' 2½" of headroom below and a host of large-boat amenities (such as a head with vanity). Despite the motorboat venue of her builders, the S&S hull and rig designs ensured that she would be a fierce competitor. The tall mast and relatively short boom allowed a single couple to handle her without strain.

One proud owner, writing from Holland, Michigan, of his race results, reported that one day his Capri engaged a 12-meter, an 8-meter, a Medalist, a Swiftsure, and a 36-foot Hinckley Custom (as well as smaller boats) in an important contest. Only the 12-meter beat him boat for boat; he won easily against all others on corrected time. Another, writing from Florida, described how "in spite of a number of mistakes typical of a crew who had never worked together, the boat took the entire fleet to weather and finished first on both elapsed and corrected time with a safe margin."

The point is that for none of these S&S production-boat owners were their boats routine. They were very special creations, worthy of prideful care and attention, deserving the same kind of rough babying that Rod had given *Mustang*, delivering the same kind of gratifying results.

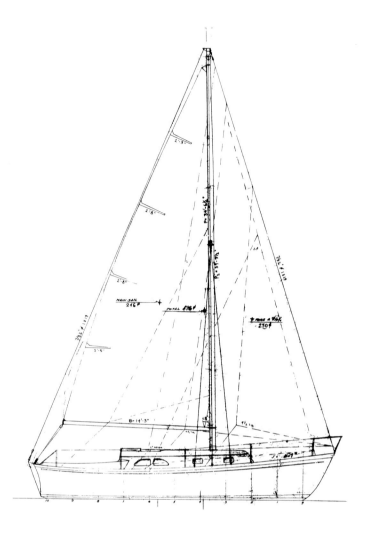

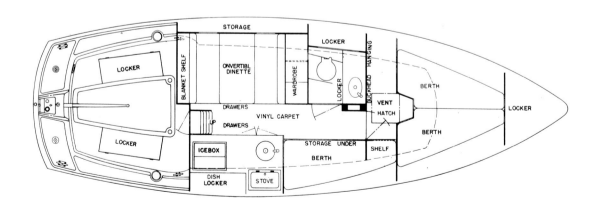

This page and facing page: Capri 30.

PJ 54 - Isanti - Design 1703

LOA: 54'   DWL: 41' 9"   Beam: 12' 9"   Draft: 5' 3"   Sail area: 1,075 sq. ft.

As the 1960s developed, boatbuilders realized that, even among production-boat buyers, there was a market for large-sized ocean cruisers. One of the first to understand that important shift—that is, that production boats sized 45 feet and above would be well received by large numbers of sailors (some of them new to the sport)—was Palmer Johnson of Sturgeon Bay, Wisconsin. Knocking on the Sparkman & Stephens door in 1962, the Palmer Johnson team requested plans for this aluminum, ketch-rigged motor-sailer.

When transferred from the drawing board to the water, *Isanti* (the prototype PJ 54) appeared to be much more of a true sailboat than a motor-sailer (even with her luxurious appointments below). The swiftness with which she moved contributed to that impression, as did her relatively low-lying house.

Indeed, there were those who said that, with the launching of *Isanti*, a new entity had been created: the fast cruiser. This was an invention that would increasingly prevail in American yacht construction; S&S would lead the way.

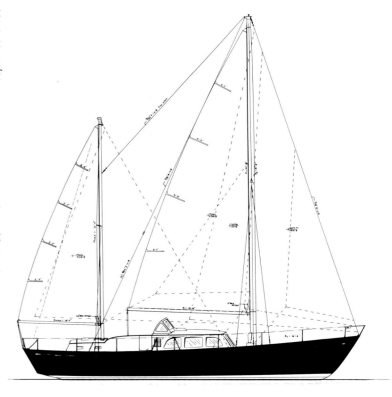

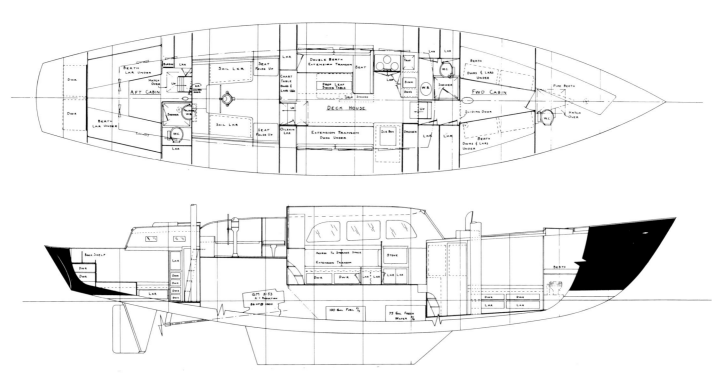

SS 34 – *Morning Cloud* – Design 1959

LOA: *33' 6"*   DWL: *24' 2"*   Beam: *10' 1"*   Draft: *5' 10"*   Sail area: *462 sq. ft.*

Perhaps the most famous of Sparkman & Stephens's production boats was the SS 34, produced in large numbers at the Winfield yard in England, beginning in 1968. She captured attention not only for her astonishing string of victories around the world (overall or prize winner in every Sydney-Hobart Race from 1969 through 1974) but also for the prominence of one of her owners: British prime minister Edward Heath.

Only a dinghy racer before his acquisition of *Morning Cloud*, Heath earned respect—for himself and for his close-winded wooden boat—by scoring class wins in every one of his first seven races. After one such punishing trial, Heath was quoted as saying, "The conditions were just about the roughest I've experienced. But she handles beautifully." She'd brought him through.

The SS 34, designed as an ocean racer, was really an updated version of the rugged Swan 36 (see next chapter). Like that splendid performer, the SS 34 keeps her engine and all other weight low; about half the weight of the boat (displacement of 22,520 pounds) is in the keel. *Morning Cloud* is also rather pinched forward (recalling the European racers of the fifties).

But in carrying her beam so far aft, she is unique and advanced for her day (1971). It should be noted that with some recent-day modifications, *Morning Cloud* is still winning races.

In her tiny forward stateroom are two pipe berths that may be folded up to make room for the impressive number of sail bags. *Morning Cloud* was equipped with a trim tab on the keel, adjustable by a separate tiller beneath the longer, regular tiller. A bit of a trick to handle.

As a result of the lavish publicity that resulted from *Morning Cloud*'s high-profile victories, and because of the boat's built-in virtues (including reasonable cost, $30,000 in 1968), SS 34 was an extremely popular boat. For the year 1969, Winfield planned to produce forty-eight of them; even before January, contracts for thirty-three had been signed, with six more pending. Yet in all this flurry of sales, S&S production supervisors allowed no slippage in quality. The managing director of Winfield wrote to an American yard, "as you know, Sparkman & Stephens are pretty tough about the people who sell their boats."

Glamour was surely visible on the surface. But it shone there because of the through-and-through quality of the product.

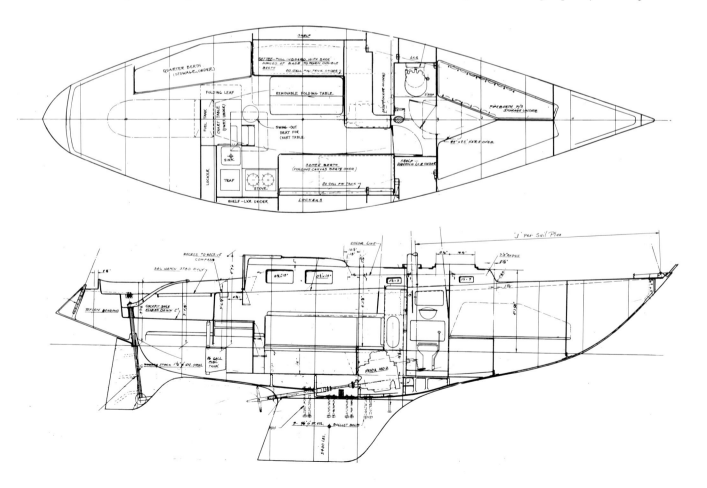

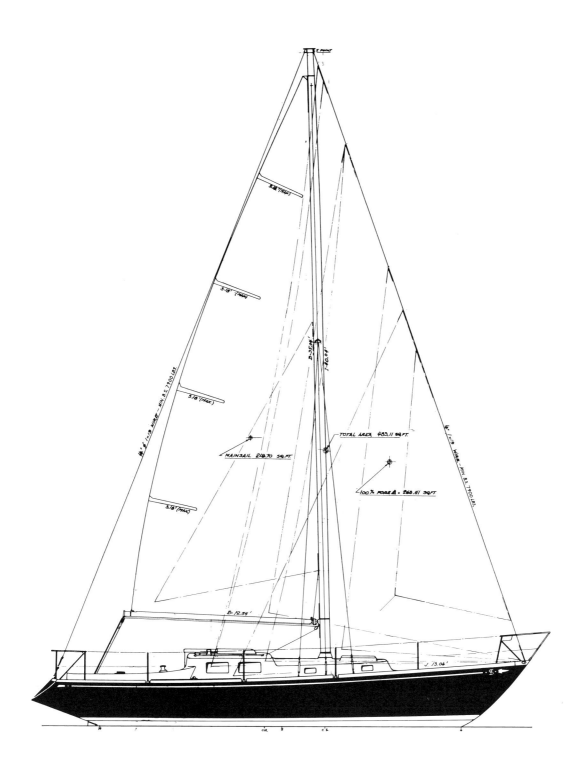

8

Fleets of Flying Swans

One day in the winter of 1966 when Rod Stephens was in Helsinki, Finland, pursuing again his long-enduring (and long-frustrated) expectation of building S&S boats in that country, he got a phone call at his hotel from Pekka Koskenkyla. He wanted to see Rod urgently. To test his seriousness, Rod explained that he was extremely busy and could only meet if the hour was set for 5:30 or 6:00 the next morning. Mr. Koskenkyla showed up promptly at 5:30; he was very serious indeed.

What he proposed was that he become the builder of a line of S&S yachts; in his little hometown of Pietarsaari on the Gulf of Bothnia there were many fine carpenters and ex–furniture makers, now unemployed, who could surely turn their talents to the building of magnificent boat interiors. Woods from Finland and Russia would be used (not always of the best quality, it must be admitted in retrospect), along with old-world craft techniques. And this could all be done at very low cost.

Rod immediately liked Pekka Koskenkyla and was willing to credit his dream. But he saw that the imaginative Finn was beginning with nothing, except a smart idea and a willingness to get up at 5:30 in the morning or do anything else necessary to sell his idea. He was not even a yachtsman or a yacht broker. He did have a bit of land up on the northern coast and he could assemble some corrugated sheds, etc. Yet along with no experience, he had no money for a complete and modern yard.

Rod concluded that the gamble was worth taking. And when he and Koskenkyla began to talk about what specific boat might be built at Pietarsaari, their thoughts turned to a dashing 36-foot S&S sloop (Design Number 1710) that, in wooden form, had already scored victories in England and the United States. Nautor—the name that Koskenkyla chose for his firm—would become the licensed builder of the fiberglass version of this boat (later called the Swan 36) throughout Europe.

When Rod traveled up to Pietarsaari to see a full-scale mock-up of the boat, he was "overwhelmed" by the excellence of the work. It was so beautiful, in fact, that Rod hesitated to make any corrections; nonetheless, urged to do so, he named a few adjustments that should be attempted, and these too were carried out with precision and style. The carpenters obviously knew their wood and their business. Under Rod's eye, the system would work.

Then another development: the management of Palmer Johnson in Sturgeon Bay, Wisconsin (one of America's most prestigious yards, whose association with S&S went back many years), having determined in 1968 that there appeared to be a market for larger-sized production yachts, came to New York and knocked on the S&S door to see what design, what yacht, might be the best to start with. At the same time, a Finnish official of Lloyds of London, named Ake Lindqvist, was in New York talking with S&S about a larger-sized yacht, perhaps 43 feet long. A coincidence was about to be turned to advantage.

Rod and Olin suggested that they knew a little yard in northern Finland which could turn out Lindqvist's boat, and that this might be the prototype of a new line for Palmer Johnson—the PJ 43s, known in Europe as Swan 43s. Koskenkyla, given a contract to build twenty-four of these tremendously popular S&S sloops, was then able to talk the government of Finland (which had always done everything possible to cooperate with Rod and his dream of Finnish S&S boats) into lending him enough money to build a state-of-the-art boatyard. Instantly, Nautor was big business.

Thus transpired Nautor's lengthy line of Swans: hundreds of handsome boats ranging from 36 to 76 feet. The most productive years for this creative partnership were between 1968 and 1973 when two Palmer Johnson engineers lived in Finland full time, working with Rod and Nautor personnel to turn out some of the finest production sailboats ever built. The molded fiberglass hulls were almost as artful as the magnificent interiors.

It might be said that Rod and the Palmer Johnson team brought the old-world craftsmen "up to speed," giving them a market in the modern yachting world. And, in the doing, they established new standards of design and execution for all modern production boats.

Even before Nautor split apart in 1983—mostly because an economic squeeze made for disharmony and increased wage demands—S&S determined that the relationship was no longer advantageous. Today, S&S is connected with that segment of the Nautor firm which became Baltic Yachts. There, too, the guiding principles worked out on the shores of the Gulf of Bothnia many years ago are still being refined, for the rest of the world to admire and perhaps to follow.

Facing page: Swan 48. See page 152.

Swan 36 - Cybele - Design 1710

LOA: 36'   DWL: 25' 6"   Beam: 9' 8"   Draft: 6'   Sail area: 545 sq. ft.

Smallest of the many S&S Swans that eventually flew forth from Finland, this swept-back keel sloop proved to be as fast in fiberglass as in the original wood, scoring impressive victories in Europe and Asia. With pleasing sheer and handsome ends (including a subtle, forward-slanting transom) she proved as sweet to watch as swift to sail.

Some threatened competitors had seen the original version as yet another "scourge of the Solent"—those recently built, S&S-designed sloops that were making mincemeat of European competition. *Clarionet* and *Roundabout* had headed that list, earning, as a type, the nicknames "Clairabouts" and "Terrible Twins." Then came *Cybele* (prototype for the Swan 36), and she was something of a surprise. She was smaller, with more sail and a number of innovative features.

The most important of those new ideas was an engine positioned lower and farther forward than normal, making better use of its weight. Access to the engine was wonderfully open and easy, directly under the aft settee cushions (as one of this book's authors remembers, appreciating not having to perform engine work in an airless locker astern). This location also freed up a generous stowage area between the quarterberths extending aft of the companionway. To gain more space in the roomy main cabin, the head was cleverly divided, with toilet to port and basin to starboard—all sealed off by sliding doors.

These radical, heavy driving sloops smashed their way through the seas and through the competition. Here's a letter from a Swan 36 owner in Hong Kong: "Although we were trailing last of the 12 yachts on the first leg, which was a spinnaker run (due to us fouling up the light spinnaker), we managed to start picking up once we were on the reach. With three quarters of the race behind, we were the leading boat, having finally passed *Reverie* (your Design Number 1254), after some windward tacking. During this duel with *Reverie*, I noticed we were able to point slightly higher than she. We were using the light genoa, with the zipper luff, which works extremely well in winds up to around 18 knots. *Reverie* managed to close the gap on the last run, but we were able to cross the line 3 minutes 2 seconds ahead, which gave us the win on corrected time of 26 minutes. The third boat was 40 minutes astern of us."

Along with scoring such sensational wins, it should also be mentioned that this power-packed sloop, as built in fiberglass by Nautor, also managed to fulfill another objective of production boats: she was a wise investment financially. Believe it or not, the Swan 36s of the 1960s cost English buyers only £8,500. Such were the blessings of Rod's Finland connection.

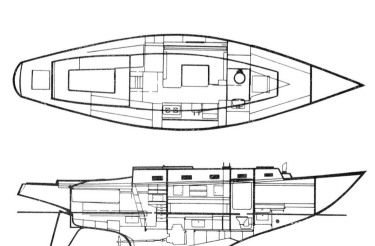

Swan 43 - *Casse Tete III* - Design 1973

LOA: 43'   DWL: 31'   Beam: 11' 8"   Draft: 6' 11"   Sail area: 807 sq. ft.

This is the boat that put Nautor and the flying Swan on the map—their very own S&S offering in Europe. She was immediately spotted as a leading contender for the Admiral's Cup. Although commentators had admiring things to say about the beauty and quality of the woodwork below, they focused mostly on her prospects as a winner—she appeared as dangerous as she was beautiful. One writer put it this way: "*Casse Tete* was designed as a fast cruiser rather than a racing machine—but she has been hotted up...."

Essentially, she carried the principles of the Swan 36—plus some new principles developed by S&S in the course of their 12-meter work—into the medium-sized racing-cruising class. And with her virtually flush deck (except for a small cabin house) and trim-tab-rigged keel, she was obviously ready to compete against the most sophisticated rivals. A very fine entry, which swells out gradually to firm bilge, and a lot of tumble-home made her seem a new, if not revolutionary, creature of the sea.

Casse Tete III was equipped with an "*Intrepid*-type" wheel mounted on the binnacle; this was in fact a double wheel which gave the helmsman fingertip control of the trim tab as well as of the rudder. Also of note was the special compartment reserved for the navigator: his own quarterberth, desk with padded seat, multiple lockers and drawers. Everything else more or less fell into place around that central helmsman-navigator axis.

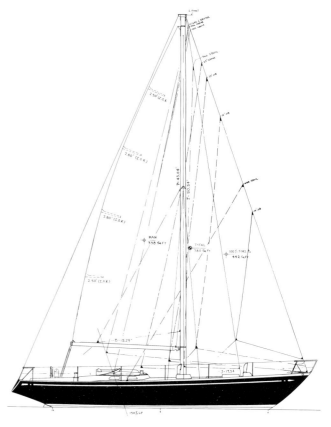

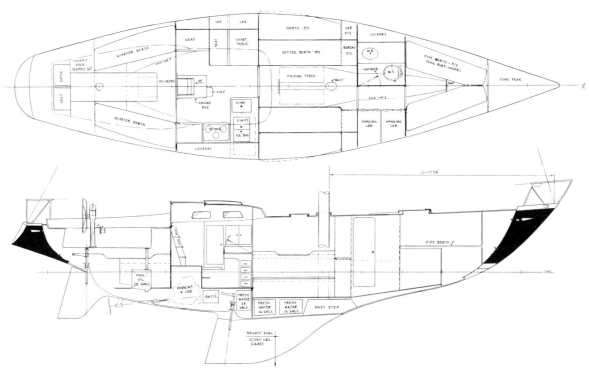

Swans 48, 38, 65, and 47 – Designs 2079, 2167, 2110, and 2201

Swan 48:   LOA: 48' 1"   DWL: 39'   Beam: 13' 7"   Draft: 7' 9"   Sail area: 1,059 sq. ft.

Swan 38:   LOA: 38'   DWL: 28' 8"   Beam: 11' 7"   Draft: 6' 4"   Sail area: 826 sq. ft.

Swan 65:   LOA: 64' 10"   DWL: 47'   Beam: 16' 4"   Draft: 9' 3"   Sail area: 1,554 sq. ft.

Swan 47:   LOA: 47' 7"   DWL: 34' 6"   Beam: 13' 6"   Draft: 7' 6"   Sail area: 1,060 sq. ft.

These extremely popular S&S designs were launched in the early and middle seventies. Common among them all is the streamlined, low-windage profile, with cabin house blending subtly into the crown of the deck. The decks seem completely uncluttered, spinnaker poles secured in recesses out of sight. Tuned up to the advanced standards and new materials of the day, the Swans were equipped with airfoil spreaders and stainless-steel rigging.

But for all their race-readiness, these are true yachts. Outer layers of varnished, hand-rubbed teak grace the edges of marine plywood structural bulkheads. Joiner work is all screw-fashioned or glued, with rounded corners. Cabin soles flatter the feet with holly-striped teak. Elegant indeed for fiberglass production craft.

Nautor offered the Swans to fortunate purchasers with either sloop or ketch rigs. And, under the watchful eyes of Rod and the Palmer Johnson team, they all met the highest standards. At the end of this period, when the economic position of Finland shifted and other factors urged change, Palmer Johnson separated from Nautor. Swans continue to fly, but the first flight has passed.

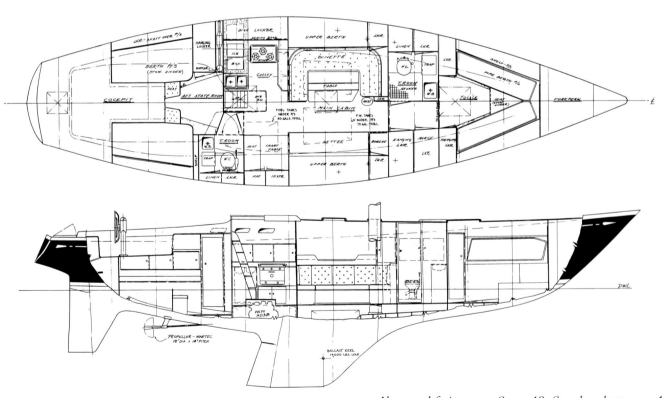

Above and facing page: Swan 48. See also photo page 146.

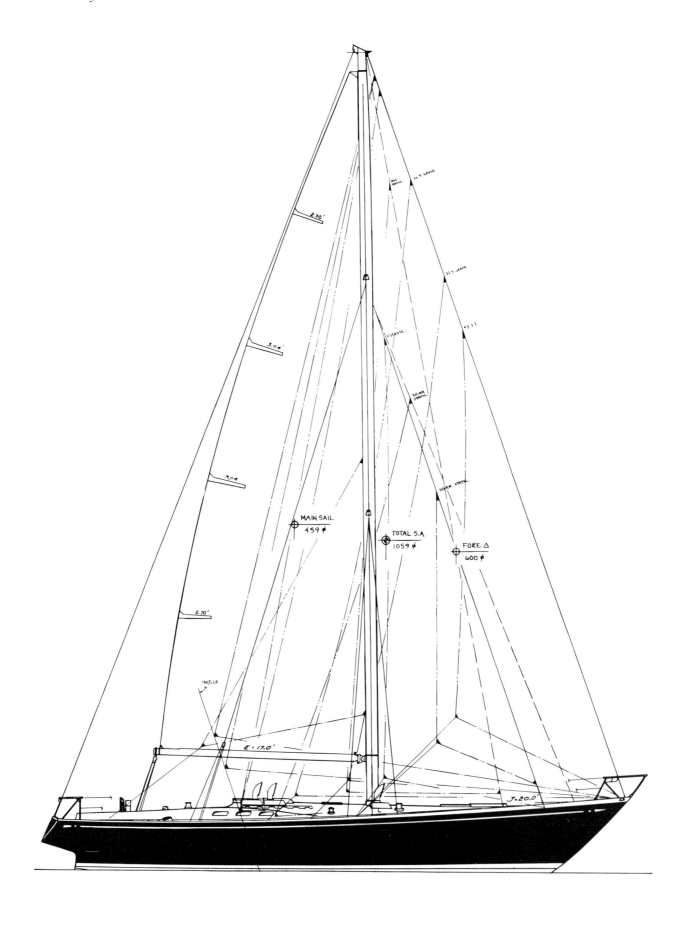

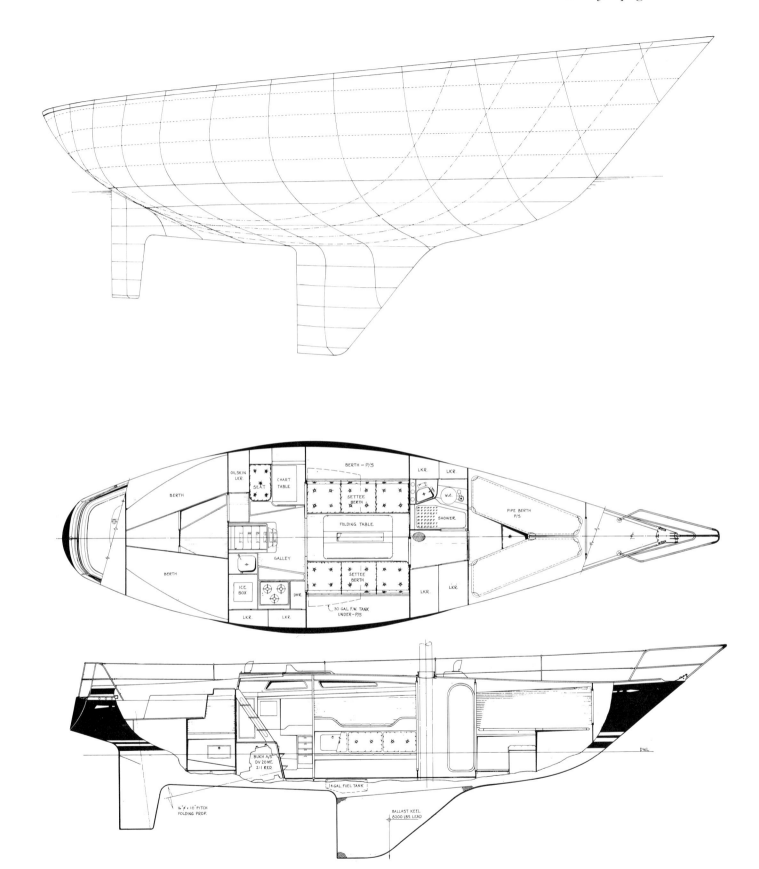

Facing page: Swan 48. This page: Swan 38.

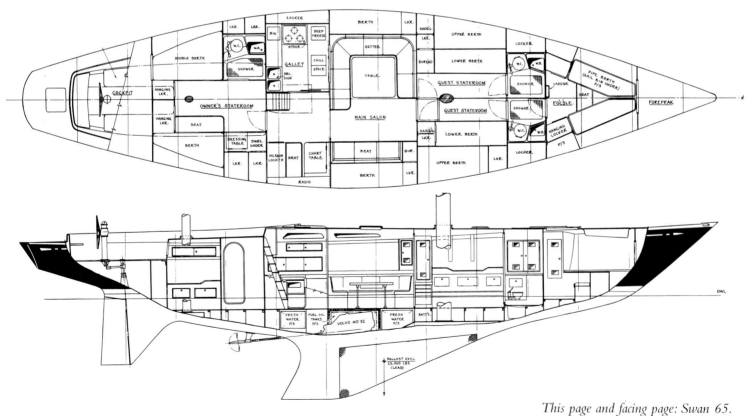

This page and facing page: Swan 65.

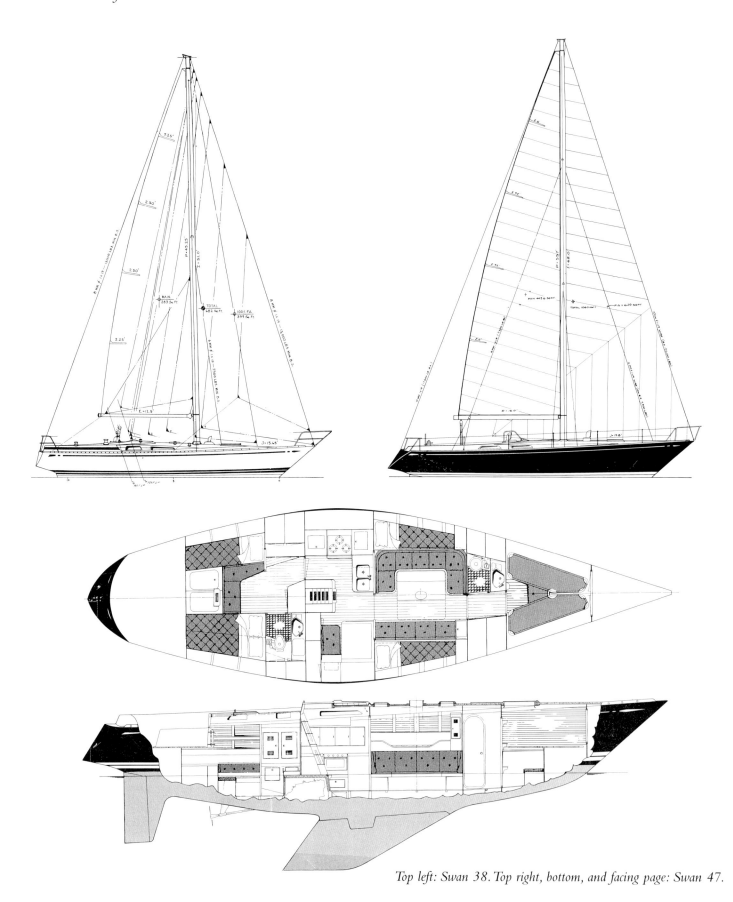

Top left: Swan 38. Top right, bottom, and facing page: Swan 47.

9

With a Surge of Power

Every summer weekday morning, after an early dip and shave and breakfast, your average Long Island millionaire of the 1920s would walk down the pier and step aboard his commuter yacht, then zoom off to Manhattan. In this delightful Gatsbyesque, prewar world, the powerboat was a necessary adjunct, if only because the railroad had not yet been completed all the way along the Island's "Gold Coast." The same could also be said for the moguls who chose to summer up the Hudson or out on the Connecticut shore: the commuting yacht, swift and elegant, was both a prerequisite and a perquisite.

For Sparkman & Stephens, designing such motor craft was a natural extension of their designing of sail yachts. And in the early thirties it seemed particularly important for the Stephens brothers to gain recognition in this prestigious part of naval architecture. Important to win prominence, it was also important to gain a part of the motorboat business, sure to grow in motor-crazy America.

Slim and opulent enough for princes, these sleek commuters are remembered as among the most refined of S&S creations. For that very reason, they seem rather unlikely as ancestors of the bulky, top-heavy craft that come to mind when "motorboat" is heard today. But, created in that earlier, gilded age, these commuter-cruisers did indeed point the way to some of the super-fast and super-glamorous yachts which Sparkman & Stephens has been designing recently. And, second, the developmental opportunity given by these early power craft to the S&S engineering staff led to the continuing brilliance of that department within the firm.

First engineer at S&S was a nearly forgotten man named Alexander George, who had come over to join Olin during the depression after the collapse of the firm where they both had worked earlier. Olin himself was far more interested in the styling and the hull shapes of the commuter yachts than in the engineering details. He left those to George—who had "his own, very interesting way of drawing." At the end of the 1930s, after the completion of the J-boat *Ranger*, the chief engineer's desk at S&S was taken over by Gil Wyland, an inspired and talented member of the team. It was on his shoulders (and those of his successor, Alan Gilbert) that S&S's reputation for engineering innovation and high-standard competence would rest.

Recognition of another sort should be given to early clients who kept returning to S&S for their motor craft and who kept those yachts parading so prominently across the yachting and society pages. Surely the most outstanding of these clients was Everett E. Dickinson, Jr., of Essex, Connecticut. Three boats designed for him are in the pages that follow. On the eve of launching, a fourth (named *Phoenix*) was totally consumed in a boatyard fire. Shocked but not discouraged, Mr. Dickinson immediately wired S&S to put in his order for *Phoenix II*.

It happens that the first S&S motor yacht (Design Number 3) was never built. Yet, because of the amazing, almost Talmudic number of detailed comments written upon her plans, it's possible to get from her a glimpse of S&S's concern that everything be exactly right. Some examples: an angle between a shelf and the inside of the hull forward was to be left "open for ventilation—very important"; the stem was to be "of white oak or hackmatack knee, or built up as shown dotted in"; on one of the few plain surfaces appear the words "this bulkhead may be paneled if desired." This meticulous exercise in contriving a dream boat led directly to the first commuter-cruiser, *El Nido*.

There is, as stated, a dramatic difference between those elegant, custom-designed and custom-built power yachts and the production motorboats of the postwar years. One obvious reason for that is sociological: the Great Gatsbys disappeared as a breed, and commuter-cruisers along with them. The new rich commuted not by sea but by land in club cars on rails.

World War II, which changed so many aspects of American life, also altered the way Americans (consumers and designers alike) thought about powerboats. They had seen miracles at sea during the war as specially created power craft stormed to victory on a number of fronts. S&S was a part of this desperate effort: Rod won the distinguished Armed Forces Medal of Freedom for his role in creating the amphibious trucks known as DUKWs. This was the distinctly non-yachty vehicle that successfully carried U.S. troops and supplies to landings in Sicily, Normandy, and a host of Pacific islands. The engineers at S&S also helped to conceive and construct a floating aluminum bridge that was something of a miracle in terms of strength and floatability per pound.

Given wonders of that magnitude, could not naval engineers now design some heavily powered pleasure boats for peacetime skippers? The answer was yes. According to Olin, the war was instrumental in encouraging the manufacture of far more potent power plants; these would be the 1,000-horsepower heavies that would drive the new generation of sailless boats.

Now bulky boats crammed with all sorts of live-aboard facilities could be made to go fast through the water; there was no longer a need to be stylishly slim. In an interview with John Trumpy, outstanding builder of postwar motor yachts, an equation was made between belowdecks volume and price per boat; the greater the interior volume, the more you could ask for the boat. Nothing else mattered much; aesthetics would have to follow along as best they could. Astonishingly, some of the cruisers from this era did achieve, particularly in the case of S&S-designed products, a chubby kind of handsomeness.

As the new era matured, it became clear that traditional naval architects, however skillful they might be at designing the details of cabin house and stern davits, were no longer the chiefs of the powerboats' creative team. That honor (when the builders stepped aside) went to the engineers. Fortunately, this catered to Sparkman & Stephens's strength: the department established by Gil Wyland, stepped up by the war and carried onward by Alan Gilbert, was prepared to build the high-speed motor yachts of the coming era.

And this they have been doing with full awareness of the traditions for excellence and stylishness set by the firm back when swiftness could only be attained by a slim and graceful hull. The new team's new hulls for clients all around the world add dynamism to grace, high-tech wizardry to eternal values of beauty at sea.

Facing page: Electron. *See page 170.*

El Nido - Design 76

LOA: 60' 2"   DWL: 58' 10"   Beam: 12' 6"   Draft: 3' 6"

The first commuter-cruiser designed for E. E. Dickinson, Jr., *El Nido* achieved a notable balance of design. In profile, she was functional but not boxy; with her unbroken sheer and raking house, she was trim but not trendily streamlined. Driven at 20 knots by her twin 275-horsepower engines, she got her owner to work on time.

No effort was made belowdecks to cram in a plethora of staterooms and facilities. Instead, two very large double staterooms occupy the whole space in the after part of the boat.

Dining saloon and "lounging room" are in the deckhouse. For those occasions when *El Nido* would be used for family cruising, a stateroom with upper and lower bunks was built in forward of the deckhouse and opposite the galley.

Upon the stock market crash of 1929 and in the depression years, economics forced Mr. Dickinson to keep *El Nido*'s trim modestly painted rather than elegantly varnished. Nonetheless, she was for many years a handsome sight on the waters of eastern Long Island Sound between Essex and Fishers Island.

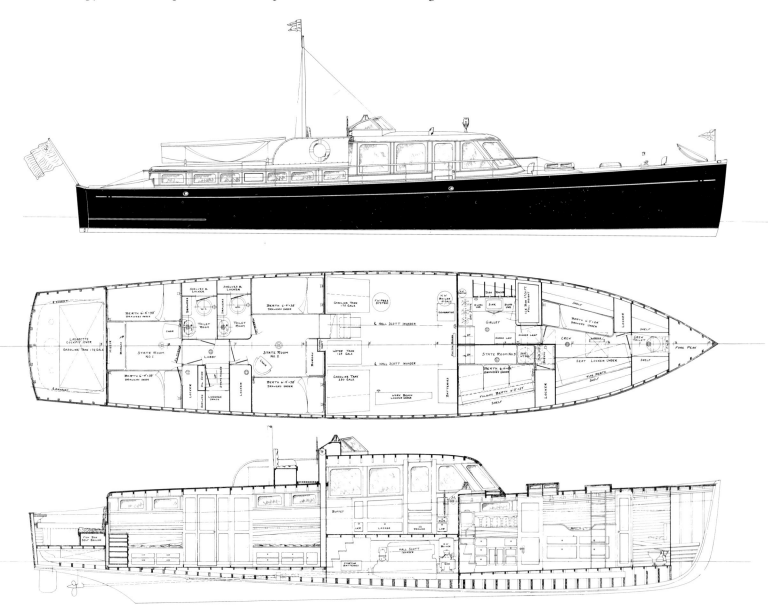

Avoca – Design 283

LOA: 68' 9"   DWL: 66' 4"   Beam: 13' 6"   Draft: 4'

Just before World War II, in 1939, E. E. Dickinson commissioned this most ambitious and speediest of *El Nido*'s younger sisters. *Avoca* resembles her predecessor in several ways, most notably in her continuous sheerline and her luxurious use of space below. Among the important differences are the available power (now the twins deliver 500 horsepower, presaging post-war plants) and the high, more commodious deckhouse.

Worth noting are the rake angles of forward windows, upper windshield, and mast. These angles play against each other in a way that has far more to do with art than science. All details of

davits, anchors, life-saving gear, etc. (including their shadows), are designed as important parts of the whole. Yet nothing is fussy or for effect alone.

Built at the Herreshoff yard in Bristol, Rhode Island, and engineered by Al George, *Avoca* proved rugged enough to achieve 31 mph in speed trials. Recognizing that it's a tough challenge for naval architect or engineer to combine light weight (so important for speed) with strength great enough to take punishment from non-compressible water, *Avoca* does indeed seem convincing evidence of George's mastery.

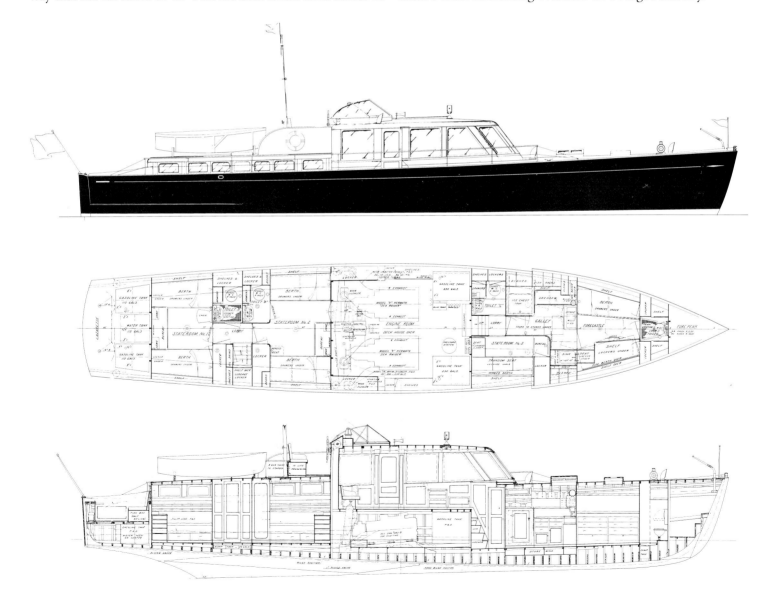

Above and below: Avoca.

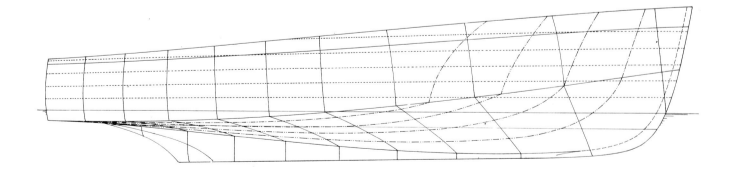

Escort – Design 334

LOA: 39' 10"   DWL: 39'   Beam: 9' 5"   Draft: 2' 9"

Escort was both a part of the tradition of the commuter-cruisers and a unique creation on her own. She served three owners well: built originally for William J. Strawbridge of Philadelphia in 1940, the handsome, 40-foot launch functioned as a naval vessel during World War II, then won renown as Briggs Cunningham's tender in the postwar years. A speedster, she was capable of whisking her owners along at 28½ mph.

Although her main purpose was to transport people on yachty errands in her capacious open cockpit, she did offer a small cabin below, with two berths, a mini galley, and head. Designed with a rounded bottom, *Escort* was easy and comfortable in a seaway; Olin admitted, however, that she might have been somewhat wetter than a vee-bottomed boat of the same size would have been.

Gleaming in the sun, correct flags snapping in the wind, she epitomized style under power.

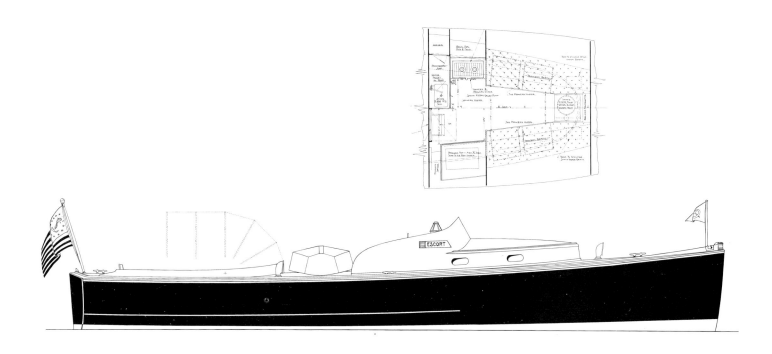

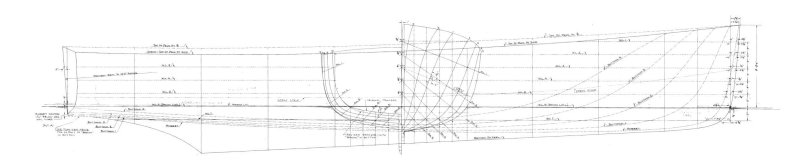

Dauntless - Design 621

LOA: 65' 10"   DWL: 62'   Beam: 17' 6"   Draft: 3' 1"

For Laurence Rockefeller, who lived up the Hudson River at Tarrytown, Sparkman & Stephens designed this extraordinary commuter-cruiser immediately after the war. Something of an anachronism—the era of the commuter having passed away in most parts of the world—she was both traditional and futuristic. That is, while harking back to the elegant, prewar *Whirlwind* (for which S&S had designed special propellers and gear boxes, for greater speed), *Dauntless* was built of aluminum and pow-ered by two PT-boat engines that delivered 1,350 horsepower each. With propellers churning at 2,400 rpm, she topped 40 knots in speed trials.

For a 65-foot yacht to have but one stateroom (plus crew's quarters) demonstrated that some Gatsby-era elegances endured from prewar years. Yet the fact that this commuter looked more like a PT-boat than a classic yacht demonstrated that change was at large.

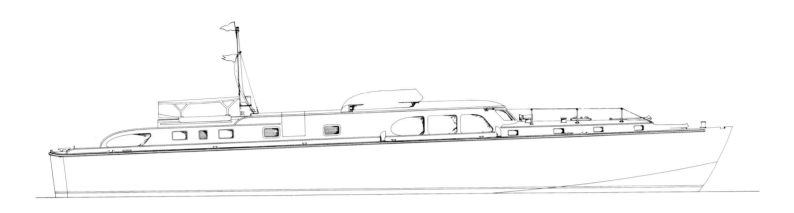

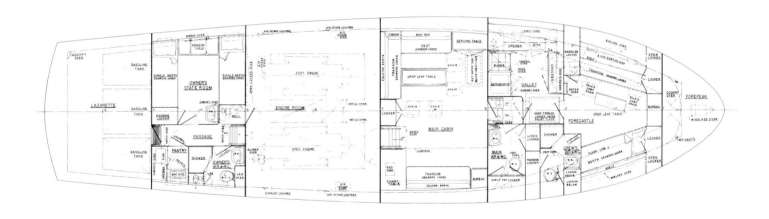

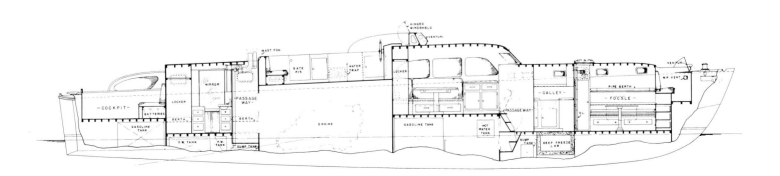

Alva – Design 809

LOA: 60'   DWL: 57' 9"   Beam: 16' 1"   Draft: 4' 1"

The last of Dickinson's S&S-designed, wooden power craft, *Alva* came off the boards in 1949. This was well after the era of the commuters; indeed, *Alva*, built by Trumpy as a cruiser, seems in many ways the embodiment of the new and less graceful power craft of the fifties and sixties. Swiftness was no longer the objective—she cruised at 12 to 14 knots—but comfort and weatherliness were.

Whereas *Avoca* was a grand launch with nice facilities, this is a live-aboard boat for long passages. And whereas *Avoca* was a delight only on calm "swordfish weather" seas, *Alva* could provide a pleasant passage under all conditions. One small flaw (presumably forced on the design team by the owner) is that the doors from the main deck to the deckhouse all swing inboard—very dangerous, as the doors could be burst open by the pressure of wind or the weight of a rogue wave.

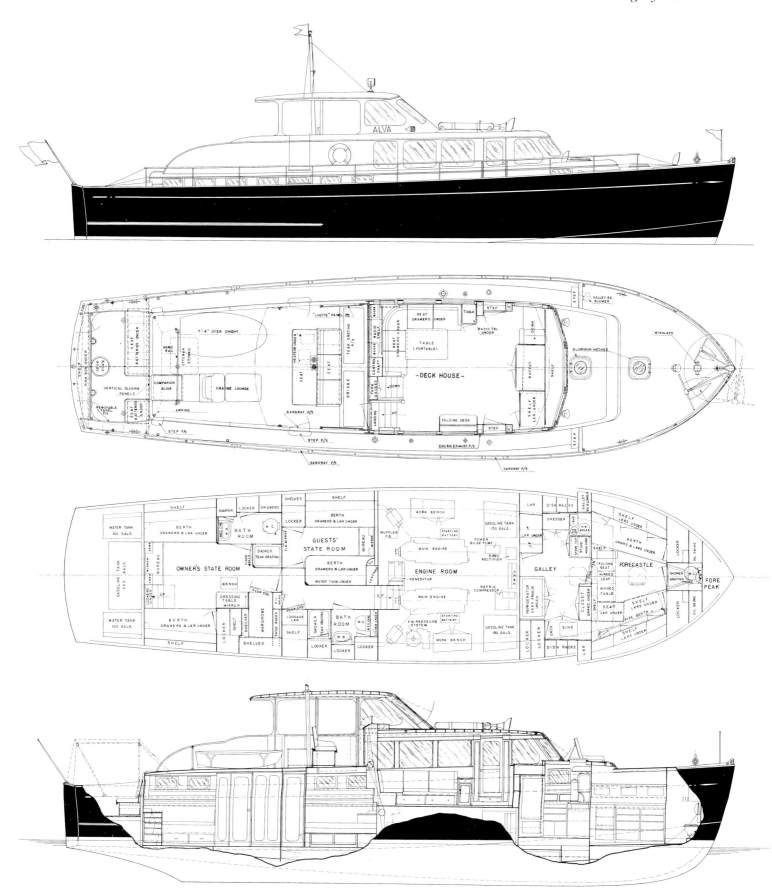

Electron – Design 1170

LOA: 82'   DWL: 77'   Beam: 18' 6"   Draft: 5'

This large power vessel is memorable because she represented a joint experiment by the Radio Corporation of America and Sparkman & Stephens to create the "Electronic Yacht." RCA was eager to have a virtual laboratory afloat in which many of its marine products could be tested. Therefore, this 1956 design was equipped with a 115-volt DC system; a rectifier for charging, starting, and lighting batteries; two generators driven by two GM 2-71 diesels; RDF with outside loop; radar, loran, and radio telephone; and a TV and hi-fi system. Perhaps it sounds a bit primitive today, but it was quite awesome then.

Renamed *Jarane* in later years, she remains an interesting yacht. All deckhouse windows have storm shutters; full air conditioning, annunciators, and an intercom telephone system complement the electronics. She has a Sperry automatic pilot and hydraulic steering for the twin rudders. Built of wood, with Philippine mahogany on white cedar for planking, her stem, keel, deadwood, and frames are of white oak.

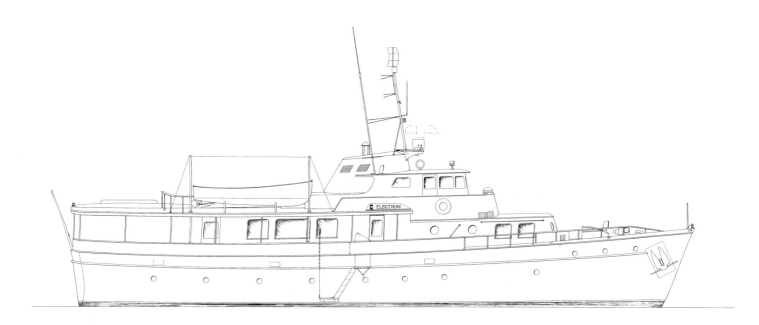

See photo page 160.

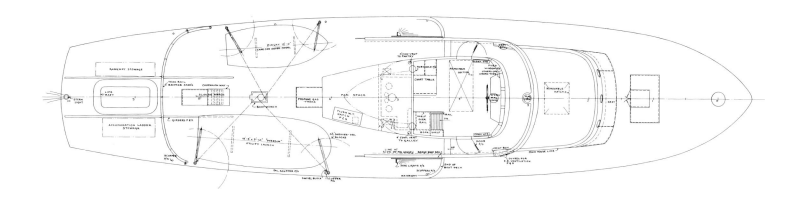

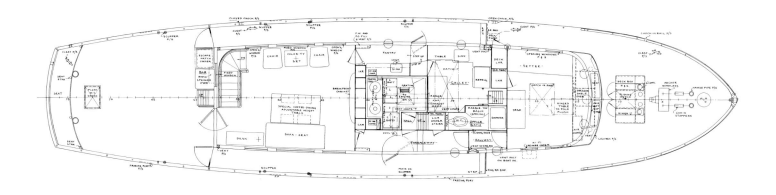

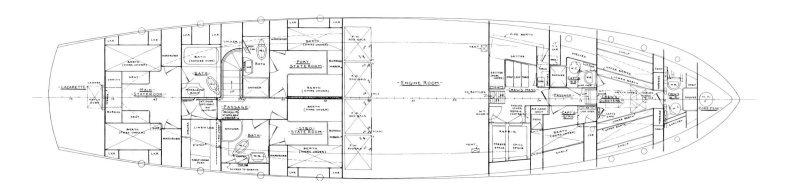

Explorer – Design 1492

LOA: 49' 1"   DWL: 45' 6"   Beam: 14' 6"   Draft: 4' 1"

This good-looking sport fisherman was intended to be a rugged and powerful offshore vessel for use in the Mediterranean. She was therefore powered by a pair of GM 4-71 diesels that could deliver a speed of 9 knots (10½ maximum) for a total cruising range of 400 nautical miles. The heavy construction of her wooden hull is emphasized aesthetically by the strong guardrail at deck level; the rail enables her to lie alongside a dock without fenders.

Explorer sleeps four in the owner's party in two staterooms—one amidships and one aft. Two crew members sleep in the generous fo'c'sle. As for any fish caught, they repose in the four refrigerated stowage boxes.

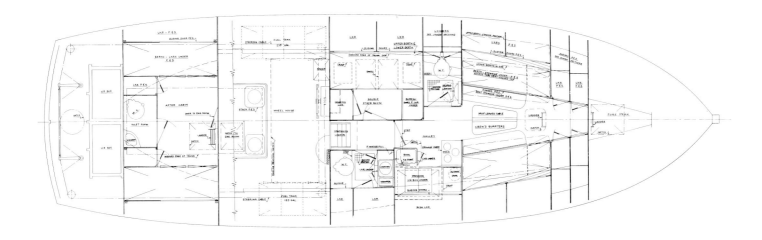

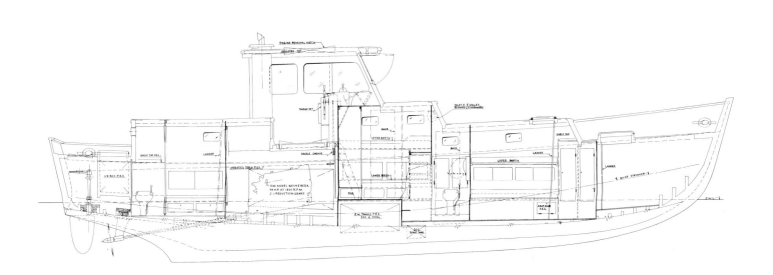

Lady Frances – Design 2512

LOA: 105'   DWL: 90' 9"   Beam: 23'   Draft: 4'

This majestic, water-jet-propelled vessel, designed in the mid-1980s, had a significant, creative effect on the mega-yachts that S&S would design in the next decade. Initially brought forth as a high-class production boat (called the Trident 105), she soon became so influenced by the unique program of her would-be owner that there was very little "production" about her. And that was the trend that would be followed into the years ahead: very big power yachts for very special and demanding clients.

Bill Langan of S&S and Paul Derecktor of the Derecktor yard in Mamaroneck shared design responsibilities, concentrating on construction integrity as much as on engineering and aesthetic design. The result—particularly when *Lady Frances* is charging along at maximum speed (30 knots)—is sensational.

Power is supplied by twin 1,960-horsepower MTU diesels driving the water jets (TB396/KaMeWa). Remarkably lightweight for her size (displacement of 110 tons), the hull has a deep vee stepped-chine that draws no more than 4 feet. The critical job of crafting the aluminum tunnels for the water jets called for precise geometry and inventive technology; the tunnels had to be fared and shaped so as to create a perfect bond between water and metal.

But for all the interior modishness and exterior dynamism, *Lady Frances* still somehow has the look of a proud S&S sailing yacht. Even Bob Derecktor said of her, "She's really built like a large racing sailboat." This is not one of your glitzy speed monsters, radical of shape and offensive of sound. From the conservative mast to the seaman-like bow and the unbroken sheer, this is a boat that continues a grand tradition.

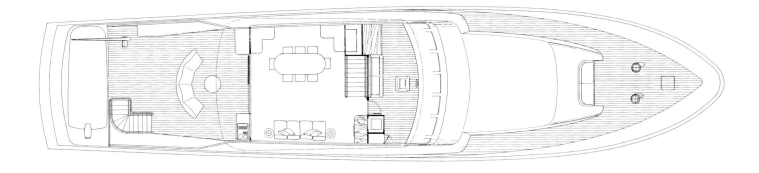

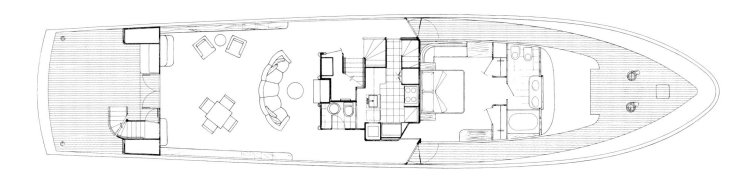

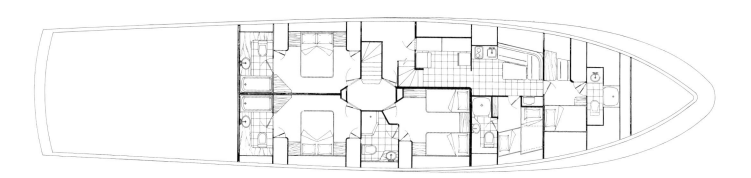

MIT-sea-AH – Design 2579

LOA: 112'   DWL: 96'   Beam: 23'   Draft: 6' 4"

Although its exterior has the aggressive, straight-lined look of a military vessel for some Great White Fleet of the future, the interior of this aluminum yacht can only be called sybaritic. A marble foyer, reached via a semicircular staircase, greets guests who have descended from the main deck (where the sauna-equipped owner's suite is located) to one or another of the four asymmetrical staterooms belowdecks. The commodious, 112-foot custom design represents the latest in the firm's thinking about how to continue honoring naval design traditions while expressing even more fully the dynamism and the rich possibilities of today's technology. In that spirit of remembered heritage and modern purpose, the vessel's name also has significance: *MIT-sea-AH* means "A Good Deal"—important to yachtsmen whether they speak Yankee or (in this case) Yiddish.

In contrast to *Lady Frances*, there is no attempt here aesthetically to recall the grand days of the tall ships or to recapitulate other classic yachts. In the manner of certain innovative modern yacht designs, a stylist was employed to work with S&S chief designer Bill Langan in order to create a distinctive look. A visitor immediately perceives the hand of such a special talent in the boat's luxurious, imaginative spaces (you can reach

the aft deck wet bar from the main saloon by passing through 6-foot, hydraulically operated glass doors)—an interior style plausibly referred to as "French deco." But that plushness does not trick up the sculpted trimness of the hull itself. "It's the outside of a boat people care about most," declares stylist Richard Liebowitz (who studied classical architecture in Rome and happens to be the son of the owner). "If a boat is going to be custom, it has to have a unique identity."

Then the problem becomes for the builder—once again the Derecktor yard—to construct that one-off creation in an accurate and efficient mode. Only by so doing will the project become, truly, a good deal for all. How well designer-builder coordination proceeded with *MIT-sea-AH* is demonstrated by her on-schedule delivery (launched in summer of 1993). It's also perceptible in the lack of vibration when her power plant is delivering either the demanded 25-knot cruising speed or the 29-knot sprint speed.

Vital to this harmonic coordination of concept and construction was S&S's highly experimental engineering program. After investigating the possibilities of a three-engine and shaft system, S&S's chief engineer Alan Gilbert settled on twin

MTU 12V396 main engines, each capable of 2,253 horse-power. Gilbert also saw to the design of special recesses in the hull for the five-bladed propellers, designed not to exceed the boat's shallow-draft requirement. The result is not only a very efficient propulsion system but one that is quiet too—even as quiet as the water-jet system of the *Lady Frances*. *MIT-sea-AH*'s owner, noting how little fuss she made when speeding along as if on an attack mission, remarked: "It's almost as if she were not moving at all."

The yacht-design industry has recognized and appreciated *MIT-sea-AH*'s unique design: the Super Yacht Society (an organization made up of builders, designers, and equipment manufacturers) awarded *MIT-sea-AH* their design award "Best Power for 1993."

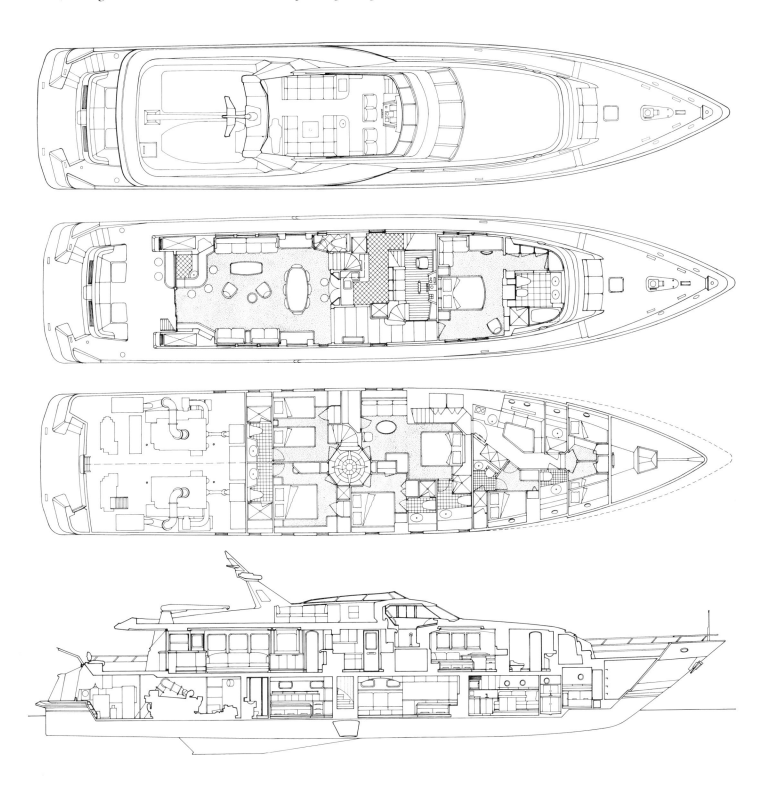

10

Rugged Motor-Sailers for Senior Sailors

We all know the type—if we are not the type ourselves. Slightly older than we used to be, anxious to keep our wives sailing with us, eager to have children and grandchildren along too, we want a sailboat that's not always over on her ear. She must have enough power to get the family home from long distances and through heavy weather. Yet she must really sail.

This type of senior sailor—the type who often came to Sparkman & Stephens requesting the design of a large but not too large powerboat that would actually be a sailboat of some panache (a motor-sailer, in other words)—seems to be somewhat on the wane today. Yet the motor-sailers that S&S produced before and after World War II for such clients have a special distinction about them that deserves to be recalled. Built mostly of wood, drawing from both seaboat and powerboat traditions, they make an impression unlike a modish sports car but like an ageless, custom-built limousine.

Olin Stephens recognizes that the rather tricky problem of designing a powerboat that sails well becomes less difficult as the size of the boat increases. That's all the truer beyond the 50- or 60-foot range. Yet Olin enjoyed the challenge in the early years, when boats were not mega-size, of creating distinctive yachts that were neither cramped nor awkward compromises.

He had before his eyes the rather wonderful, older line of motor-sailers named Bonnie Dundee, designed for Clifford Mallory, Sr. Although the first of these craft, designed for the senior Mallory by Nathanael Herreshoff, was a bit "brutal,"

with plumb ends and high freeboard, the second, designed by Luders, was an extremely handsome yacht. She served as an inspiration for both Olin and competitive designer Philip Rhodes. Another admirable line of American motor-sailers had been created by William H. Hand, who (according to Olin) had "one of the best eyes in the business." These Hand-designed classics tended to be for clients more interested in fishing well than in sailing well.

For that reason, the general run of motor-sailers came to be scorned in salty quarters—scorned as "fifty-fifties" because of their compromised rigs and hulls. But the best motor-sailers would go on to win respectability. The astonishing thing about the boats within this category designed by Olin and the S&S team in the fifty years between 1933 and 1983 is not only how competitive some of them have been as racers but also how varied many of them are, as boats for families and for sportsmen in the United States and abroad. They demonstrate, perhaps more than any other category, how (to repeat Rod Stephens's words) "Olin had a way of giving clients what they wanted."

The authors' suggestion, then, is that the following selected yachts be viewed as gifts—gifts from Sparkman & Stephens to the senior class of yachtsmen. We're speaking here of sailors of the stature of Irving Johnson and Harold Vanderbilt, yachtsmen who clearly deserved to be given the best of the best.

Facing page: Tamerlane. *See page 180.*

Tamerlane – Design 21

LOA: 65' 9"   DWL: 53'   Beam: 17' 2"   Draft: 5' 2"   Sail area: 1,517 sq. ft.

Regarding this handsome, early ketch, Rod Stephens would tell the following story. Her owner, George P. Knowles, Sr., was seen sailing along in the distance. When Rod caught up with *Tamerlane*, greetings were exchanged, as well as the unwelcome news that the motor-sailer had broken her drive shaft. To Rod's amazement, Mr. Knowles, having expressed once more his happiness with the design, proceeded to sail away on a new course. The fact of having no engine capability didn't seem to bother him at all on that balmy day.

By her sailability as well as many other features, *Tamerlane* established herself as the paradigm of the S&S lines of motor-sailers. Her distinctive profile—the low trunk cabins ahead and astern of the deckhouse; the nearly flush, gently rising deck—would be seen on many granddaughters to follow. And because these progeny could be rather heavy displacement boats (as opposed to powerboats of the same size), the accommodations could be kept low down and heavily constructed.

Typical of subsequent motor-sailers, *Tamerlane* had short spars and a shallow keel. An initial thought had been to provide her with a centerboard, but that was overruled in the interest of one less thing to worry about. And although Olin had feared that that would mean the owner would have to use the engine to bring her through the wind on a tack, that maneuver proved to be no problem under normal conditions.

Beyond her gracious deckhouse, the glory of *Tamerlane* was her roominess below. Access to the owner's cabin forward was via a separate scuttle. Another interesting feature was the location of the galley—aft, between the deckhouse and the crew's quarters.

Produced at the Lawley yard in 1933, *Tamerlane* would go on to provide many decades of good sailing (and 9-knot powering) for successive owners.

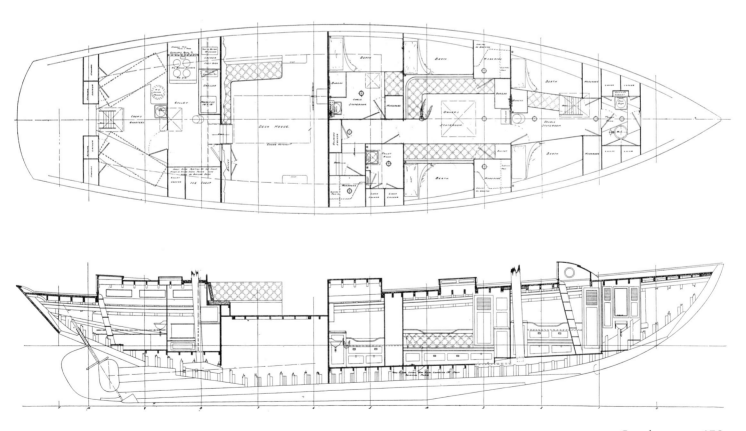

See photo page 178.

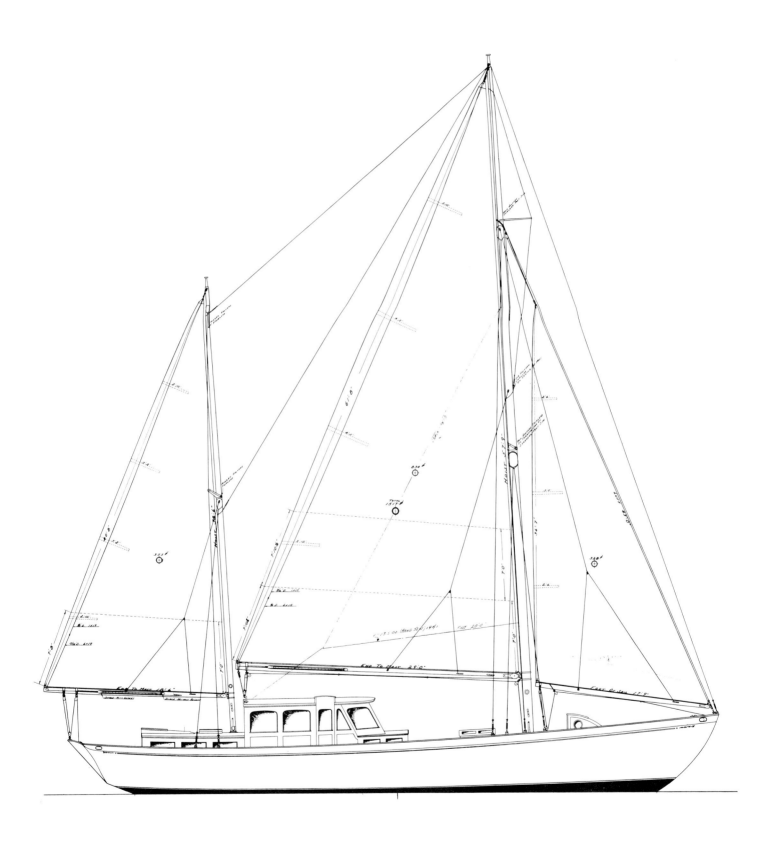

Versatile – Design 873

LOA: 88' 9"   DWL: 74' 6"   Beam: 20' 6"   Draft: 7'   Sail area: 2,475 sq. ft.

For the distinguished yachtsman Harold S. Vanderbilt, with whom the Stephens brothers had enjoyed so much sailing, S&S designed this formidable motor-sailer. Built in 1949, she represented Mr. Vanderbilt's return to sea after ten years of wartime service and being "on the beach." With lingering affection, Olin recalls this very individualistic creation as "more of a trawler than anything else."

Double-ended, and with a high-rising sea bow, she does indeed look as if she were setting forth to the Grand Banks. But, in fact, she's a highly sophisticated pleasure yacht, with bridge table built into the lounge. Aft of the partially sunken deck-house is a kind of open verandah. Forward of the palatial master stateroom (with tub) are two commodious guest staterooms.

The ketch rig has sufficient power to drive the husky, sea-going hull; the ten tons of ballast on the keel helps assure that those sailing runs will not be at much of an angle. Mechanical power is supplied by twin GM diesels, delivering enough horsepower (185) to keep *Versatile* surging along at 10 knots. Unusually capacious tanks make sure that she can cruise some 1,750 miles at sea before needing to refuel.

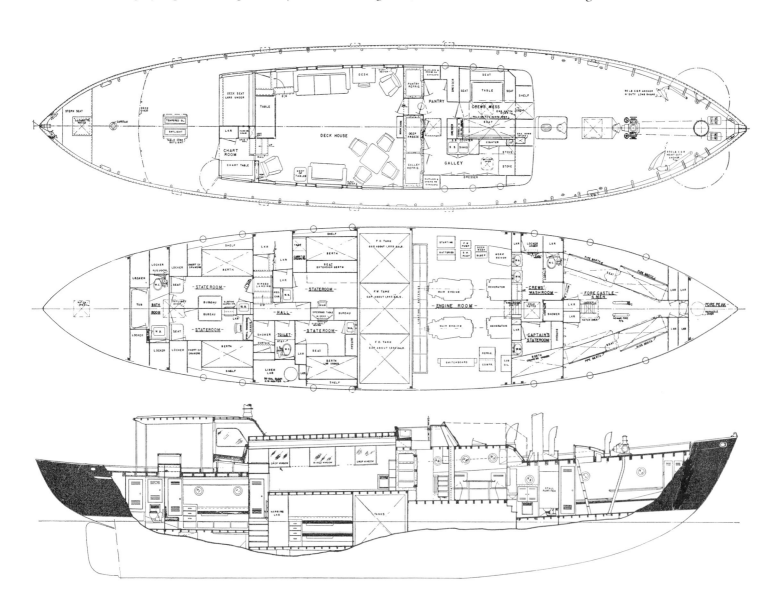

Anna Marina – Design 915

LOA: 63' 10"   DWL: 46' 6"   Beam: 14' 6"   Draft: 8'   Sail area: 1,909 sq. ft.

Rod Stephens concurred with Olin that this motor-sailer is perhaps the best cruising boat to come off the S&S boards. Built for a Swedish client at the Bengt Plym yard in 1950 and equipped with a tall rig, she proved almost embarrassingly fast, slipping past even some of S&S's own European racers.

Like the ancient *Tamerlane*, *Anna Marina* has a long, shallow keel. But unlike *Tamerlane*, she is narrow as an arrow, along the lines of *Refanut* (whom she beat). Accordingly, her accommodations below seem rather tight—with the exception of the generous, "sunken" deckhouse. Note that, here too, the galley is aft, beneath the bridge deck.

When she was first built, a GM diesel engine moved her at a cruising speed of 8.5 knots—at those rare times when sail did not suffice.

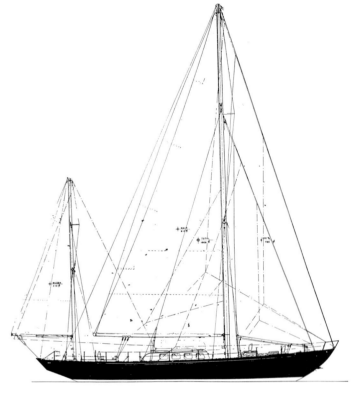

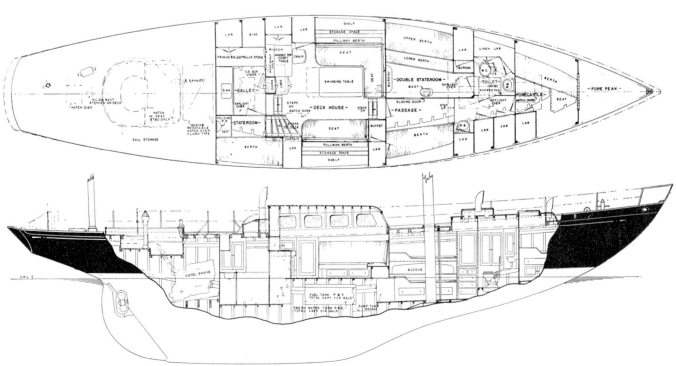

Palawan – Design 991

LOA: 47' 3"   DWL: 32' 6"   Beam: 11' 3"   Draft: 6' 8"   Sail area: 1,065 sq. ft.

This is the sixth boat of the same name designed for Thomas J. Watson, Jr., by S&S—each one of them suited to the racing/cruising style that that yachtsman favored at the time. By 1983 when *Palawan* was designed, Mr. Watson was more interested in having a proper vessel for children and grandchildren than in single-handed adventures or racing victories.

Though completely modern in appearance, *Palawan* still carries on the *Tamerlane* theme. But, more like *Anna Marina*, she is long and lean and easily driven by her lofty rig. Constructed of aluminum, she displaces 53,000 pounds; more important, her displacement/length ratio is only 285, comparable to that of fast cruisers.

After all his years of cruising, Mr. Watson felt that "in order to put the guests on an equal footing with the owners, they should be given a large stateroom and head with shower." The forward stateroom is therefore as large as the master cabin. But because this *Palawan* was also designed in anticipation of several grandchildren being aboard, the forward stateroom is equipped with a divider that allows it to be split in two, each compartment provided with upper and lower bunks. Additional children and grandchildren may be accommodated in the main cabin.

With family and crew aboard, the first cruise planned on *Palawan* was from Helsinki down the Baltic Sea, through the Gota Canal and the Danish islands, then through the Kiel Canal and on to Cowes. Under discussion was whether to sail home via the Atlantic or Pacific. With this kind of boat, there's no need for adventures to end.

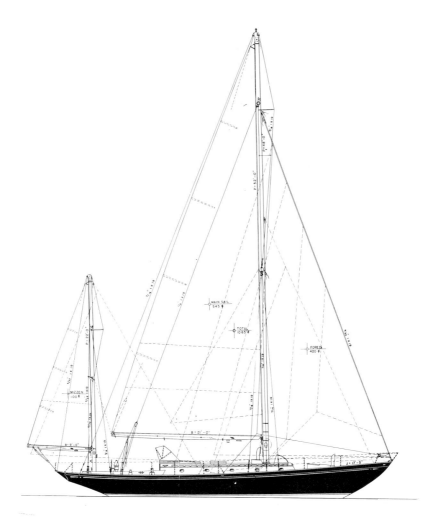

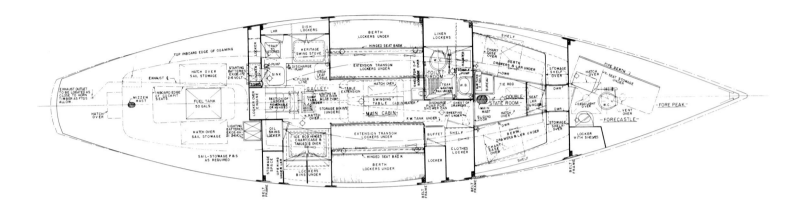

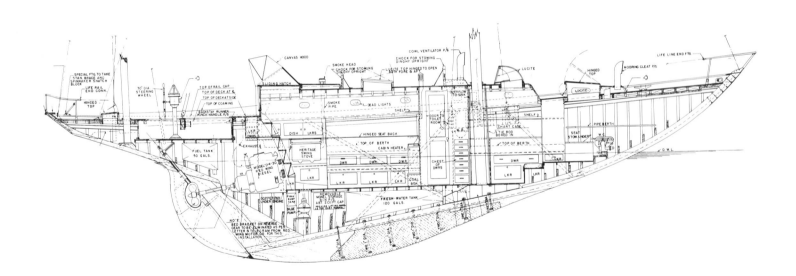

This page: Palawan.

Yankee – Design 1278

LOA: 50' 7"   DWL: 42' 6"   Beam: 15' 4"   Draft: 4'   Sail area: 1,323 sq. ft.

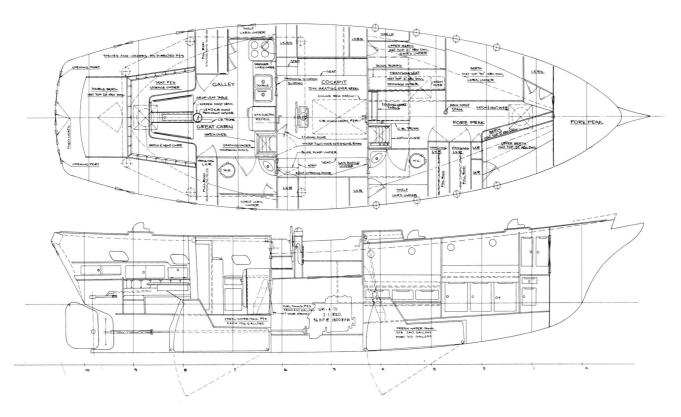

After you've sailed around the world seven times and spent uncountable days at sea on square riggers and ocean voyagers of all kinds, where do you want to go on what kind of boat? The answer for renowned seaman Irving Johnson was inland cruising on board the steel motor-sailer ketch *Yankee*, a project on which he worked with Olin and Rod Stephens—and his wife, Electra—for many months and years.

The Johnsons were convinced after much experience that the pleasure of inland cruising would be "vastly increased by having a boat that was built to run aground." Though that might seem a contradiction to a seaman, to this couple (with eyes set on the waterways of Europe) it was a tremendous practicality. Furthermore, the two centerboards, desirable for better boat handling at sea, could also be useful at a canal lock for digging into the bottom when it was necessary to hold fast.

A radical and unusual vessel, *Yankee* is nonetheless as traditionally good-looking as a character boat can be, with her clipper bow and raised poop deck. Below, the main feature is the "Great Cabin," lighted by ports in trail boards and transom. Johnson joked that what he'd asked Olin to design for him was "a cross between *Finisterre* and the *Mayflower*."

The masts, stepped in on-deck tabernacles, can be lowered when passing through the tunnels and bridges of the European canals. When raised, the masts can carry a fair spread of sail, including the "mule" which is set on the main backstay and sheeted to the head of the mizzen. Power is supplied by a GM 3-71 diesel with hydraulic clutch and two-to-one reduction, turning a three-bladed, single screw.

Ever the adventurer, Irving Johnson found it entertaining to climb to the spreaders and steer from there with a remote control device. This allowed him to look over the canal and river banks and see the exotic lands through which he passed.

This page: Yankee.

Egret – Design 1331

LOA: 56' 6"   DWL: 47'   Beam: 15' 3"   Draft: 4' 7"   Sail area: 1,361 sq. ft.

This rugged, beautifully proportioned wooden ketch was designed for C. Porter Schutt, member of the Du Pont family and the New York Yacht Club. She was thus, intensely, a family boat and a club racing boat.

Despite her pedigree as a descendant of non-competitive *Tamerlane*, *Egret* proved herself a very competent racer. For example, in the 30-mile Nassau Cup race of 1961 (which featured a 15- to 18-knot easterly, mostly abeam), she finished second in the fleet, only two and a half minutes on actual time behind the famous, 73-foot *Ticonderoga*. On corrected time, *Egret* was fourth in the fleet. Not bad for a motor-sailer.

An English writer wrote of *Egret* that, because she was not a "motor boat with a sail," she was a "most interesting example of a type of yacht of which there are very few in Britain." He went on to say: "A large centreplate [board] will help her to windward, but the most significant fitting is the coffee grinder winch on the counter which proves, if proof were necessary, that *Egret* does not carry masts for decoration; despite the 167 b.h.p. diesel engine."

In American terms, that engine's a four-cylinder, 151-horsepower GM 4-71 diesel, driving a 28-inch wheel through two-to-one reduction gears. *Egret*'s speed under power is about 8.5 knots. When in a cruising mode, and with 560 gallons of fuel aboard, *Egret* has a range under power alone of 780 miles.

In keeping with the family purpose of the vessel, there's a large-sized stateroom with head forward in addition to the owner's stateroom aft. Hardly the layout of a stripped-down racer. But look out.

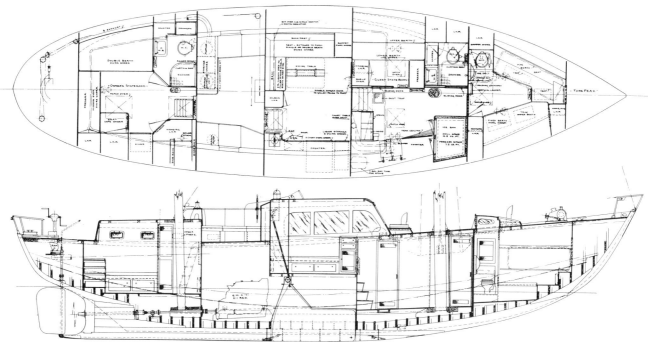

Pavane II – Design 1428

LOA: 52' 11"   DWL: 43' 4"   Beam: 14' 6"   Draft: 4' 4"   Sail area: 1,194 sq. ft.

This steel sloop, launched in 1959, might be considered the epitome of motor-sailers of that period. She presents many special features, such as the small cockpit far astern (intended primarily for fishing) and deep centerboard for increased windward performance. Nonetheless, the basic *Tamerlane* pattern of trunk cabins fore and aft of the deckhouse can be glimpsed—almost as traces of the unforgettable past. As Olin expresses it, "I was working within a kind of tradition, but I always wanted to give the owner something different, something right for him."

Another unique feature of *Pavane II* is the backing rudder, located just above and in front of the propeller. This extra steering aid, derived from river towboats, throws the reverse propeller wash to port or starboard, as desired, enabling the helmsman to back into marina slips with added agility. When the engine is in forward drive, this backing rudder is locked fore and aft.

Pavane's sail plan shows a roller-reefing boom and a crow's nest on the mainmast at the height of the lower spreaders. While useful for fish-spotting purposes, this perch, accessible by ratlines, is also helpful when threading through rock-littered straits.

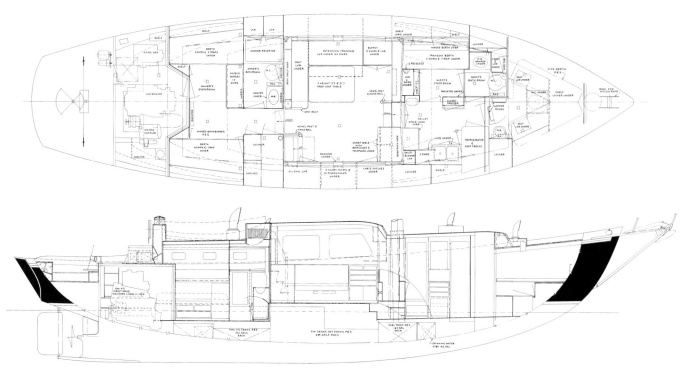

11

The Saga of the Twelves

"I don't really see why there's all this fuss about 12-meters," said the stately woman sitting beside one of this book's authors at a Newport dinner a couple of decades ago. "When I was a girl, everyone had a twelve; we just sailed them against each other, and nobody thought anything about it." Perhaps then, but times have changed since 1930.

By 1938, Harold Vanderbilt recognized that, with the apparent decline of the really big boats (like *Ranger*, his peerless J), the 70-foot-long twelves were where the action was. That was true both in this country (where active fleets sailed Long Island Sound, Block Island Sound, and many other sounds of the wealthy) and abroad (where both England and Germany and other nations competed in twelves even as war clouds gathered). For Vanderbilt, S&S designed the brilliant *Vim* (profiled in this chapter), clearly the best of her prewar generation.

But then there occurred a curious blank in the pages of 12-meter history. This was occasioned not only by the disruptions of war but also by the new spirit of yachtsmen in the late forties and fifties: as mentioned earlier, these sailors were more inclined to go cruising or racing with their families in husky boats like *Revonoc* and *Finisterre* than to charge around the buoys in fragile, large-sized one-designs. So for nearly a dozen years after the launching of *Vim*, no one saw a place for her or other twelves in the yachting spectrum. *Vim* herself stayed laid up at the Nevins yard, wrapped in canvas and forgotten.

What changed all this, what turned the 12-meters into the most exciting class in the world, were two factors: first, the mounting enthusiasm of certain leaders within American racing who rediscovered the virtues of these grand yachts; second, the maneuver by the New York Yacht Club to change the deed of gift of the America's Cup so that challenges for the cup would be raced in twelves. That legal alteration was accompanied by the important provision that challengers no longer had to sail from their own countries to this one on their own bottoms (which would be very difficult for twelves).

Yet there's another answer to the question of the Newport woman about the sudden and unexpected appearance of twelves as the most important racing boats in the world. As the excitement of competition for the America's Cup increased in the fifties, sixties, and seventies (with all but one of the select-

ed defenders being designed by S&S), the spin-off benefits to other racing craft increased too. The press for ever more innovative, ever more high-tech solutions seemed to be most intense at the level of the twelves...so the world watched.

The glamour of this class also contributed to the broadened appeal of the entire sport of racing. Joining the Old Guard of yachting families were new sportsmen determined to win recognition for themselves and their countries. Publicity about the personalities who raced the twelves and about the fortunes spent on designing and outfitting the twelves made sailing seem like what a prince or a prime minister or a media king must do to win fame.

Premier designers of the twelves during this exciting, experimental era were the imaginative team at Sparkman & Stephens. Press stories of how Olin Stephens used the test tank to derive helpful data for 12-meter designs—and how Rod Stephens plotted new deck layouts—leaped from the sports pages to the front pages. In the fifties, the world's attention focused on *Columbia*, the first S&S twelve of the postwar period. After *Columbia*'s clean-sweep victory over the British *Sceptre* in 1950, *Constellation* came forth from the boards at S&S in the early sixties. And after her thrashing of the British *Sovereign*, the snub-nosed, innovative *Intrepid* was unveiled in 1967, to score a total wipeout of the Australian *Gretel*. Olin and the brilliant young team of designers who worked under his tutelage seemed incapable of designing anything but winners.

Nor were Olin's contributions restricted to the design boards. Just as Rod was an active presence on the front line, making sure that rig and layout and crew all functioned perfectly, so Olin provided personal inspiration for the racing team. He not only served often as helmsman in the fifties and sixties but also functioned as manager of the prima donnas and true geniuses (like Briggs Cunningham and Bob Bavier) who were involved in the defense effort. A part of the secret of the Stephens designs' victories was that Olin got the most from the skippers and crews who sailed them.

Then came the embarrassment of the S&S 12-meter *Valiant* (1970), which sportswriters instantly branded a "dud." In Olin's terms *Valiant* "was too extreme"; it seemed to him that she bombed because she was a departure from the "reasonable bal-

Facing page: Intrepid. *See page 202.*

ance" that S&S designs had always represented. Perhaps, he mused, he had been lured into that extreme by too much devotion to the test tank results and to computer-drafted solutions. Henceforth he would stay away from those deviations.

His next twelve, the lovely and light (aluminum) *Courageous*, was a total redemption: she obliterated the Australian *Southern Cross* in 1974 and went on to beat *Australia* in 1977. In 1980, with Olin in semi-retirement, *Freedom* (designed in collaboration with S&S's new chief, Bill Langan) scored new triumphs for the country and the firm.

But leadership of the defense of the America's Cup had then fallen to such bold personalities as Dennis Conner. When he vetoed S&S cooperation on designing *Liberty*—a new twelve slated to compete against *Spirit of America* (designed by Olin and Bill Langan) and another boat for the honor of defending the cup—it was clear that an organized attempt to move the

defense away from S&S was afoot. "I've never seen Olin so mad," Bill Langan recalls. "And Rod said that he'd only seen him angry three times before in all their seventy years together!"

It should be noted that *Liberty* (designed without S&S) was the U.S. twelve fated to lose the cup to Australia in 1983. Also that, in all the years before and after the loss to Australia, not one S&S twelve has lost a single match to any foreign twelve in America's Cup competition. This record-making defense of a national treasure (as well as the concepts tested and the standards established by S&S twelves) speaks for itself. As new generations polish and repolish the cup, and as S&S staff members continue to consult with creators of cup contenders of the new classes, the historic contribution of Sparkman & Stephens seems to shine ever more brightly.

Nyala and Vim – Designs 214 and 279

Nyala: LOA: 68' 4"   DWL: 47'   Beam: 11' 5"   Draft: 9' 2"   Sail area: 953 sq. ft.

Vim: LOA: 69' 7"   DWL: 45'   Beam: 12'   Draft: 8' 11"   Sail area: 1,916 sq. ft.

These memorable twelves were built in 1938 and 1939, respectively, at the height of the prewar flowering of the class. As mentioned above, Harold Vanderbilt's *Vim*, a design project calling for some forty-one completed drawings, won renown soon after launching as "the fastest 12-meter in the world." She was also the first twelve to have bar rigging and an aluminum mast—premonitions of high-tech improvements to come.

But *Vim* had to go through the indignity of many years under a tarpaulin before she emerged as a force in the postwar yachting world. In the fall of 1949, W. M. Dickerson chartered her from Vanderbilt and completely updated her. There's the oft-told story here of how, the very day after *Vim* was moved into a secure shed for the rebuilding, the site where she'd been resting all those years was totally wrecked by a storm of near-hurricane force. This boat was clearly destined to survive.

Engelina Dickerson has written of what it was like to be aboard in those exciting years after *Vim* was recommissioned. "I remember particularly the day in Buzzard's Bay when *Vim* was jockeying for position before the race for the Astor Cup. The renowned Sou'wester was up to a steady 15. One other twelve sailed in the same class, as did *Bolero*, *Baruna*, *Windigo*, and *Cotton Blossom*, all over 70 ft. long, plus a few more of well over 50 ft. A minute and a half to our start and suddenly the

tension was there! Every headstay carried its largest genoa; every hull approached its top speed; every skipper was dedicated to be on the line as the gun went off. Not more than a boat length, and in many cases, less, separated boat from boat. The absolute silence was broken only by the surge of the seas past the shining topsides, the harping of the wind in the rigging and an occasional 'Room! Room! You've got to give me room...' But there was no room. One mistake at the helm, one sheet let go too soon, one instant's loss of control could precipitate an unimaginable tangle of rigging, crashing spars, crumbled topsides and crushed bodies—disaster. In that minute and a half I suddenly understood the lure of the big boat and the thrill of knowing that you have under you the fastest of them all."

It was a spectacle that entranced more than the onboard participants: the sophisticated sporting world loved it, with its gleaming grandeur. It was on the basis of this very special appeal that New York Yacht Club commodore Henry Sears was able to convince the officials that the struggle for the America's Cup should henceforth be waged in 12-meter yachts. *Vim*'s role in the years immediately to follow was that of the supercompetent elder sister. Beat me if you can, you youngsters!

Harold Vanderbilt once had written: "Mistakes are made frequently in yacht races. Fortune smiles on the yacht that

Facing page: Vim.

makes the fewest." So *Vim*'s now-owner John Matthews, having been informed that it was possible in modern times for someone to design and build a boat perhaps 3 percent faster than *Vim*, determined to make her just as fast as possible. In a mid-fifties rebuild, she was lightened and stripped internally to the minimum required by the 12-meter rule. Furthermore, on Rod Stephens's advice, chain plates were strengthened, sail area slightly reduced, and ballast increased; new bar standing rigging was installed, all running rigging replaced, and old winches modernized plus new coffee grinders added. She was all set to race against the new generation.

And it was by but a whisker that *Vim* (sailed by Bus Mosbacher) lost the defender contest of 1958 to the innovative S&S contender *Columbia* (sailed by Briggs Cunningham).

Specifically, that whisker of superiority was the improved training on board *Columbia*; forsaking earlier casualness, the *Columbia* crew realized it had to shape up, to fight harder than the *Vim* crew. They finally fought so hard in the multiple-tack exchanges that exhaustion was recognized as a mentionable problem.

Though *Vim* lost this all-America contest, she won her final challenge of readying an American boat to slaughter the foreign opponent. For many years thereafter *Vim* served as the grande dame of all twelves, American and foreign. She was a design, a system, a myth that would sustain the sport. And, to the joy of all who have seen or known of her in her prime, she is being carefully restored today.

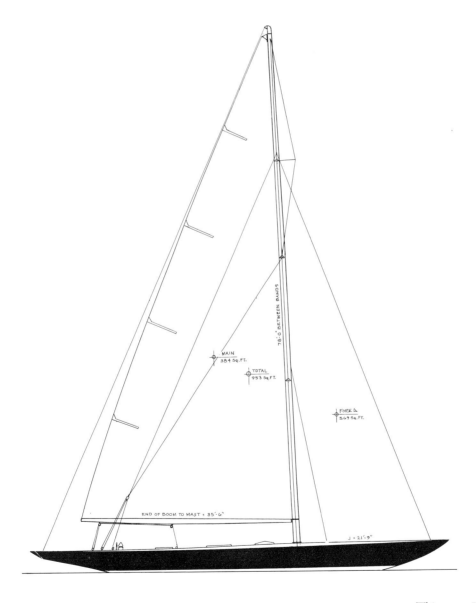

This page: Vim. *Facing page:* Nyala.

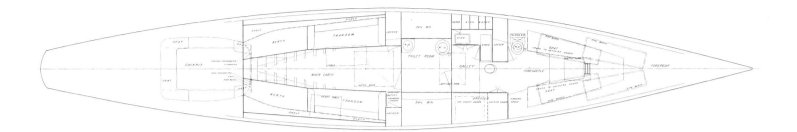

Columbia and Constellation – Designs 1343 and 1773

Columbia: LOA: 65'   DWL: 46'   Beam: 11' 2"   Draft: 8' 11"   Sail area: 1,985 sq. ft.

Constellation: LOA: 68' 4"   DWL: 45' 6"   Beam: 12' 4"   Draft: 9' 1"   Sail area: 1,783 sq. ft.

Although Olin Stephens has called *Columbia* "really an improved *Vim*," this reverse-transom twelve of 1957 did represent a step toward modern design. And the subsequent S&S twelve, *Constellation* of 1964, with her remarkably short keel, was even more obviously an advance into the future.

During this period, Olin, who gradually withdrew from active racing, was competing intellectually. He was experimenting and testing how the wetted surface of a hull could be reduced (for less drag and greater speed) without endangering the seaworthy qualities of the boat. And he made an important discovery (which he insists on calling "just textbook stuff"): "I had the feeling that wetted surface aft was not as harmful, perhaps, as it was forward because the water by then was already going with the boat."

This discovery allowed him to add a kind of "kicker" or bustle to the afterquarters of *Constellation*—a boat which

This page and facing page: Columbia.

sportswriters referred to as "another S&S landmark." Olin also dared to reshape *Constellation*'s keel as a result of his experiments; the keel is vee-shaped at the bottom, an innovation that improved windward performance by reducing leeway.

But at the same time as these two successful cup defenders were winning their headlines (and apparently demonstrating that tank tests were the best aid to successful design), Olin was beginning to wonder if other, more scientific systems might not be available. When the rival Australian boats came along after 1970, he perceived that "aircraft type applications of fluid dynamics had been well employed." There was still much to be learned.

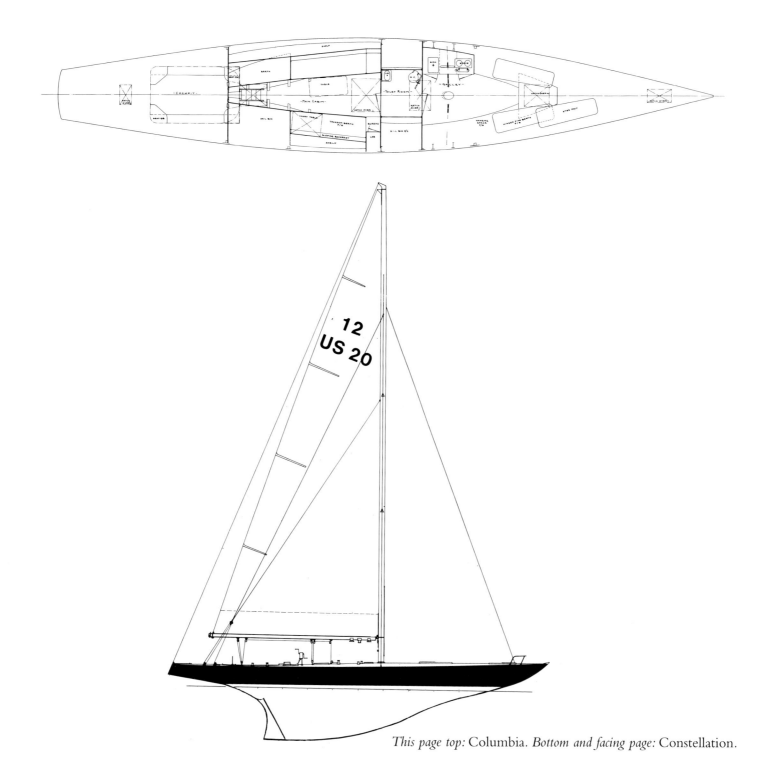

This page top: Columbia. *Bottom and facing page:* Constellation.

Intrepid and Courageous – Designs 1834 and 2085

Intrepid: LOA: 64' 3"   DWL: 45' 6"   Beam: 12'   Draft: 9'   Sail area: 1,770 sq. ft.

Courageous: LOA: 65' 6"   DWL: 51' 5"   Beam: 11' 11"   Draft: 8' 11"   sail area: 1,774 sq. ft.

Constantly striving to produce more slippery, more advanced twelves for the defense of the cup, the S&S team came up with *Intrepid* in 1967 and *Courageous* in 1974. Both were dazzlingly successful.

Olin regards *Intrepid* as his "most innovative twelve," from the somewhat awkward-looking, knuckle bow (an attempt to cut down weight) to the trim tab. Although such tabs had been introduced on smaller racing hulls, this was the first twelve to risk the innovation. On *Intrepid*, the steering system is really a matter of two rudders in tandem, a deep one on the keel and a shallow one on the skeg. The former, the trim tab, is used to drive the boat to windward, and to help her turn quickly in

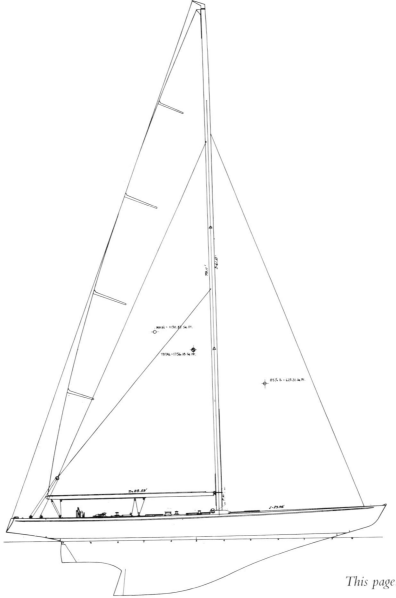

This page: Intrepid. *See photo page 192.*
Facing page: Courageous.

tacking duels. The skeg rudder is for steering. Both are controlled by three concentric wheels on the pedestal. The outer one turns the rudder, the middle one turns the tab, and the small one locks both rudders so they can turn together.

As well as the most innovative, *Intrepid* (at an estimated $750,000) was the most expensive twelve in those days of the inflated dollar. Some of the total went into the two coffee-grinder winches ($20,000 each), some into the $22,000 sail inventory, some into the even more expensive and fragile aluminum-titanium masts. But many of the dollars went into the

planning and mocking up of the deck layout—a collaborative effort on which skipper Bus Mosbacher and his colleagues worked, according to S&S standards.

Rod Stephens was deeply concerned that the two forward hatches desired by the crew (for better access to the sails stored below) would be dangerous because of waves crashing aboard and filling the forward compartment. The crew, however, determined to carry out their assignments swiftly, argued that *Intrepid* was not being designed for the Bermuda Race or for a *Dorade*-type Atlantic crossing; the two hatches would be fea-

This page: Courageous.

sible. They won their case—but later admitted that the boat was "very wet going."

To Olin, one of the most interesting features of this twelve was the very low boom, made possible by moving all winches, etc., belowdecks. He recalls that this lower boom developed from experiments being carried out on an S&S boat for United Aircraft. One of that company's engineers had a hunch that a mainboom right down at deck level would serve as a kind of "end plate"; the "induced drag" of the sail would be reduced and the sail's effectiveness greatly improved. He proved to be correct—this same effect is seen on the low-cut jibs for such S&S designs as the Tartan 10s.

With all these improvements (and later alterations, including a "pie plate" astern to reduce turbulence caused by the trim tab), *Intrepid* completely dominated the 12-meter scene, until the arrival of the lighter and faster *Courageous*. Besides her

aluminum construction (allowed by a revision of America's Cup regulations), *Courageous* departed from *Intrepid* in the increasingly dolphin-like shape of her underbody. As with *Constellation*, *Courageous* had a remarkably short keel. Despite her lightness and trimness, she was a tremendously powerful boat, delivering most of the drive that Olin's diagrams had predicted.

After her successful 1974 defense of the cup, she was challenged by a number of younger U.S. rivals in 1977. Having been slightly modified by Ted Hood, she succeeded in defeating them all. Then, with Ted Turner at the helm, she went on to wallop *Australia*. Not until 1980 was she defeated by a youngster—the S&S twelve *Freedom*. A valiant campaigner, last of the twelves to be designed by Olin Stephens alone, *Courageous* seemed to recognize that, for her too, the time had come to retire.

Freedom – Design 2368

LOA: 62' 2"   DWL: 44' 9"   Beam: 12' 2"   Draft: 8' 10"   Sail area: 1,767 sq. ft.

This was the adventurous twelve that successfully defended the America's Cup in 1980. Demonstrating the linked talents of Olin Stephens and Bill Langan, she was a relatively heavy, accident-prone ship—but she got the job done.

On the first of the five races of that contest, sailed in a shifting, 10-knot easterly, *Freedom* suffered the indignity of having her rudder linkage break on the second windward leg. On the next downwind leg, lack of rudder control proved no large problem, as the skipper (Dennis Conner) could steer with the trim tab. But for the final upwind leg, it was necessary to try wrapping a line around the rudder post and leading this to a genoa winch. Steering by this winch device and the trim tab proved manageable but clumsy: *Freedom* was forced to feather upwind and to make a major operation of each tack. Nevertheless, her crew performed these maneuvers with such skill that Conner, after winning the race, saw no need to mention the breakage. Instead, he dodged questions about why he

had sailed the final leg the way he did, admitting only that his tactics had been "unorthodox."

Thus developed a theory that the canny skipper was really holding *Freedom* back in an effort to conceal her real speed. This theory fell apart when the real story came out, and was rarely heard again when *Freedom* lost the second of the five races.

As a total work of design and construction (including superior, Kevlar/Mylar sails), *Freedom* proved herself to be a redoubtable yet devilish competitor. On the third race she blew a spinnaker into two pieces, one streaming irretrievably from the halyard; she tore the head out of her jib and had to stagger jibless along the last quarter mile to the second windward mark; she then hoisted her spinnaker under her pole lift, lost her jib overboard, dropped her pole overside, and nearly wrapped her spinnaker around the headstay—all in one climactic, five-minute display of free-spiritedness. But she won.

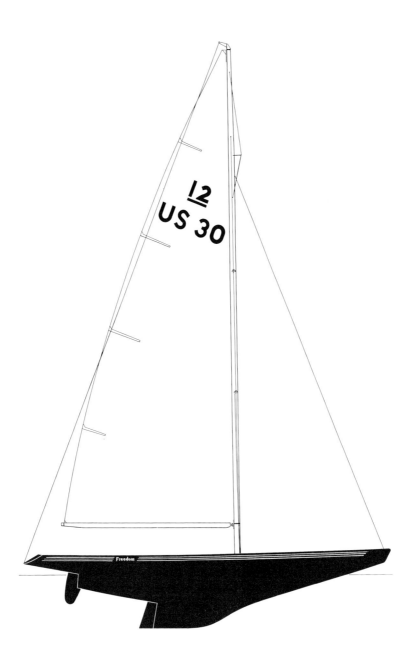

12

The Flat-Out Racers

During the exciting decades when competition for the America's Cup was getting increasingly fierce, and when Sparkman & Stephens's reputation as the premier designer of twelves was being challenged by a new generation, a special group of yachts came forth from the S&S boards.

These were flat-out ocean racers—which tended to live or die according to the whims of the International Offshore Rule (see Chapter 6). Although the S&S ocean racers within this category were impressively successful, inspired by many of the innovations developed on the twelves, they represented a kind of moral-intellectual dilemma for the emerging design team at S&S. The issue was: how central to good design (and to clients' safety) were the IOR regulations, favoring light-displacement boats as they did? So, as these dynamic racers succeeded each other and scored their victories, Olin and the S&S design team struggled to break away and design boats that were, of themselves, admirable seaboats. Not slanted in the IOR directions, they would win races on their own merits.

These boats, reflecting modern tastes, look quite different from previous Sparkman & Stephens winners. Above the water they seem angular, sleek, less sweeping in their lines; below the water they appear porpoise-like, with big, bulging "bustles"

between keel and rudder. Although this avoirdupois in the stern (favored by CCA and IOR measurement standards) seemed to give the boats an extraordinary sea-keeping ability upwind, it made for less satisfactory results downwind. Skippers occasionally felt that they were "dragging the whole ocean" behind them.

With their almost flush decks and massive coffee grinders, the flat-out Sparkman & Stephens ocean racers were obviously out to punish opponents and to win trophies. There is, nonetheless, nothing aesthetically offensive about them, with every detail contributing to the total effect. They reflect the Stephens brothers' philosophy that handsome, winning boats make for the sale of more handsome, winning boats. And as they evolved—from the racers of the middle and late sixties through the seventies—they earned a special place in the affections of a new generation.

Best of them all was the magnificent *Running Tide*, which Olin has difficulty denying is his favorite creation. Indeed, it's hard not to view this whole era as about *Running Tide*, what caused her to come into being and what came after her as a result. She holds that central position with appropriate grandeur, queen of the fleet.

Facing page: Obsession. *See page 218.*

Equation and Lightnin' – Designs 1938 and 1938.1

Equation: LOA: 56' 8"   DWL: 40'   Beam: 12' 4"   Draft: 8' 1"   Sail area: 1,333 sq. ft.

Lightnin': LOA: 56' 9"   DWL: 40'   Beam: 12' 4"   Draft: 8' 2"   Sail area: 1,325 sq. ft.

These virtually identical, trim-tabbed aluminum sloops, one with fractional rig and the other mast-headed, were designed just before the IOR regulations were adopted. Yet *Equation* and *Lightnin'*, along with their near sister ship *Palawan* (one of Olin's favorite boats), performed brilliantly against the competition in many an ocean thrash to a distant shore. It's no wonder that, after yet another victory by these Sparkman & Stephens racers in Bermuda, a sports columnist wrote (with some apparent world-weariness) that "U.S. Yachts Again Sweep Sailing Trophies."

Why these clean sweeps? One answer: because of S&S's awareness of checkpoints examined under new regulations, judges could easily measure S&S boats (which were often the mainstay of U.S. teams racing abroad). The writer quoted above then went on to say, "The opposition was in a rut. For the third straight time, the teams from Argentina, Bermuda, and England had not the foggiest idea of where they stood in the official standing because none had measurement certificates for all their boats. It's a problem that is wide-spread in this year [1970] of the great transition to the new International Offshore Rule for establishing handicap ratings."

Yes, it was a problem for some, but not for these efficient, hard-driving S&S sloops. In the second year of *Equation*'s life she scored the tremendous victory of overall winner in the 370-mile St. Petersburg to Fort Lauderdale Race. And, by overcoming such famous veterans as *Windward Passage* and *Ondine*, she demonstrated that these S&S speedsters—the IOR to the contrary not withstanding—had become the boats to beat.

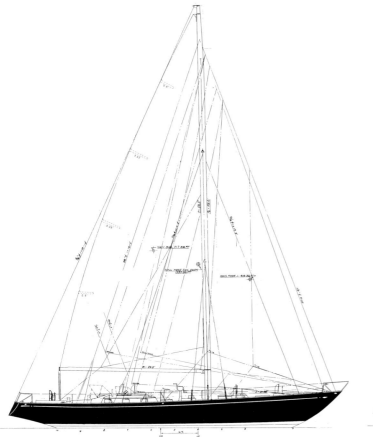
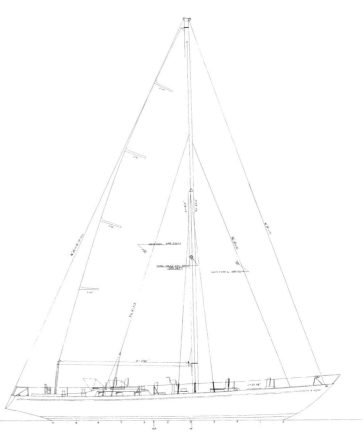

Above left: Equation. *Above right and facing page:* Lightnin'.

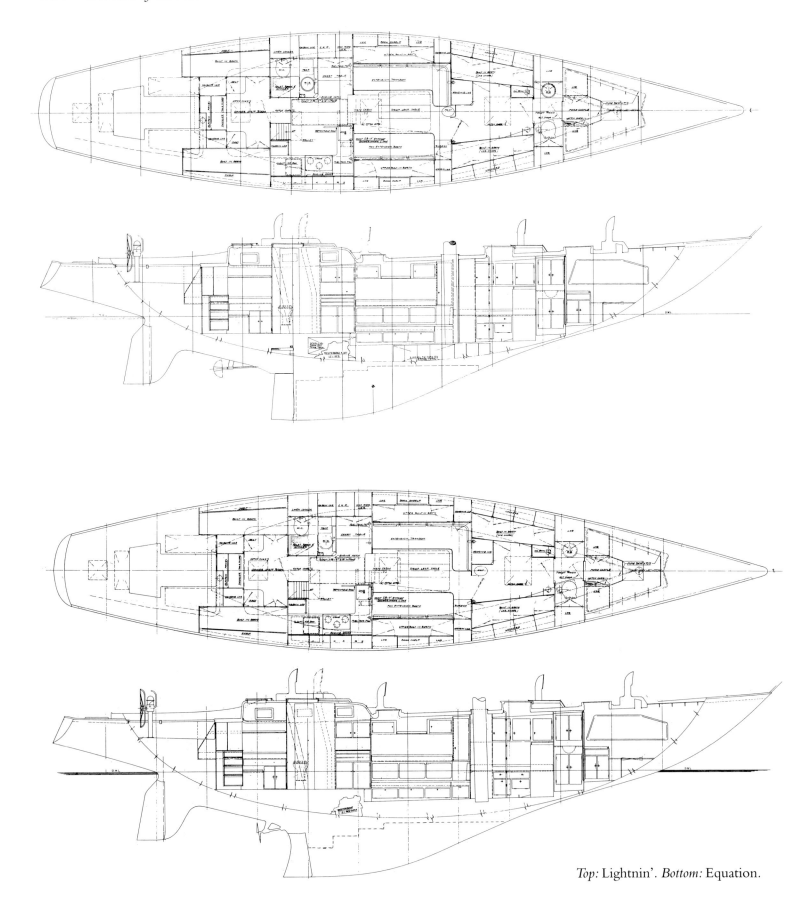

Top: Lightnin'. *Bottom:* Equation.

Running Tide – Design 1969

LOA: 60' 6"   DWL: 45'   Beam: 14' 3"   Draft: 9'   Sail area: 1,515 sq. ft.

Right after her christening, *Running Tide*'s owner (shipping magnate Jakob Isbrandtsen) charged out and won class honors in the 1970 Bermuda Race and placed first in the 1971 Southern Ocean Racing Circuit. That was the pace setter for this mighty offshore racer, which had been the first aluminum yacht built by the Royal Huisman shipyard in Holland. As the years and the victories rolled on, much consideration was given to the fact that she had been designed for her own virtues, before the inviting temptations of the IOR lured clients and designers alike toward lighter boats.

A glance at the accommodations below will reveal that *Running Tide* was hardly a pleasure cruiser: no magnificent staterooms here; only spare accommodations for the battered seamen engaged in driving her to victory. The only features that appear to be generous are the oilskin locker and the navigator's station. The entire forward section of the dimly lit hull is devoted to sail bins, plus a couple of no-weight pipe berths. A yachting writer of the time used the phrase "skinned out."

Nonetheless, for the Van Metres (who came into possession of the boat after a bidding war in 1972), *Running Tide* became

a family boat, campaigned from Chesapeake Bay. Real estate developer Albert G. Van Metre and his son Beau soon went on to win the 1973 Storm Trysail Club Week, the 1973 Miami to Palm Beach Race, the 1974 Nassau Cup, and were overall winners of the 1976 Bermuda Race—which was only a beginning.

In addition to her basic strengths, the secret to *Running Tide*'s success as the decade of the seventies advanced was that the Van Metres were dedicated to upgrading her in all possible ways. Keeping the lady competitive was their passionate desire, even as the lighter, more easily driven (and less seaworthy) rivals appeared on the starting line. The first major modification came when a 7-foot section was spliced into the 69-foot aluminum mast, penalty poles added, and the winch layout redesigned. "It was a disaster, the rig was way out of balance," said Van Metre. He then set about installing a more balanced, improved rig, plus a slimmer keel designed by S&S.

Running Tide responded by winning the 1976 Bermuda Race. But as the eighties dawned, it became evident to the Van Metres that newer, lighter, faster yachts could no longer be overcome. Respecting their grand vessel, however, the family had no intention of parting with her. The pasture out to which they put *Running Tide* consisted of family cruises to Europe and other, sunnier climes. She would never disappoint them.

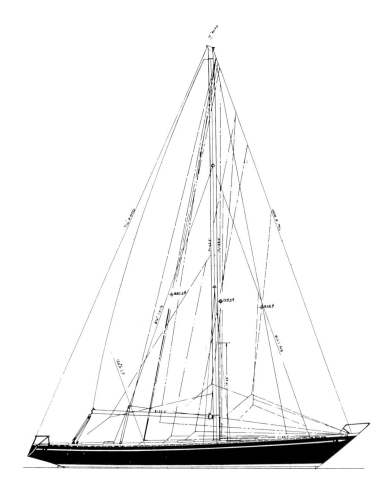

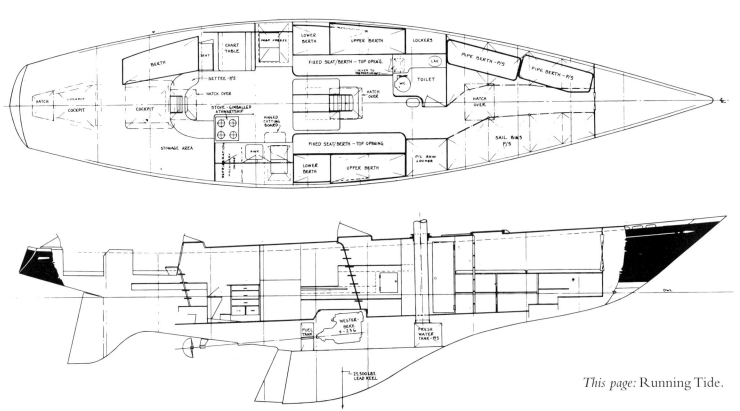

This page: Running Tide.

Flyer – Design 2273

LOA: 65' 2"   DWL: 49' 9"   Beam: 16' 4"   Draft: 10'   Sail area: 1,827 sq. ft.

Another famous competitor produced by Sparkman & Stephens in the critical era of the late 1970s was the global racer *Flyer*. A high-sided ketch, she was specifically designed for the Whitbread Round the World Race. Following in the footsteps of the S&S-designed *Sayula* (a Swan 65) which won the Whitbread in 1973, *Flyer* went on to take first place in 1977 and in 1978.

Though seemingly light and tall-rigged, *Flyer* is constructed of marine-grade welded aluminum for ultimate strength and easy maintenance. Some 25,000 pounds of lead ballast were poured into her fin keel, a tricky procedure where the temperature of the aluminum cannot be allowed to exceed 300 degrees Fahrenheit lest changes in the temper of the plating occur. *Flyer* also shows typical S&S concern for seaworthiness and habitability. As remarked in the in-house description, "Special care is taken to ensure dry sleeping facilities for all hands."

While racing, *Flyer* carries a crew of ten or eleven, for whom there is room in the cabins aft and amidships; under those circumstances, the "root berth" space forward is given over to sail stowage. The long passageway along the boat's center line proves useful for stopping light sails. A sewing machine is located there for any emergency repairs.

Flyer is presently cruising the coast of California and the Hawaiian Islands, while being used as a training boat for the Orange Coast College.

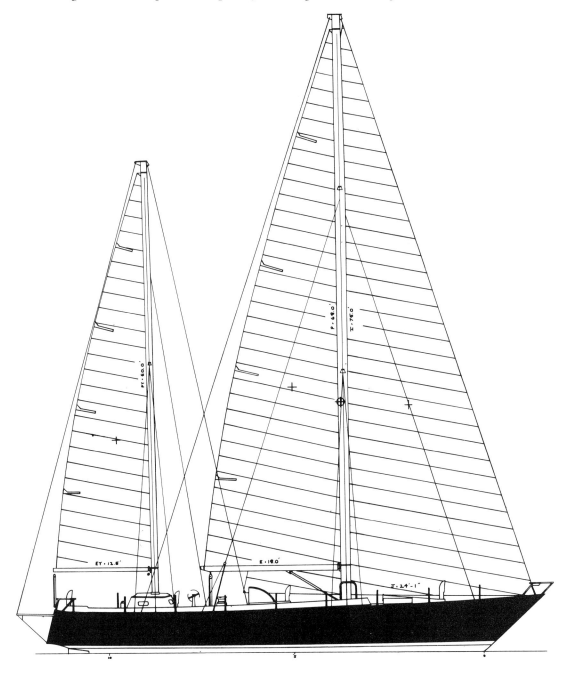

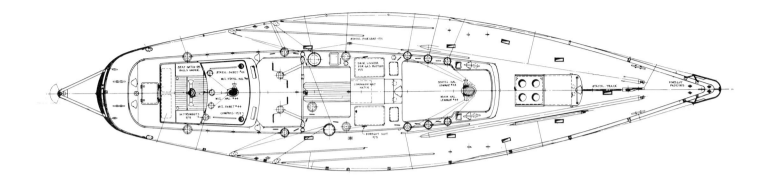

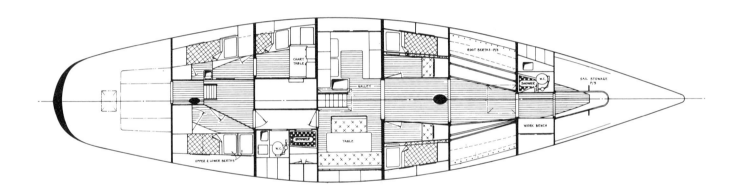

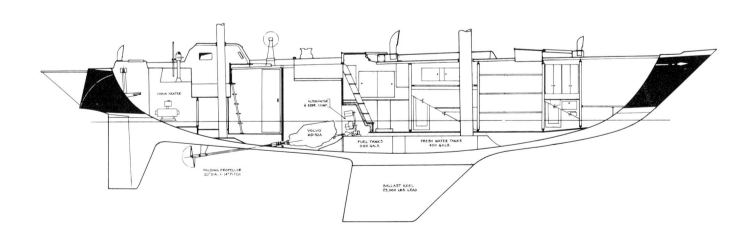

Obsession and Challenge – Designs 2333 and 2381

Obsession:	*LOA: 45' 8"*		*DWL: 64' 10"*		*Beam: 14' 3"*	*Draft: 8' 1"*	*Sail area: 935 sq. ft.*	
Challenge:	*LOA: 45' 7"*		*DWL: 36' 6"*		*Beam: 14' 4"*	*Draft: 8'*	*Sail area: 1,067 sq. ft.*	

In the late 1970s, Sparkman & Stephens designed two IOR-conformed sloops which competed triumphantly against the most successful of their contemporaries. Named *Obsession* and *Challenge*, they continue to demonstrate the beauties and the hazards of such tall-rigged, lightweight, flat-out racers.

Challenge was commissioned by an Australian yachtsman who, impressed by the record of *Obsession*, ordered a near-duplicate for himself, to be entered in the 1979 Hitachi Southern Cross Cup Series. The problem was that the builders (Maas Brothers of Melbourne) were given but four months in which to produce the boat—a challenge worthy of her name.

Working twelve hours a day for seven days a week, they completed the aluminum-alloy boat on schedule. Subsequently she was, as hoped, selected for the Victorian Southern Cross team.

One of the interesting changes in *Challenge* over *Obsession* was that the rig was reduced from masthead to 80 percent. This proved to be very fast for reaching and running, and had no detrimental effect on upwind and light-air speed. As a result, she won convincingly in the Southern Cross Series and was victorious in the subsequent King of Derwent Race, and in 1983 she won the Sydney-Hobart Race.

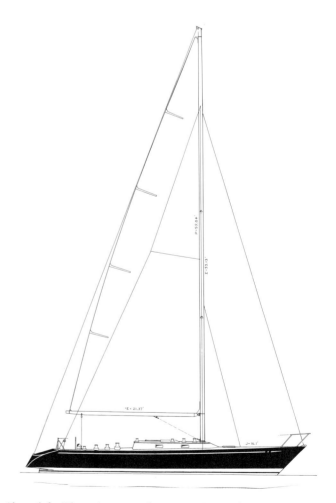

Above left: Obsession; *see photo page 208. Above right:* Challenge.

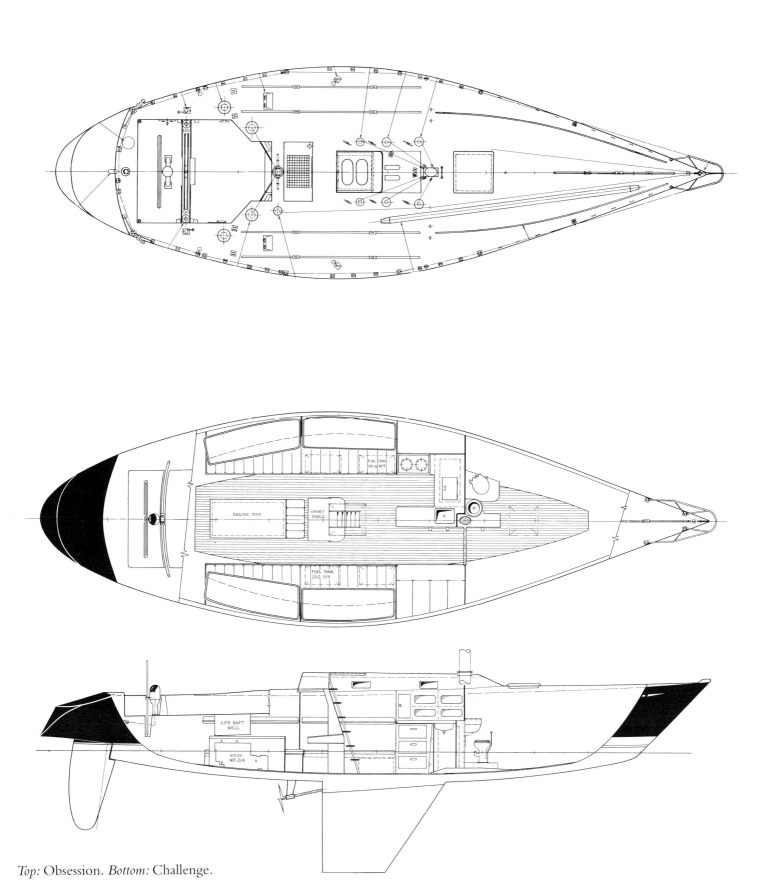

Top: Obsession. *Bottom:* Challenge.

13

High-Performance Cruisers of the Eighties

When it comes to the keels and rudders of the new-style boats S&S created in the 1980s, Bill Langan and Alan Gilbert agree, self-mockingly, "They look as if those appendages had been nailed on!" No such engineering madness actually occurred, of course. Instead, what's seen here is a carefully thought-out evolution of design from the "flat-out racers" of the previous decade—whose every purpose was to finish first and whose very shape was determined by IOR standards—to the new generation of cruising boats whose purpose and shape responded to different demands.

This transition can be best understood by examining even more closely the underbodies of the new high-performance cruisers versus those of their predecessors—studying the "hierarchy of generic shapes," in Bill Langan's lingo. No longer are the leading edges of the keels gradual developments of the forward sections; no longer are the generous bustles molded and pinched into the rudders. Now the "back-ends" (Bill's language again) are smooth and simple, with rudder and keel very much on their own.

In terms of S&S designs, the point at which this switch occurred was Design Number 2331—the Swan 76, renowned for her bustle. Thereafter, that piece of stern sculpture is diminished, if not totally absent. More important, after the Swan 76, the mission at S&S became even more focused on engineering the details of a proper racing yacht and even less on shortcuts for flashy, rules-favored winners.

Indeed, a deliberate choice was made—which business managers might call a "mature-company decision"—no longer to follow the fast track of attention-getting racers but the more rewarding track of superior, high-performance cruisers. This choice, this turning-away from the hot action areas where their fellow professionals competed, involved no little agony for the young inheritors of Olin and Rod Stephens's mantles.

But obviously times were changing, and so was the business. A reduction in costs of advanced construction materials (such as aluminum alloys and exotic composites of reinforced fibers and plastics) and new methodologies in design and construction encouraged radical rethinking. That led to the application of computer-aided design (CAD) and computer-aided manufacture (CAM) systems to the design process. Naval architect and yacht builder alike then had sharper tools for more advanced results.

The success achieved by S&S's first new-line products—the high-performance cruisers *Zimba* and the Sequin 44 (profiled in this chapter)—soon let the design team know that they were on the right azimuth. These boats, designed somewhat differently in terms of both technology and philosophy, are undoubtedly must-includes among the best of the best.

Facing page: Encore. *See page 231.*

Zimba - Design 2365

LOA: 50' 10"   DWL: 40' 9"   Beam: 15'   Draft: 8' 6"   Sail area: 1,120 sq. ft.

The decade of the eighties began, from the S&S perspective, with the delivery of *Zimba* to her owner, the experienced off-shore sailor Paul E. Luke of East Boothbay, Maine. There was so much innovation aboard the newly delivered boat that she startled observers who had expected the well-known, S&S look. For example, where did the cockpit (or cockpits) begin and end? And was she flush deck or did she have a cabin house? Hard to tell. (In fact, the aft cockpit is for steering and sheet handling, while the forward cockpit is the control center for halyards and reefing winches.)

Zimba's true radicalism, however, cannot be understood by a quick glance at profile or plan; it lies underwater. There, aft of the jut-jaw bow, hangs a nearly spade keel of generous size. In the stern, a deep rudder swings from a slender skeg. This "partially balanced" rudder arrangement had been tried on a modified Swan 44 and had proved remarkably easy to handle. With these clean underbody lines (and a low displacement/length

ratio of 210), she's obviously ready for fast passages at sea.

Much new thinking on the part of the designers also went into the cabin layout, where the emphasis is on clean and open efficiency. The cross-ship bulkhead between the main cabin and the side-by-side forward staterooms is actually two sliding panels, which can be slid back to port and starboard, opening up the whole central part of the boat. Similarly, the dividing bulkhead between the staterooms can be folded back. Space has been made on the port side of the main cabin for a work bench—that facility so often sought but so rarely found by oceangoing bosuns.

The tall cutter rig is set up to give tremendous power to the light, easily driven hull, even in gentle airs. Another advantage of the cutter rig is the variety of headsails that may be set. Given these advantages, *Zimba* immediately began turning in coastwise and blue-water performances that confirmed S&S's expectations.

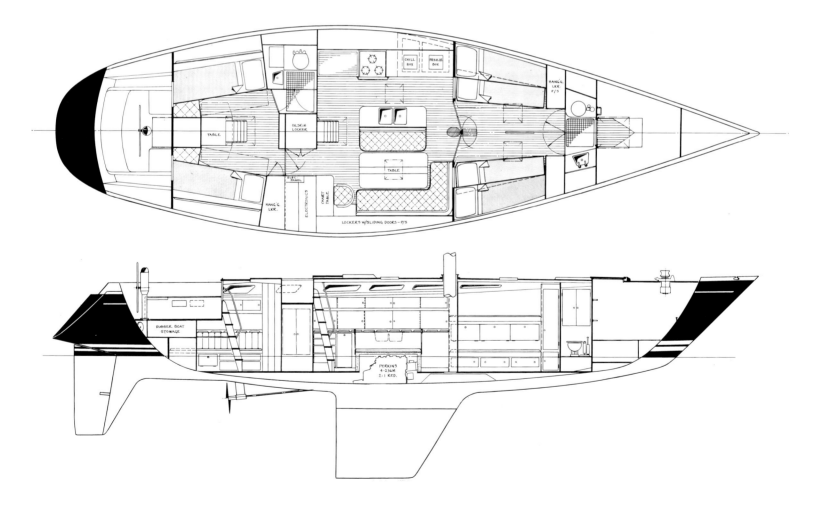

Stevens 47 and Sequin 44 – Designs 2390 and 2396

Stevens 47:   LOA: 46' 10"   DWL: 37' 9"   Beam: 14' 4"   Draft: 6'   Sail area: 1,144 sq. ft.

Sequin 44:   LOA: 44' 6"   DWL: 33' 6"   Beam: 12' 10"   Draft: 6' 3" (racing keel: 7' 9")   Sail area: 873 sq. ft.

These two yachts, the one but a few feet longer than the other, both designed in 1980, show how varied the new cruisers of S&S could be, even while the basic hull configuration was being thought through and developed. Whereas the Sequin 44 was conceived as the right boat for a traditionally minded individual yachtsman and his family, the Stevens 47 was designed as a charter boat. Actually she was conceived to outmatch another charter boat that had proved very popular in the Caribbean, the Gulf-Star 50.

Both the Stevens and the Sequin met their objectives brilliantly, with the Sequin earning an outstanding reputation as an offshore passage maker and the Stevens becoming so successful on the charter circuit that more than eighty of them were built. Nor was the Stevens any less of a speedster, for all the be-gentle inhibitions of a charter craft. Rod Stephens took justifiable pride when he saw her performing in the Islands. "I knew this was going to be fast when I saw the designs. Then I sailed on it during the Antigua Race Week and was just delighted. Each day we showed we had it, especially when we got on the wind." The Stevens went on to win six trophies in the series.

She remains, nonetheless, a beamy, spacious vessel, ideal for lounging and relaxing (now, updated, she's known as a Hylas 49). The raised, midships cockpit, as well as providing a good position for dining al fresco, offers the helmsman unobstructed

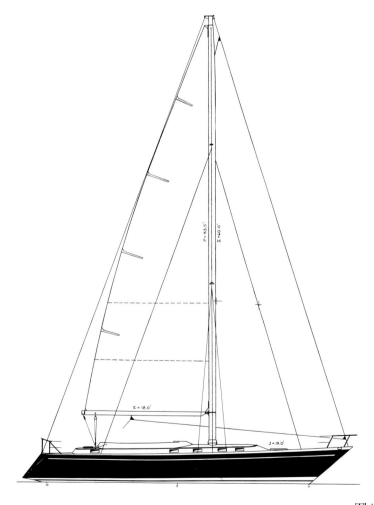

This page and facing page: Stevens 47.

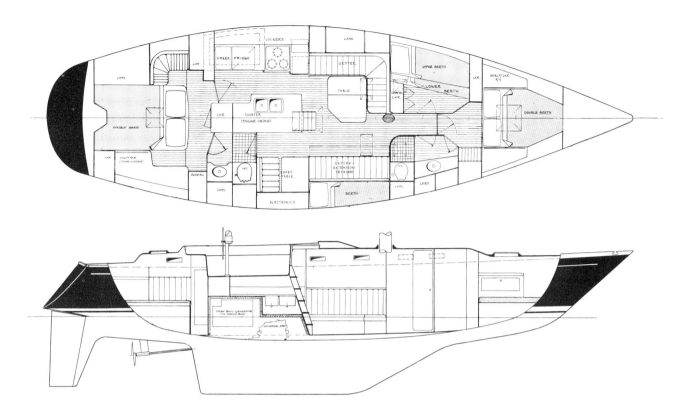

views of sails, deck area, and surrounding water. In order to facilitate nudging into shoal harbors, the keel has been kept as shallow and long as possible.

By contrast, the Sequin's keel is shorter and deeper, her hull slimmer and more spare of space, her styling more traditional. She was ordered by the Lyman-Morse Boatbuilding Company of Maine. Its president, Cabot Lyman, figured that his clients would want a boat of "distinguished pedigree," designed to go fast but according to no specific rule which might, one day, make the boat obsolete. He put much emphasis on the flexibility of interiors, inviting the owners to select what was truly best for them in the manner of custom architects.

Both of these boats are fiberglass with Airex core. But, in keeping with her more aristocratic destiny, the Sequin's fiberglass deck structure is covered with teak. Reflecting the engineering interests of the new S&S team, the diesel engines in both craft are in central locations, approachable from all sides.

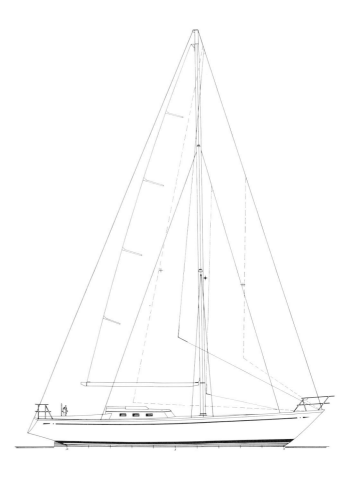

This page and facing page: Two variations of Sequin 44.

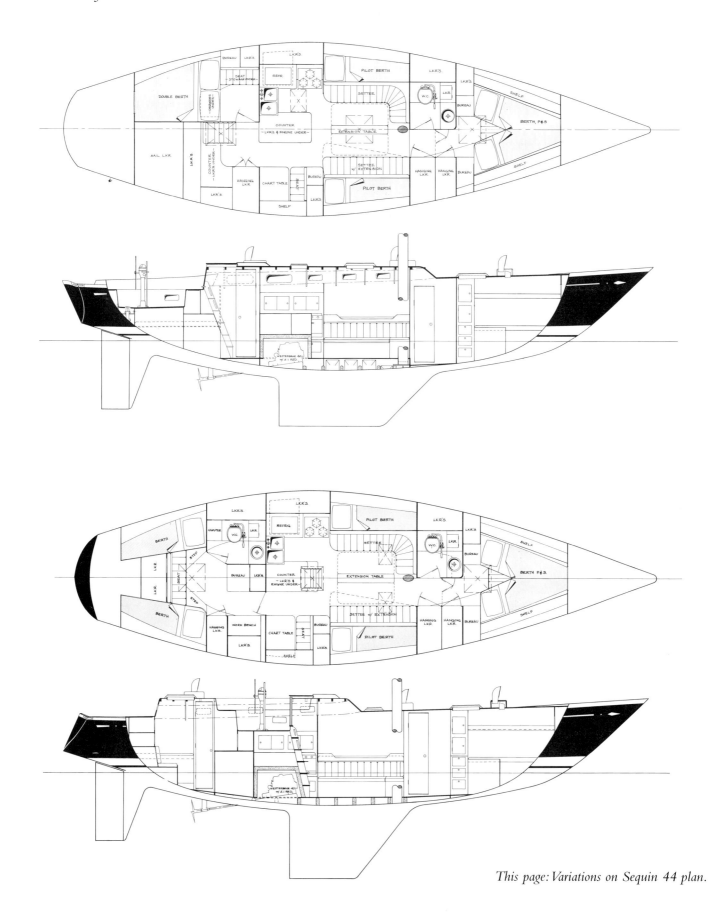

This page: Variations on Sequin 44 plan.

Karyatis – Design 2475

LOA: 69' 7"   DWL: 54'   Beam: 17' 10"   Draft: 10'   Sail area: 2,040 sq. ft.

As the Sparkman & Stephens designers gained confidence with the success of their new line of high-performance yachts, they moved into the realm of more elaborate, even sumptuous contenders. Surely the best example is *Karyatis*, a 70-foot, aluminum cruising sloop, launched in 1985.

Nothing was spared here to create a luxurious craft: the owner's stateroom has, in addition to standard features, a gun locker, a safe, a private head with separate shower stall plus onyx countertop and tile sole; the interior seems unusually bright and airy because of the ash and other light woods used.

Despite such cruiser-style comforts, *Karyatis* was by no means burdened down with her amenities. The year after her launching, she won line honors in the IMS division of the Newport–Bermuda Race. In fact, she finished only eight hours behind *Condor*, the IOR Maxi Division winner. She would never spend much time looking at another boat's stern.

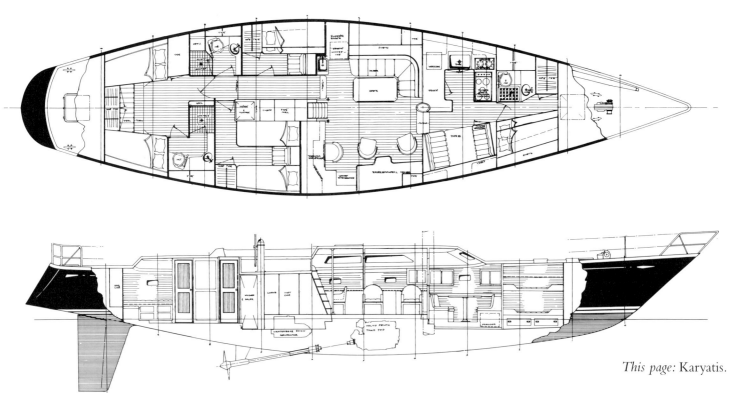

This page: Karyatis.

Encore – Design 2527

LOA: 73'   DWL: 58'   Beam: 18' 6"   Draft: 7' 10"   Sail area: 2,435 sq. ft.

Ten years after the disastrous Fastnet Race of 1979, and also after the IOR had been replaced by the International Measurement System, this large, rugged racer was designed by Sparkman & Stephens and built of aluminum at the Derecktor yard. Sailed by a father-and-son team, she immediately established herself as a winner in the Annapolis-Newport Race, the Marblehead-Halifax Race, the Antigua Race Week, and the Monhegan Race of 1990. In that year she also placed second in the Bermuda Race. Three years later she was the overall winner in the 1993 Fastnet Race.

What's also remarkable about *Encore*—and what makes her a high-performance cruiser rather than a flat-out racer—is that she has an insertable/removable cruising interior, an interior reflecting the old-world standards of a more leisurely time. In the words of her owner, "*Encore*'s outside is like a Ferrari and her interior is like a Rolls Royce."

Because Derecktor had commenced building innovative S&S designs, including a number of the 12-meters, immediately after World War II, *Encore* also represents the happy culmination and future thrust of a forty-year-long partnership.

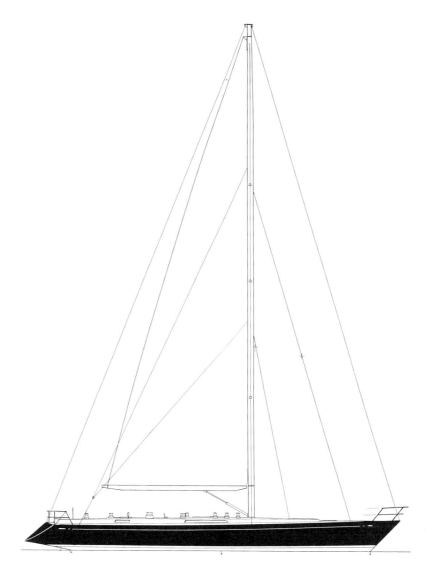

See photo page 220.

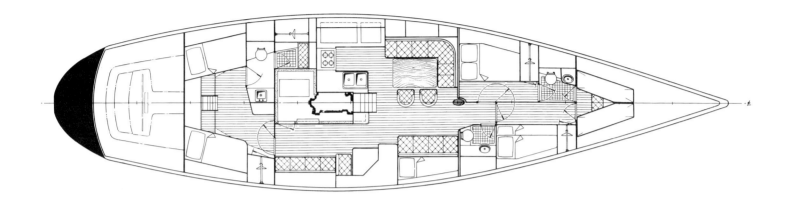

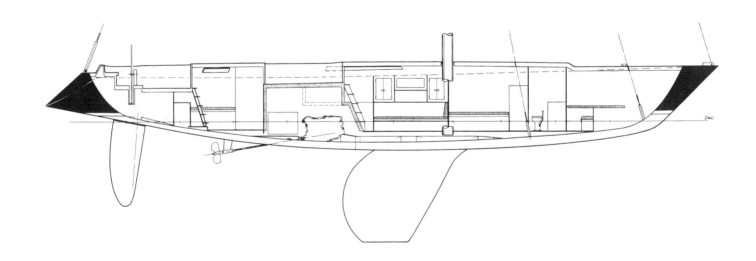

This page: Encore.

Baltic 52 – Design 2544

LOA: 51' 6"   DWL: 41' 11"   Beam: 15' 5"   Draft: 6' 6"   Sail area: 1,310 sq. ft.

The young design group at S&S in the 1980s had the advantage not only of computers and other technically advanced systems to aid their computations ("numbers, numbers, numbers"), but also of exciting new materials that were revolutionizing hull and rig design. Thus science came increasingly to the fore—though perhaps not as a total reversal of the "90 percent art, 10 percent science" formula that Olin Stephens had once worked out to describe naval architecture. The Baltic 52, with its vacuum-bagged, balsa-cored hull made of Kevlar

and glass laminates (50 percent lighter and two or three times stronger than most cruising hulls), is a good demonstration of the new technologies at work afloat.

Accompanying this sophisticated hull design is a rather surprising rig. In contrast with the lofty cutter rigs often seen in the 1980s, this is relatively low, with the mast rather far forward. All efforts have been made to ensure that, for all her raciness, the Baltic 52 will be easy for a cruising family to handle. One such skipper described the rig like this: "I suppose that

some might say we've gone back to mainsail profile popular about twenty years ago. Frankly, I like it that way offshore because I think it works better." Rod Stephens, ever the advocate of a long-boomed, reefable main and single jib, would heartily agree.

The Baltic 52 has benefited from the novel approach of interior designer Tor Hinders: almost nothing is lined up in the old-fashioned, fore-and-aft manner. To port in the main saloon are a wraparound galley and spacious dinette; to starboard are navigation station, head, and the door to one of the three commodious staterooms.

But as with other S&S cruisers produced during this era, the most remarkable aspect of the design is (in Bill Langan's words) "how the appendages hang down without support." Here, too, advanced engineering is required to achieve the necessary strength for an independent keel and rudder.

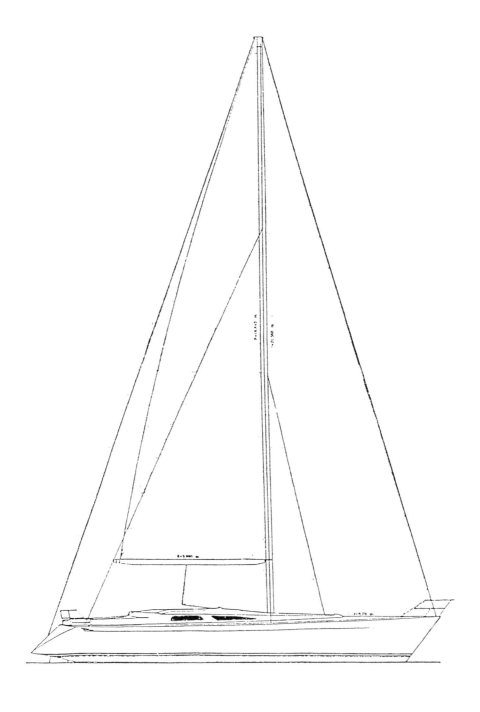

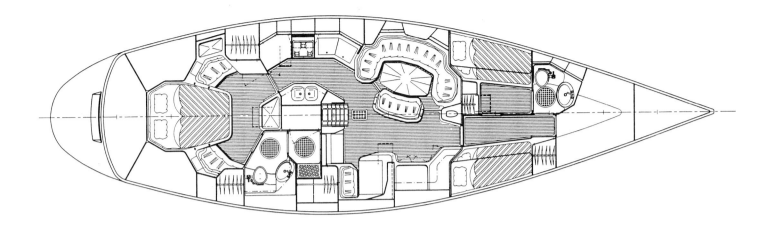

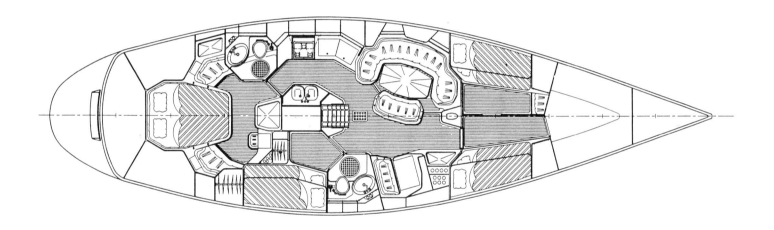

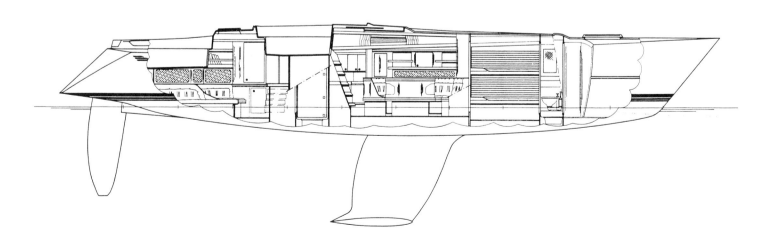

Victoria of Strathearn – Design 2551

LOA: 90' 7"   DWL: 71' 10"   Beam: 20' 8"   Draft: 10' 1"   Sail area: 3,140 sq. ft.

One of the most notable boats designed by S&S during the 1980s, this sensational, 90-foot ketch may be regarded as the acme of the new-style cruisers. Camper & Nicholsons, British builders of the yacht, quoted Bill Langan as saying, "The exterior appearance is one of the most important aspects of any design, and it was especially true for this owner. The sheerline, cabin house, and overhangs have been carefully balanced to achieve a combination of power and grace that we hope will turn heads when *Victoria of Strathearn* sails into harbour."

Bill also remarked that the hull design was a development of S&S's new, fast-cruising philosophy. "The lines are quite fair for speed with balanced ends for an easy sea motion. To gain performance at shallow draft, a wing keel has been fitted…far simpler than the alternative of a centreboard, particularly for a yacht of this size." The result: a boat that sails as beautifully as she looks. The owner is particularly pleased with the "feedback" he gets from the wheel—calling it almost as sensitive as a tiller.

With a crew of four housed almost as comfortably as the owner's party, *Victoria* represents a successful overseas translation of the new S&S ideals for a competitive boat that need be neither brutal nor dangerous. She also dramatically leads the way to the "mega-yachts" that characterized the work of S&S at the end of the 1980s and beginning of the 1990s (see following chapter).

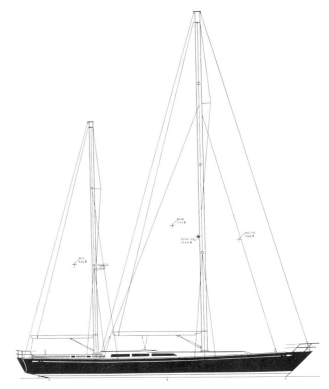

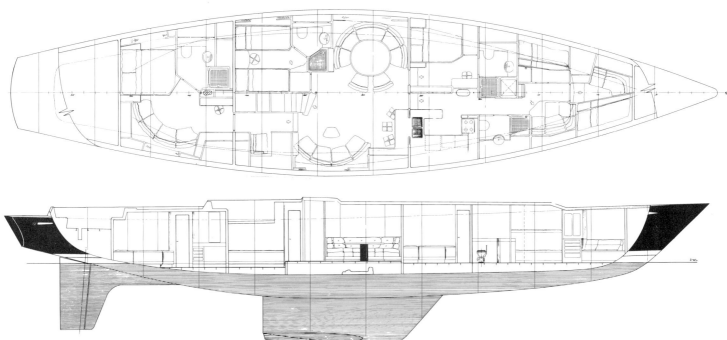

14

Globe-Girdling Mega-Yachts

Even today, when the enormous yachts that Sparkman & Stephens has been designing so successfully for a decade and more have demonstrated their superior sailing abilities, Bill Langan is asked whether these aren't just nice, big motor-sailers. And he rises to the bait: "These people look at the cabin house and assume the boat can't sail!"

Then he starts to teach: "In a motor-sailer, powering characteristics are as important as sailing characteristics, but here primary attention is given to sailing. The power is essentially auxiliary." He ends up talking about "available technology"—these enormously complex, independent, floating cities can now be conceived, built safely, and affordably crewed, whereas that was not the case in foregoing generations.

Clearly another factor is a new type of client. The owners are not only very rich, they are also very eager to present themselves as world-sailers (whether they've had much previous experience sailing or not). For family pleasure or for business, the boat allows them to be anywhere around the world, privately, without having to book a suite or rent a villa. Instead of several expensive summer and winter places here and there, they have this one "movable asset," always in the right place. Nelson Doubleday, a mega-yacht owner, claims that it's the less expensive way to go. Then, having sailed to that very right place, it appears ipso facto you're a prince of a seaman when you're ashore.

To point out one particular example of this new breed of Magellans—who represent a great market for naval architects—there's Bill Simon. Once secretary of the treasury under President Nixon and presently owner of the S&S yacht *Freedom*, he had not had much experience beyond his Sunfish. Now he says in a knowledgeable way: "I am very pleased, not only with *Freedom*'s engineering and superior workmanship, but also with the yacht's outstanding handling characteristics."

As with *Victoria of Strathearn*, every effort is made to give owners the best possible sailing experience. This includes a fingertip sense of how the boat is responding to wind and water. While some designers urge their clients into more and more

hydraulics, S&S favors steering systems worked by cable and wire—the same, trusted mechanical device which the firm has always advocated.

Mega-yacht clients tend to be systems people, as eager to manage complexities as they are to sail. The key system at the heart of this whole "mega" business is the rather humble-appearing, hydraulic sail stowage system. It was this invention that allowed big yachts to do away with big crews. In the 1890s, seasoned crewmen numbering a dozen or more had to be supplied for large yachts; in the 1990s, four or five youngsters can do the trick, at captain's command.

Beyond such inventions, however, there have to be assurances of reliability—for these floating palaces need to be operationally independent of everything but food and fuel. Therefore, a remarkable shift occurred at Sparkman & Stephens: the majority of time spent on a given yacht changed from shaping and testing the hull and rig to designing and perfecting the complex inner systems. Such intricate problems as freshwater makers and entire electronic systems had to be resolved for such waterborne spaceships. The systems had to be totally reliable.

Furthermore, room had to be made in the interior design for sizable engine rooms, complemented by space for replacements for all equipment. A comparison of the difference between the engine and stowage rooms of *Victoria of Strathearn* (see Chapter 13) and *Sea Angel* (see this chapter) shows this generic difference between big cruiser and mega-yacht, though the boats are approximately the same size.

As the theory and practice of mega-yacht design have developed, Bill Langan and Alan Gilbert have discovered that there are, really, two breeds. One of these, including *Osprey*, *Astral*, and the quasi-motor-sailer *Queen Nefertiti*, is less performance oriented. The second, the lineage extending from *Sea Angel* and *Freedom* through *Galileo* and *Maysylph*, is high performance without reserve. But they all are magnificent carriers-on of the S&S traditions for sailability and style—the best that money can buy.

Facing page: Astral. *See page 250.*

Osprey – Design 2391

LOA: 96'   DWL: 72'   Beam: 23'   Draft: 10'   Sail area: 3,717 sq. ft.

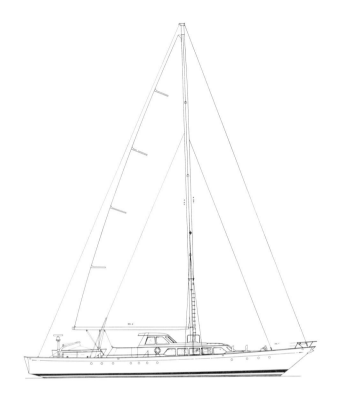

Designed in 1980, *Osprey*, at 96 feet, was one of the first true mega-yachts. Since her owner and his family intended to cruise the world in pursuit of their own aquatic sports and marine-biology activities, only a small crew was desired. Therefore, the key to this cutter's success was the Hood stow-away mainsail, complemented by an electrically driven furling headstay and inner forestay. These systems can also be operated manually.

The cockpit is set up for fishing and scuba diving with a large stern door, provision for a bait tank, and stowage for some twenty scuba tanks (chargeable at that location). In order to facilitate fish-spotting and navigation from above, operation of the yacht from a position in the crow's nest is possible—in the mode of *Yankee*. While the main steering station on *Osprey* is in the main cockpit, other supplementary steering stations are located in the enclosed bridge station and the aft cockpit.

Hull construction is aluminum alloy; the profile bears some relationship to such handsome S&S yachts of former times as *Pavane II*, though on a far grander scale. Power is supplied by a 267-horsepower Caterpillar diesel, but even more extraordinary are the desalinization system, the four refrigerator systems, the Jacuzzi whirlpool, and the elaborate small-boat handling equipment. Because of them all, S&S designers were quoted as having said that *Osprey* provided "every comfort and entertainment imaginable—a veritable magic carpet of the sea."

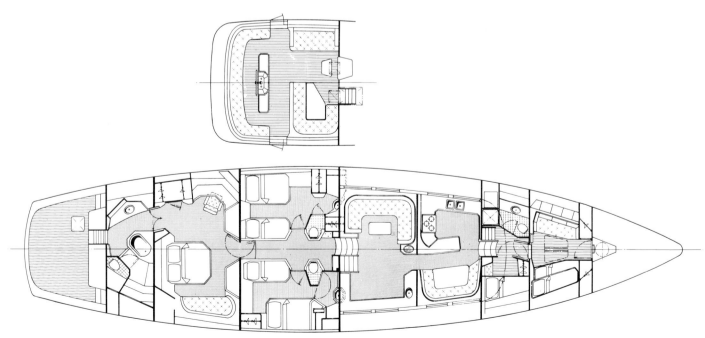

Sea Angel and Freedom – Designs 2455 and 2483

Sea Angel: LOA: 88' 3"   DWL: 68'   Beam: 20' 6"   Draft: 8'   Sail area: 2,890 sq. ft.

Freedom: LOA: 123'   DWL: 98'   Beam: 26'   Draft: 10'   Sail area: 4,819 sq. ft.

These two superketches are big and little sister, so similar in profile and general purpose that you have to look again to see which one is in fact larger. Though smaller, *Sea Angel* (in the words of Bill Langan) "started it all—this particular line of mega-yachts." They both have all the sail and engine power to go anywhere in the world, as well as all the systems to give owner's party and crew alike a safe but thrilling sea adventure.

Of special note are the immensely powerful winches employed in adjusting the roll-away sails. On *Sea Angel* (which was designed for the owner of an electronics company, eager to try out his systems across the seas), five of the deck winches are driven by Lewmar hydraulic power packs. On *Freedom*, Lewmar hydraulic "Commander" units integrate winch operation and roller furling operations; each unit can handle any two functions simultaneously. *Freedom*'s headstay furling unit is one of the largest of its kind ever manufactured.

Whereas *Sea Angel* was constructed at Stephens Marine in Stockton, California, *Freedom* was built by the Picchiotti yard in Viareggio, Italy, and launched in August of 1986. Both are of aluminum and employ centerboards housed within long, shallow keels.

Above left: Freedom. *Above right and facing page:* Sea Angel.

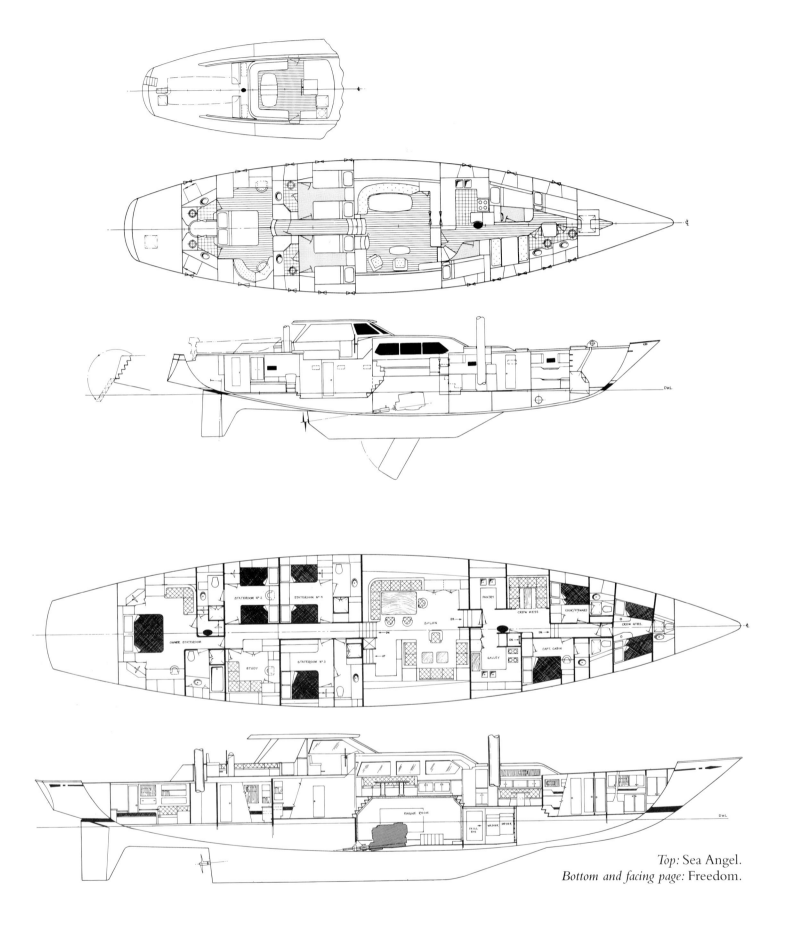

Top: Sea Angel.
Bottom and facing page: Freedom.

Queen Nefertiti - Design 2477

LOA: 123' 6"   DWL: 96'   Beam: 26'   Draft: 12'   Sail area: 4,944 sq. ft.

The owner of this clipper-bowed schooner, more interested in the classic lines of yachts at the earlier end of the century than in contemporary styling, nonetheless wanted a fully modern yacht. Built of aluminum in Bilbao, Spain, she was sailed to Antibes for delivery to the owner in May 1985.

The two levels for living and entertaining are connected by a circular stairway. Engine noise and propeller noise are reduced in the living quarters by positioning the engine room as far aft as possible. Equipment in the galley (placed forward, with the crew's quarters) includes a garbage compactor, a dishwasher, a microwave oven, an icemaker, and a clothes washer/dryer.

Above the cockpit—and the two sport boats on the after deck—rises a lofty mainsail, powerful enough to drive the schooner as fast as a clipper. Mechanical power is supplied by a DD 16V-71 diesel, turning a controllable-pitch propeller.

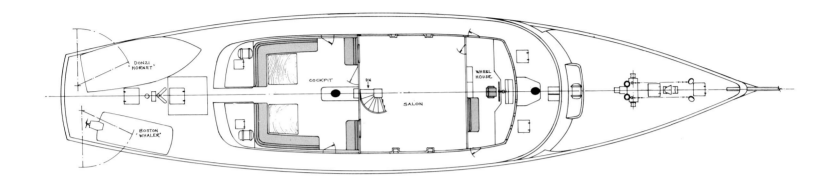

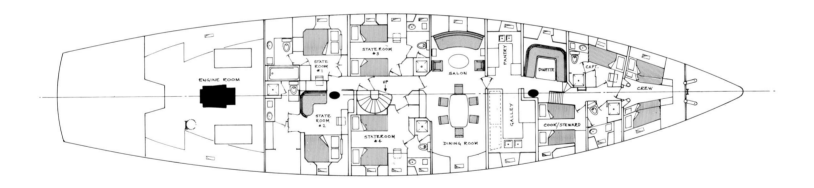

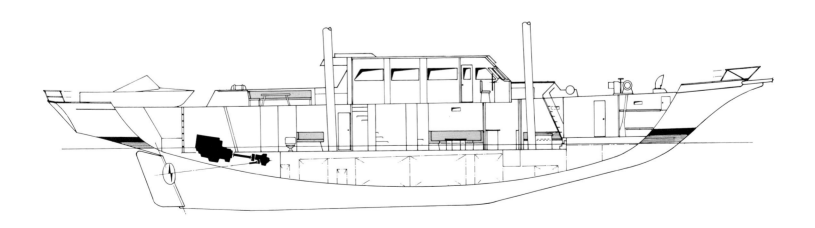

Galileo – Design 2510

LOA: 123' 4"   DWL: 96'   Beam: 26' 1"   Draft: 12' 8"   Sail area: 5,161 sq. ft.

Though a continuation of the *Sea Angel–Freedom* line, *Galileo* represents many new departures. For one: her sensational size. When completed in 1989 at Palmer Johnson's Sturgeon Bay yard, she was the largest sailing yacht built in the United States since the 1930s.

But *Galileo*'s main departure from *Freedom* is her underbody. Instead of the centerboard to permit cruising in shoal waters, *Galileo* has a unique wing keel. This feature, selected by Bill Langan after many tests, makes for amazing speed and upwind efficiency—the sailing excellence which the owner desired. That requirement caused "a lot of creative thinking," Langan admitted, "leading to the '*Galileo* wing'; it proved superior to all other typical shallow-draft alternatives."

Other new features include a virtually soundproof interior. This is explained by Alan Gilbert as an objective long pursued by S&S: "Ever since our work with the 93-foot [power cruiser] *Kalamoun* fifteen years ago, our clients have been increasingly interested in carrying out polite conversation while the yacht is under way." Now that attribute of leisurely civilization was possible, even at high speed.

As with her predecessors, *Galileo*—so rightly named for one of the world's scientific geniuses—offers a wonderfully true feel at the helm. Supplementing the direct steerage linkage is a trim flap on the rudder; this reduces steering loads during rough conditions and is hydraulically operated from the steer-

ing station. And even while that system provides such fine sailing, other systems are at work backing up the experience: on a Tracor Marcon monitor, the helmsman can check all the vital signs of the vessel on a video screen.

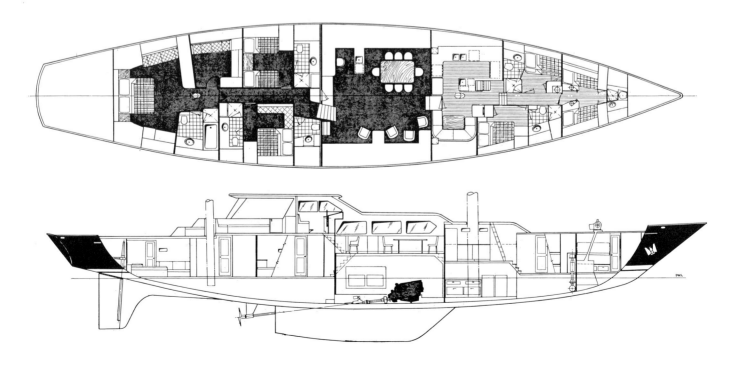

Astral – Design 2536

LOA: 115'   DWL: 88'   Beam: 25'   Draft: 12' 7"   Sail area: 4,292 sq. ft.

Though planned as a yacht that could be chartered, and which should thus not be too specially tailored, *Astral* has the admirable features of the most spectacular, private mega-yachts. Built by Palmer Johnson in Sturgeon Bay, Wisconsin, she has been given the most beautiful woodwork interior that American craftsmen trained in old-world traditions can create. She also (in the words of Palmer Johnson president Mike Kelsey) represents a "refinement in shape and detail" over the mega-yachts which had preceded her.

The 115-foot yacht's layout is both logical and elegant. At the touch of a button, a pneumatically operated hatch draws forward, the companionway door hisses smoothly aside, and one steps down into a magnificent deck saloon. Down three steps and to port is a formal dining area. The remainder of the boat forward is given over to a large galley, and crew quarters for six. Aft of the saloon and below the pilothouse are two double guest staterooms and the full-width owner's stateroom aft.

For owner or charterers alike, *Astral* has proved to be a model of stability and comfort—even in extreme conditions. During the boat's first sailing trials she performed without a hitch on all points of sailing in four days of 30-knot winds on Sturgeon Bay. Bill Langan, who was on board during those trials, reported, "it was extremely gratifying, because we had plenty of wind to prove that our design effort had paid off." A further demonstration: *Astral* won the informal but notable Nantucket Bucket Race in 1993.

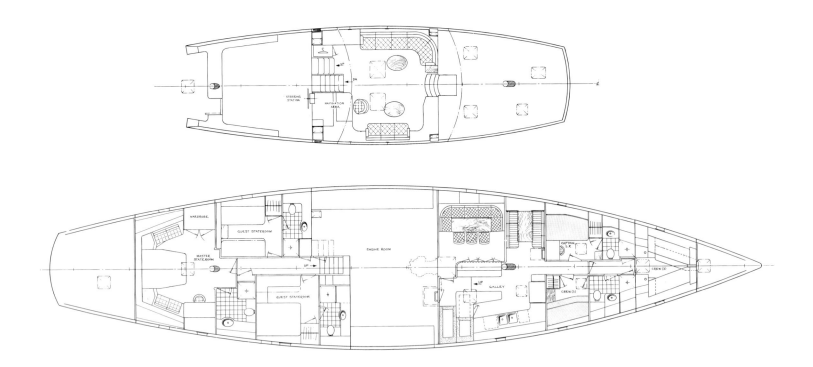

See photo page 238.

666 FT²
MIZZEN

1619 FT²
MAIN

4318 FT²
TOTAL

2033 FT²
100% F.D.

Maysylph – Design 2550

LOA: 123' 5"   DWL: 96'   Beam: 26' 6"   Draft: 12'   Sail area: 5,158 sq. ft.

Because she was launched in 1990 and because she's the largest of her line, *Maysylph* is considered the climax of a decade of mega-ketch designing. She's also extraordinarily beautiful—perhaps because of her somewhat thinner masts.

These masts result from the untypical decision to abandon the self-stowing sail rig of the other megas and to gain the best possible sail shapes by means of full-battened main and mizzen. For the team that made the sails, North Sails of Italy, this was a tremendous challenge, compelling them to invent new hardware as well as sails specially confected of heavy-duty "soft" Norlam. This cloth incorporates a layer of Mylar laminated between two outside layers of pre-stressed Dacron.

Sparkman & Stephens sought to improve *Maysylph*'s sailing qualities even beyond those of *Galileo*, thoroughly reviewing the hull's underwater appendages. After much study, the wing keel was refined and extended by the addition of 6 inches of draft, taking it to a depth of 12 feet.

In the traditional S&S manner, Alan Gilbert made sure that *Maysylph*'s European owner was aware of the risks implicit in these refinements and innovations. The boat was put to the test immediately after launching when, during the run passage from Newport to St. Thomas, captain and crew encountered a 50-knot gale that lasted for two days. The crew found it surprisingly simple to reef—and even to furl—the big, full-battened sails under these extreme conditions. The luff-and-leech reefing operation was assisted by lazyjacks (a wondrously old-fashioned addition to the newfangled rig).

In the subsequent sailing through the Caribbean, owner and captain were delighted to find that, under almost any wind conditions, *Maysylph* kept surging steadily along at about 10 knots. And she could go to windward like a J-boat.

S&S mastery of sailing features had brought forth a yacht that was as great in performance as in size and technological wizardry. The firm was, as always since the 1920s, in a leadership position in worldwide naval architecture.

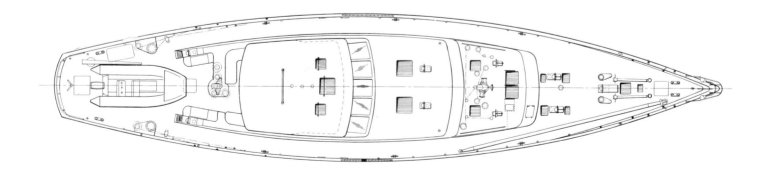

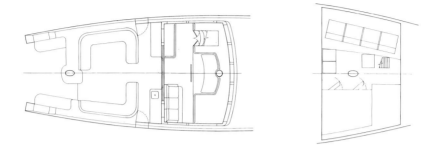

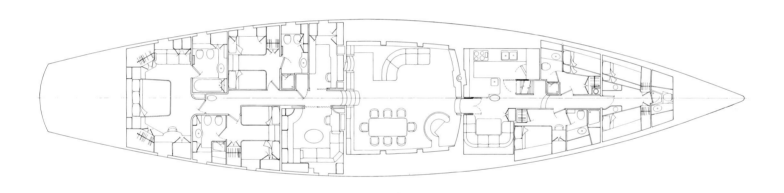

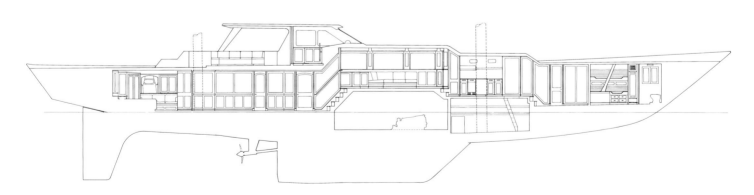

This page: Maysylph.

Appendices

Sparkman & Stephens Designs*

Design	Date	Client	Name/Class	Job Description	LOA	DWL	Beam	Draft	Type
1	1928	J.Y.R.A. of L.I. Sound	Manhasset Bay OD	Class One Design	21.50	15.00	5.83	3.50	Sloop
2	1928	Arthur P. Hatch	Kalmia	Cruising sloop	30.00	20.00	7.50	4.75	Sloop
3	1928	B. C. Hart	45-foot powerboat	Not built	n/a	n/a	n/a	n/a	Power
4	1930	S. W. Labrot, Jr.	Salabar/Balkis	Ex–Cynara	37.50	27.17	8.42	6.00	Cutter
5	1929	Lewis Young	Thalia	6-meter	36.67	22.75	6.25	5.25	Sloop
6	1937	John K. Roosevelt	Mist	6-meter	37.50	23.00	6.00	5.33	Sloop
7	1936	Rod Stephens, Sr.	Dorade	Fast cruiser	52.00	37.25	10.25	7.62	Yawl
8	1930	John P. Wilson	Comet	6-meter	37.50	23.00	6.00	5.33	Sloop
8.1	1930	Oscar Johnson	Meteor	6-meter	37.50	23.00	6.00	5.33	Sloop
9	1930	Walter Farley (syndt.)	Conewago	8-meter	49.67	30.67	7.92	6.50	Sloop
10	1930	Herman Whiton	Cherokee	6-meter	37.25	23.25	6.00	5.42	Sloop
11	1930	Dave Morris	Alsumar	Cruising aux.	44.00	30.00	9.00	6.25	Sloop
12	1932	Walter Barnum	Brilliant	Aux. schooner	61.50	49.00	14.17	8.83	Schooner
13	1931	R. Meyer	Bob Kat II	6-meter	36.75	23.50	6.25	6.67	Sloop
14	1931	H. W. Buck	Nortada	43-foot power cruiser	43.00	40.00	12.00	4.50	Power
15	1931	W. O. Becker	Velero	26' 6" sloop	38.25	26.50	8.75	5.58	Sloop
16	1931	J. Seward Johnson	Jill	6-meter	36.38	23.42	6.50	5.32	Sloop
17	1932	Van S. Merle-Smith	Nancy	6-meter	36.70	24.20	6.70	5.50	Sloop
18	1932	Bedford	Power tender	Not built	50.00	47.33	12.75	5.08	Power
19	1933	H. B. Nevins, & S&S	Gimcrack	23-foot sloop	34.37	23.00	7.04	4.48	Sloop
21	1933	George Knowles	Tamerlane	Motor-sailer (ketch)	66.17	53.00	17.10	5.19	M/S
22	1936	R. G. Morrison	Desert Water	Powerboat	51.00	49.50	12.50	3.67	Power
23	1934	Nassau	Not built	14-foot One Design cats	14.00	n/a	5.04	9.04	Catboat
24	1934	Lawrence M. Ballierr	Aweigh	35' 8" wl. sloop	47.12	35.67	11.79	5.98	Sloop
25	1934	Frank E. Richmond	Blue Heron	43' 5" yawl	43.47	30.00	11.29	4.33	Yawl
26	1934	Dave Morris	Alsumar	52' 6" wl. yawl	79.75	50.00	15.89	6.33	Yawl
27	1934	Philip LeBoutillier	Stormy Weather	39' 8" wl. yawl	53.92	39.75	12.52	7.89	Yawl
28	1934	R. C. Lockton	Roon II	32' 3" ketch	38.54	32.25	11.33	5.30	Ketch
29	1934	F. S. Pratt	Eaglet	20' 8" c/b sloop	29.13	20.67	8.17	3.50	Sloop
30	1934	J. Seward Johnson	Jack	6-meter	37.50	23.00	6.50	5.25	Sloop
35	1934	R. J. Schaefer	Edlu I	40-foot wl. aux. yawl	56.17	40.00	13.00	7.85	Yawl
36	1934	R. M. Willet	Swallow	6-meter	37.17	23.50	6.00	5.33	Sloop
37	1934	Clarence S. Postley	Kiboko	56' 9" wl. motor-sailer	59.95	56.75	16.71	6.75	M/S
40[1]	1934	Herman F. Whiton	Erne	6-meter - design aid	40.08	23.75	6.58	5.42	Sloop
41[2]	1936	G. V. Vetlesen	Vema III	Alterations (12-meter)	n/a	n/a	n/a	n/a	Sloop
44[2]	1934	Briggs Cunningham	Lucie	6-meter - alterations	37.00	23.00	6.50	5.25	Sloop
46[2]	1934	G. W. Ferguson	Sprig	6-meter - alterations	36.92	23.00	6.25	4.75	Sloop
48[2]	1934	No record	Gray Dawn	Re-rig	n/a	n/a	n/a	n/a	n/a
49[2]	1934	Chandler Harvey	Weetamoe	J-boat alterations	125.75	83.00	19.83	15.00	Sloop
50	1934	proposal	Not built	Prop. 28-foot wl. aux. cutter	n/a	n/a	n/a	n/a	Cutter
51	1934	proposal	Not built	Prop. 19' 8" aux. sloop	27.00	19.67	7.75	4.33	Sloop
52	1934	Royal Corinthian Y. C.	Trenche-Mer	Competition later built	72.00	53.50	14.83	10.58	Yawl
53	1934	Donald B. Abbott	Not built	Prop. 26' 6" wl. cutter	33.92	27.50	8.92	5.50	Cutter
54	1934	Guy W. Rex	Landfall	32-foot wl. aux. yawl	44.00	32.00	9.75	6.50	Yawl
55	1934	F. T. Moses	Not built	Cruising ketch	52.67	40.00	13.25	7.00	Ketch
56	1934	J. Holmes	Not built	Prop. fishing boat	70.00	69.00	15.00	n/a	Power
57	1934	R. J. Reynolds	Not built	Prop. 66-foot wl. schooner	87.83	66.50	18.83	11.00	Schooner
58	1934	Charles Jencks	Werdna	30-foot wl. aux. yawl	40.25	30.00	10.42	6.08	Yawl
59	1934	William L. Stewart	Santana	55-foot wl. schooner	55.17	40.33	12.50	7.92	Schooner
60	1934	G. Ottley	Not built	Prop. 56-foot schooner	71.92	56.50	16.50	9.67	Schooner
61	1934	J. Rupert Schalk	Linwood	67-foot wl. power	76.92	75.50	15.50	4.00	Power
62	1934	Babson	Not built	Prop. 47-foot wl. yawl	n/a	n/a	n/a	n/a	Yawl
64[2]	1934	Mrs. Barklie Henry	Skylark	Alterations	n/a	n/a	n/a	n/a	n/a
65	1934	J. M. Nelson	Penrith	32-foot wl. aux. sloop	43.92	32.00	10.92	5.94	Sloop

*Gaps in this list could not be filled without further delays in the publication of this book. We hope to complete the historical record for future printings.—The Editor.

[1] This design done by Herman Whiton and S&S, as a joint effort.
[2] Not an S&S design.

Design	Date	Client	Name/Class	Job Description	LOA	DWL	Beam	Draft	Type
66	1934	Albert Fay	*Starlight*	32-foot wl. aux. cutter	44.00	32.00	10.50	6.50	Sloop
67	1934	N. G. Loud	Not built	20' 8" prop. sloop	29.71	20.75	8.08	4.21	Sloop
68	1934	Islesborough	*Dark Harbor*	One Design	30.00	20.00	6.50	4.17	Sloop
69	1935	J. Gordon Gibbs	Not built	Prop. 39-foot wl. yawl	56.17	40.00	13.00	7.92	Yawl
70[2]	1934	No record	*Vega*	New spar	n/a	n/a	n/a	n/a	n/a
72	1935	Tawas Boat Works	One design	Class One Design	27.08	17.50	6.09	3.73	Sloop
73	1935	Proposal	No record	Prop. ice boat	n/a	n/a	n/a	n/a	n/a
74	1934	W. R. Greenwood	Not built	Prop. ketch	n/a	n/a	n/a	n/a	Ketch
75	1935	Casco Bay Lines	Not built	Prop. passenger craft	n/a	n/a	n/a	n/a	Power
76	1935	E. E. Dickinson	*El Nido*	Burned during constr.	58.00	56.67	12.50	3.50	Power
77	1935	F. M. Haines	Not built	Prop. 32-foot wl. aux. sloops	n/a	n/a	n/a	n/a	Sloop
77C[3]	1937	H. S. Vanderbilt	*Ranger*	J-boat	135.00	87.00	20.92	15.00	Sloop
78	1935	Proposal	Not built	Prop. 27-foot wl. daysailer	n/a	n/a	n/a	n/a	Sloop
79[2]	1935	No record	Comet OD cl	New mast	16.00	n/a	5.00	n/a	Sloop
81	1935	L. Lee Stanton	*Kretzer*	Kretzer boats – 6 built	29.96	22.33	8.17	4.33	Sloop
82[2]	1935	H. Havemeyer	*Mouette*	12 meter - alterations	67.58	44.33	11.83	8.75	Sloop
83	1935	R. P. Baruch	Not built	Prop. 37' 6" wl. cutter	n/a	n/a	n/a	n/a	Cutter
85	1935	Walter Rothschild	*Avanti*	40-foot wl. aux. yawl	55.69	40.00	12.45	7.74	Yawl
86[2]	1935	No record	*Sally Ann*	New rig	n/a	n/a	n/a	n/a	n/a
87[2]	1935	No record	*Ace*	Catboat	n/a	n/a	n/a	n/a	Catboat
88[2]	1935	E. Sturges	*Cleon*	New rig	n/a	n/a	n/a	n/a	n/a
89	1935	J. W. Steube	*White Swan*	28-foot wl. aux. sloop	35.00	28.00	9.33	5.42	Sloop
90	1935	William McCoy	Not built	Shoal-draft schooner	75.27	66.50	19.17	5.00	Schooner
91[2]	1935	No record	*Tar Baby*	Prop. new rig	n/a	n/a	n/a	n/a	n/a
94	1935	Albert D. Phelps	*Sonny*	39-foot wl. aux. cutter	53.50	39.00	12.54	7.62	Sloop
95[2]	1935	No record	*Game Cock*	Alterations	n/a	n/a	n/a	n/a	n/a
96	1935	B. Wilford	Not built	Prop. gyro boat	n/a	n/a	n/a	n/a	n/a
97	1935	John U. White	*Babe*	25-foot wl. aux. sloop	30.50	25.08	7.87	5.33	Sloop
98	1935	R. B. Benedict	Not built	Prop. 37' 6" wl. yawl	n/a	n/a	n/a	n/a	Yawl
99	1935	James R. Lowe	*Manitou*	44-foot wl. aux. yawl	62.00	44.00	13.75	8.50	Yawl
100[2]	1935	Van S. Merle Smith	*Seven Seas*	New rudder (twelve)	68.50	45.42	12.00	8.92	Sloop
101	1935	J. W. Dart	Not built	Prop. 41-foot cutter	n/a	n/a	n/a	n/a	Cutter
102	1935	H. G. Hoster	*Tejeria*	33' 6" wl. aux. sloop	44.87	35.50	11.33	6.00	Sloop
103	1935	Calvin Tomkins	Not built	Prop 23-foot wl. aux. sloop	n/a	n/a	n/a	n/a	Sloop
104	1936	Herman Whiton	*Bobkat III*	6-meter	35.75	23.42	6.17	5.37	Sloop
105	1935	H. N. Slater	Sport fisherman	Prop. 36-foot wl.	36.00	35.25	9.50	n/a	Power
106	1935	*Dark Harbor*	Not built	Prop. 16' wl. One Design	21.81	16.00	6.00	3.67	Sloop
107	1935	W. G. McCullough	Not built	Prop. 28' wl. aux. cutter	n/a	n/a	n/a	n/a	Cutter
108	1935	Carl Moses	*Dorado*	57-foot wl. fisherman	55.39	54.83	12.71	4.17	Power
109	1935	Squibb	Not built	Prop. 41-foot wl. aux. m/s	47.42	41.00	13.00	5.00	Cutter
110	1935	R. Harte	Not built	Prop. 72-foot wl. aux. m/s	n/a	n/a	n/a	n/a	n/a
111	1935	William Bross Lloyd	Not built	Prop. 50-foot wl. m/s	65.58	55.75	16.00	6.33	n/a
112	1935	Walter S. Gubelman	*Windigo*	Aux. yawl	71.50	50.00	15.50	9.12	Yawl
112.1	1935	John Shethar	*Ptarmigan*	50-foot aux. yawl	71.50	50.00	15.50	9.12	Yawl
114	1936	Mortimer N. Buckner	*Pampero*	Yawl rig for N.Y. 32	n/a	n/a	n/a	n/a	Yawl
116	1935	Adrian Iselin	*Redhead*	42-foot wl. aux. yawl	59.45	42.00	13.33	8.33	Yawl
119[4]	1935	Wyatt	*Bloodhound*	Bermuda yawl	63.25	44.58	12.50	9.08	Yawl
120	1935	Junius S. Morgan	Not built	Prop. aux. ketch	44.33	35.83	11.42	6.50	Ketch
121	1935	Langhorne Gibson	*Diana*	57' 6" wl. motor sailer	60.50	57.50	16.33	6.25	Ketch
122	1936	Alan Grago	*A. Grago* - not built	35-foot wl. aux. cutter	35.00	27.33	8.58	5.96	Sloop
124	1935	William C. Appleton	*Rainey*	30-foot wl. aux. sloop	36.75	30.00	9.90	5.00	Sloop
125	1935	Various	New York 32	New One Design class	45.33	32.00	10.58	6.50	Sloop
126	1936	C. Bruynzeel	*Zeearend*	40-foot wl. aux. yawl	54.62	40.00	12.00	8.33	Yawl
127	1936	Various	Not built	Prop. new One Design	n/a	n/a	n/a	n/a	Sloop
128[2]	1936	P. W. Howard	*Valkyrie*	Rig alterations	38.00	23.33	7.75	5.33	Sloop
129	1936	Dexter Lewis	*Hersilia*	New rig	n/a	n/a	n/a	n/a	Sloop
130	1936	Schooner Yacht	*Gilnockie*	Alterations (new rig)	69.08	28.58	11.67	5.83	Power
131	1936	No record	*Siwash*	Aux. yawl	39.83	n/a	n/a	n/a	Yawl
132	1936	No record	*Shearwater*	New sail plan	n/a	n/a	n/a	n/a	n/a
133	1936	S. G Saunders	*Noreg*	6-meter alterations	36.25	24.50	6.00	5.50	Sloop
134	1936	No record	Not built	Prop. One Design class	n/a	n/a	n/a	n/a	n/a
135	1936	No record	*Seafather*	Alterations	n/a	n/a	n/a	n/a	n/a
136	1936	Henry B. Nevins	Not built	Prop. One Design class	45.75	32.00	10.58	6.50	Yawl
137	1936	George A. Whiting	*White Cloud*	New rig	60.52	42.75	13.08	8.53	Sloop
138	1936	No record	*Anitra*	New rig	n/a	n/a	n/a	n/a	n/a
139	1936	No record	*Vamarie*	Sail plan alterations	n/a	n/a	n/a	n/a	n/a
140	1936	No record	*Venturon*	New rig	n/a	n/a	n/a	n/a	n/a
141	1936	Briggs Cunningham	Not built	Prop. fishing boat	n/a	n/a	n/a	n/a	n/a
142	1936	No record	N.Y.Y.C. 32'	Re-rig	49.33	32.00	10.58	6.50	Sloop
143	1936	J. Thornton Baker	*So Fong*	54-foot wl. aux. schooner	70.29	54.00	16.17	9.75	Schooner

[2] *Not an S&S design.*
[3] *Design by W. Starling Burgess and Sparkman & Stephens, Inc.*
[4] *Bloodhound hull by Camper/Nicholson; rig and interior by S&S.*

Design	Date	Client	Name/Class	Job Description	LOA	DWL	Beam	Draft	Type
144	1936	Raymond Paige	*Prelude*	8-meter sloop	46.75	31.00	8.00	6.56	Sloop
145	1936	E. E. Dickinson	*Phoenix*	Powerboat	64.67	63.33	12.50	3.50	Power
146	1936	Donald B. Ayres	*Vryling*	38-foot wl. aux. yawl	53.13	38.00	12.00	7.58	Yawl
147	1936	Col. Edwin L. Chance	Not built	Prop. 45-foot wl. m/s	n/a	n/a	n/a	n/a	n/a
148	1936	Baxter	Not built	18-foot canoe	n/a	n/a	n/a	n/a	n/a
149[2]	1936	No record	*Ariel*	New rig	n/a	n/a	n/a	n/a	n/a
150	1936	R. J. Reynolds	*Elizabeth McCaw*	45-foot wl. aux. yawl	63.33	45.00	14.00	8.00	Yawl
152	1936	Bechtel	Not built	Prop. 33-foot wl. cutter	n/a	n/a	n/a	n/a	n/a
153	1936	Harold T. White	*Spookie*	32-foot wl. aux. cutter	45.33	32.00	10.25	6.50	Sloop
155	1936	Barclay Henry	*Odyssey*	32-foot wl. aux. yawl	88.56	62.00	18.00	10.67	Yawl
156	1936	No record	*Medora*	Re-rig	n/a	n/a	n/a	n/a	n/a
157	1936	Van S. Merle-Smith	*Nancy Pat*	Express cruiser	55.33	54.50	11.75	3.50	n/a
160	1937	Palmer Scott	*Baltica*	Boston office	38.42	29.00	10.17	5.42	Ketch
162	1937	Kenneth Boyd	C/B yawl	Boston office	75.00	53.00	17.25	5.50	Yawl
163	1937	Dexter L. Lewis	Aux. sloop	Boston office	44.39	32.00	11.00	6.67	Sloop
164	1938	Various	Islander class	One Design (Boston)	30.00	23.00	8.33	4.75	Sloop
165	1938	Dr. Chas. L. Swan, Jr.	Aux. ketch	Boston office	57.58	42.00	14.00	7.75	Ketch
166	1939	Kenneth Boyd	*Solution*	Boston office	46.17	34.00	12.25	5.50	Sloop
167	not used	n/a	n/a	n/a	n/a	n/a	n/a	n/a	n/a
168[2]	1936	No record	*Cressida*	New sail plan	n/a	n/a	n/a	n/a	n/a
169	1936	No record	Not built	One Design proposal	n/a	n/a	n/a	n/a	Sloop
170[2]	1936	No record	*Sheerness*	New rig and rating	n/a	n/a	n/a	n/a	n/a
171	1936	Rumson Country Club	Arrow OD cl	One Design	21.69	18.17	6.00	2.31	Sloop
172	1936	Porter Buck	*Nugget*	26-foot wl. sloop	33.14	26.00	10.04	5.00	Sloop
173	1936	James C. Kimberly	Not built	Prop. 85-foot diesel cruiser	85.00	83.50	16.50	4.00	Power
174[2]	1936	No record	*Sextet*	Alterations	n/a	n/a	n/a	n/a	n/a
175	1936	Boeing Airlines	None	Design airplane galley	n/a	n/a	n/a	n/a	n/a
176	1939	Penn Yann	*Seabird*	Seawanhaka	23.94	15.00	5.77	3.48	Sloop
177	1936	P. M. Sturges	Tender – not built	30-foot power tender	30.00	29.17	7.25	2.25	Power
179	1935	Briggs Cunningham	*Lulu*	6-meter	36.75	23.33	6.00	5.33	Sloop
180	1937	F. T. Bedford	*Fun*	6-meter	37.00	23.75	6.00	5.25	Sloop
181	1935	David Macdonell, Jr.	*Mary Clyde*	C/B gaff-headed yawl	33.87	26.33	10.00	3.00	Yawl
182[2]	1936	DeCoursey Fales	*Niña*	Re-rig schooner	59.00	50.0	15.17	6.92	Schooner
183[2]	1936	Huntington Hartford	*Joseph Conrad*	New arrangement	118.50	102.17	25.33	12.50	Ship
184[2]	1936	Henry Sears	*Actea*	Keel alterations	61.83	44.75	13.33	8.83	Cutter
185	1936	John J. White, Jr.	*Souvenir*	34-foot wl. aux. cutter	47.50	34.00	11.33	6.17	Sloop
186	1936	C. S. Postley	Not built	Prop. 63-foot wl. class	63.00	n/a	n/a	n/a	Ketch
192	1937	W. A. Lippincott	*Fair wind*	Aux. cutter	44.19	31.67	10.92	6.75	Cutter
193	1937	P. H. Hazelton	Tender	Power tender	32.00	31.00	8.33	2.33	Power
196[2]	1937	Charles Belsky	*Sea Lure*	Re-rig	40.00	31.50	11.00	5.50	Schooner
197	1937	Proposal	Proposal	Prop. "L" class	n/a	n/a	n/a	n/a	Sail
198	1937	S. A. Mitchell	Nassau class	28' 8" wl. aux. sloop	34.50	28.67	11.00	4.00	Sloop
199[2]	1937	Unknown	*Typhoon*	Larchmont "P" new rig	46.00	35.00	12.00	7.33	Schooner
200[2]	1937	Unknown	*Chinook*	N.Y. 40 – new rig	59.00	40.00	14.42	8.00	Yawl
201	1937	Henry Sears	Not built	Prop. fisherman	40.25	38.83	10.00	3.67	Power
202	1937	C. A. Tomkins	Not built	26-foot wl. aux. sloop	32.92	26.00	8.00	5.58	Sloop
203[2]	1937	Tomas Robbins, Jr.	*Hopwell*	Alterations	n/a	n/a	n/a	n/a	n/a
204	1937	F. A. Jenkes	*Orient*	44-foot wl. aux. cutter	63.42	44.00	14.08	8.54	Cutter
205	1937	H. Nelson Slater	Not built	Prop. 65-foot wl. ketch	n/a	n/a	n/a	n/a	Ketch
206[2]	1937	L. Wasey	*Phantom*	Powerboat revisions	n/a	n/a	n/a	n/a	Power
207	1937	Walter L. Todd	*Onaire III*	44-foot wl. cutter	63.35	44.00	14.08	8.53	Cutter
208	1937	Various	Weekender	Cruising class	35.04	27.00	9.50	5.58	Sloop
209	1937	K. B. Noble	Not built	Prop. 40-foot wl. yawl	n/a	n/a	n/a	n/a	Yawl
210	1937	Unknown	Newport raceabout	Not built	n/a	n/a	n/a	n/a	Sloop
211	1937	Dave Morris, Jr.	Not built	Prop. 45-foot wl. m/s	n/a	n/a	n/a	n/a	M/S
212	1937	Pemberton Whitcomb	*Onkahya*	C/B yawl	59.50	42.00	14.17	5.83	Yawl
213	1937	B. E. Ruys, Jr.	*Atalanta*	Aux. cutter	55.42	39.00	11.67	8.00	Cutter
214	1937	F. T. Bedford	*Nyala*	12-meter	70.16	45.00	12.00	8.75	Sloop
215	1937	Henry Sears	*Actea*	44' 9" wl. aux. cutter	61.83	44.75	13.33	9.08	Cutter
216[2]	1937	W. A. Labrot	No record	Re-arrangement plan	n/a	n/a	n/a	n/a	Yawl
217[2]	1937	J. E. Plumb	*Nam Sang*	Re-rig	66.25	50.00	14.25	9.00	Ketch
218	1937	R. J. Schaefer	*Edlu II*	48-foot wl. aux. yawl	68.00	48.00	14.50	9.25	Yawl
219	1937	Edward Rosenberg, Jr.	*Azura*	30-foot wl. aux. yawl	42.08	30.00	10.08	6.50	Yawl
220	1937	Harkness Edwards	*Wakiva*	48-foot wl. aux. yawl	70.25	49.50	15.12	9.00	Yawl
221	1937	R. J. Reynolds	*Blitzen*	C.C.A. racing cutter	55.27	40.00	12.45	7.74	Cutter
222	1937	Henry C. Taylor	*Baruna*	50-foot wl. aux. yawl	72.00	50.00	14.83	9.50	Yawl
223	1937	C.G.A.S. Parre	Not built	48-foot wl. schooner	n/a	n/a	n/a	n/a	Schooner
224	1937	William Gundlach	Not built	Prop. bridgedeck cruiser	n/a	n/a	n/a	n/a	Power
225[2]	1937	William P. Barrows	No record	Accommodation plan	n/a	n/a	n/a	n/a	Yawl
226	1937	Thomas H. Hefferan	*Tomahawk*	34-foot wl. yawl	48.25	34.00	11.00	6.83	Yawl
227	1937	George H. Townsend	Cruisailer 41	Class m/s 41	40.92	35.83	11.33	4.96	Ketch
227.1	1946	H. Boone Porter	*Gray Mist*	Revisions to rig	41.00	35.83	10.33	5.00	Ketch

[2] *Not an S&S design.*

Design	Date	Client	Name/Class	Job Description	LOA	DWL	Beam	Draft	Type
228[2]	1937	Harry Wagner	Unknown	Studies - 36-foot yawl	n/a	n/a	n/a	n/a	Yawl
229[2]	1937	Gulfport Boiler Works	Harb. & coast. tanker	230-foot diesel tanker	234.25	n/a	42.00	n/a	Power
230	1937	Col. Edwin M. Chance	*Far Cry*	Motor-sailer	47.33	42.00	13.04	4.50	Ketch
231	1937	Dr. Hans Collignon	*Mitchel II*	6-meter	36.96	23.35	6.00	5.02	Sloop
232	1937	Eugene DuPont	Motor-sailer	Sketches only	n/a	n/a	n/a	n/a	M/S
234	1938	Gilbert Ottley	*Falcon*	Motor-sailer	53.14	46.50	13.67	5.58	Ketch
235	1937	Smith & Johnson	Not built	165' pass./cargo/oil boat	171.50	165.00	26.00	8.00	Power
236	1938	R. J. Reynolds	*Kit Jones*	Diesel tugboat	60.33	56.00	16.00	4.50	Power
238	1938	Henry S. Morgan	*Djinn*	6-meter	36.84	23.63	6.02	5.40	Sloop
239	1938	Alfred L. Loomis	*Northern Light*	12-meter	70.00	45.00	11.84	8.75	Sloop
239.1	1956	Stavros Niarchos	*Nereus*	Re-rig 12-meter	70.00	45.00	11.84	8.75	Sloop
241	1938	Anonymous	*Typhoon*	New sail plan	n/a	n/a	n/a	n/a	Schooner
242	1938	C. A. Wright	Not built	Prop. motor-sailer (ketch)	56.33	49.25	14.17	5.83	M/S
243	1938	George Nichols	*Goose*	6-meter	37.00	23.67	6.05	5.42	Sloop
244	1938	H. W. McGregor	*McGregor*	32-foot wl. aux. cutter	47.55	33.50	10.92	6.75	Cutter
245[2]	1938	Anonymous	*Latifa*	Re-rig	n/a	n/a	n/a	n/a	Yawl
247	1938	George H. Townsend	Cruisailer 55	Class 55-foot motor-sailer	54.65	46.50	13.69	5.23	Ketch
248	1938	George H. Townsend	Not built	Prop. 65' 9" wl. m/s	n/a	n/a	n/a	n/a	Ketch
249	1938	Powell Crosley, Jr.	Not built	Prop. 39-foot wl. m/s	n/a	n/a	n/a	n/a	Ketch
250	1938	Anonymous	34-foot wl yawl	New sail plan	n/a	n/a	n/a	n/a	Yawl
251	1938	Van Merle-Smith	*Seven Seas*	Rudder alteration	68.00	44.50	12.00	8.92	12-meter
252	1938	C. E. Davis	*Tasmania*	30-foot wl. aux. yawl	44.25	30.13	10.58	6.00	Yawl
253	1938	Branigan	Not built	60-foot harbor tanker	62.83	60.00	18.00	6.50	Power
254	1939	Sandy Hook Pilots	Not built	Profile & arrang. plans	n/a	n/a	n/a	n/a	Power
255	1938	William L. Stewart	*Chubasco*	46' 6" wl. aux. yawl	67.25	46.50	13.83	9.12	Yawl
255.2	1966	Donald Haskell	*Chubasco*	Updated (re-rig)	67.25	46.50	13.83	9.12	Yawl
256	1938	Albert Fay	*Corinthian*	Class 20-foot One Design	20.20	18.00	6.33	3.33	Sloop
257	1938	U. S. Navy Dept.	Not built	110-foot submarine chaser	n/a	n/a	n/a	n/a	Power
258	1937	Gulfport Boiler Works	Not built	705-ton dw. tanker	n/a	n/a	n/a	n/a	Power
259	1938	Dave Hennen Morris	Not built	Centerboarder	36.75	28.50	10.75	3.67	Sloop
260	1938	U.S. Naval Academy	U.S.N.A. yawl	30-foot wl. aux. yawl	44.18	30.33	10.87	6.03	Yawl
261	1938	Thomas Robins, Jr.	Not built	41' 6" wl. aux. yawl	n/a	n/a	n/a	n/a	Yawl
262	1938	U.S. Navy Dept.	Not built	70-foot torpedo boat	79.78	77.00	14.33	4.33	Power
263.1	1938	George H. Townsend	Not built	63-foot wl. m/s	n/a	n/a	n/a	n/a	Ketch
263.2	1938	Irving A. Sartorius	Not built	46-foot wl. aux. ketch	n/a	n/a	n/a	n/a	Ketch
264	1938	Various	Voyager class	Class sloop or yawl	44.23	30.08	10.58	6.29	Sloop
265	1938	Various	Lightning class	19-foot wl. One Design class	19.00	16.00	6.50	1.42	Sloop
267	1938	American Yacht Club	Not built	Prop. One Design class	26.25	19.42	6.50	4.25	Sloop
268	1938	Various	S&S plans	Type details	n/a	n/a	n/a	n/a	n/a
269	1938	Various	S&S design	Dynamometers	n/a	n/a	n/a	n/a	n/a
270	1938	Anonymous	Not built	7' 9" pram dinghy	n/a	n/a	n/a	n/a	Sloop
271	1938	William J. Strawbridge	Not built	35-foot wl. aux. sloop	n/a	n/a	n/a	n/a	Sloop
272[2]	1938	Anonymous	*Mariette*	Alterations	n/a	n/a	n/a	n/a	Sloop
273	1938	W. H. Vandervorm	*Zwerver I*	39-foot wl. aux. cutter	60.05	43.00	12.79	8.69	Cutter
274	1938	Phillip Roosevelt	Not built	Five-meter sloop	n/a	n/a	n/a	n/a	Sloop
275	1938	Ronald Tree	*Iskareen*	8-meter sloop	48.75	31.00	8.00	6.50	Sloop
276[2]	1938	American Yacht Club	Unknown	Launch alterations	n/a	n/a	n/a	n/a	Power
277	1938	Skaneateles Boats	Skiff	11' 6" skiff (One Design)	11.46	n/a	4.69	n/a	Sloop
278[2]	1938	Arthur Peck	Pratt launch	Renov. 35' fishing boat	35.00	33.33	10.21	2.58	Power
279	1938	Harold C. Vanderbilt	*Vim*	12-meter	70.22	45.50	11.83	8.86	Sloop
279.1	1951	Harold C. Vanderbilt	*Vim*	Engine installed	70.22	45.50	11.83	8.86	Sloop
279.2	1957	Harold C. Vanderbilt	*Vim*	New mast	70.22	45.50	11.83	8.86	Sloop
280	1939	A. E. Fuller	*Cirrus*	26-foot wl. aux. sloop	33.50	26.00	8.83	5.50	Sloop
281	1938	Floyd Noble	*Clemencia*	42-foot wl. aux. yawl	59.71	42.00	13.25	8.25	Yawl
282	1938	Philip Roosevelt	Seawanhaka 21	One Design class	31.00	21.00	6.58	4.50	Sloop
283	1938	E. E. Dickinson, Jr.	*Avoca*	66-foot express cruiser	68.79	66.37	13.50	4.00	Power
284	1938	A. Altman	Proposal	45-foot fast ferry	n/a	n/a	n/a	n/a	Power
285	1938	Morris Floyd	Proposal	28-foot wl. sloop	36.50	28.00	9.75	5.50	Sloop
286	1938	Robert H. Moore	*Perroquet*	32' 10" wl. cutter	46.95	32.09	10.92	6.75	Sloop
287	1938	Fishers Island	Proposal (not built)	27-foot One Design	n/a	n/a	n/a	n/a	Sloop
288	1939	Spencer Goodwin	Not built	30-foot wl. aux. cutter	n/a	n/a	n/a	n/a	Cutter
289	1939	David H. Morris, Jr.	*Pelican*	25-foot wl. cutter	29.50	23.00	9.10	2.83	Cutter
291	1939	Robert W. Johnson	*Good News*	45-foot wl. aux. yawl	64.50	45.00	13.42	8.83	Yawl
291.1	1966	Jakob Isbrandtsen	*Good News*	45-foot wl. aux. sloop	64.50	45.00	13.42	8.83	Sloop
292	1939	J. Veltjens	6-meter	6-meter sloop	n/a	n/a	n/a	n/a	Sloop
293[2]	1939	Anonymous	*Seven Seas* (12-meter)	Keel alteration	68.00	44.50	12.00	8.92	Sloop
294	1939	Ray Alan Van Clief	Not built	200-foot seag. yacht 22 kn.	210.00	200.00	29.00	11.25	Power
295[2]	1939	Goddard	*Ramallah*	New rig	n/a	n/a	n/a	n/a	Yawl
296	1939	Cape Cod Shipbuilding	Mercury class	C/B or keel	15.00	13.00	5.42	3.25/2.42	Sloop
297	1939	Various	Privateer	Privateer class	35.33	24.50	8.89	5.44	Sloop
298	1939	Frank E. Richmond	*White Heron*	47-foot motor-sailer	55.17	47.00	14.17	4.00	Ketch
299	1939	Arthur Iselin	Not built	Motor-sailer	73.08	58.50	16.75	7.00	Ketch

[2] *Not an S&S design.*

Design	Date	Client	Name/Class	Job Description	LOA	DWL	Beam	Draft	Type
300	1939	Platzer Boat Works	Proposal	70-foot cargo schooner	n/a	n/a	n/a	n/a	Schooner
301	1939	Jose Duarte	*Vendaval*	46-foot wl. aux. sailer	64.67	46.00	14.31	8.46	Yawl
302	1939	Henry P. DuPont	Proposal	65-foot wl. motor-sailer	70.33	65.00	18.67	7.00	Ketch
303	1939	Adrian R. Allan	Not built	68-foot wl. diesel yacht	70.67	68.00	16.00	4.67	Power
304	1939	John Parkinson	Not built	23' 7" wl. penthouse slp	23.94	23.58	7.85	4.35	Sloop
305	1939	Speculations	Proposal	Police and fireboat	47.50	46.00	12.00	3.25	Power
306	1939	Dr. Francis W. Soyak	Not built	47-foot wl. aux. cruiser	48.00	47.00	12.50	3.33	Sloop
307	1939	Naviere Columbia	Proposal	Passenger boat - river	220.00	n/a	48.00	3.50	Power
309	1939	L. K. Jennings	*Timber Doodle*	Diesel cruiser	52.58	51.00	13.08	4.00	Power
319.1	1939	Pert Lowell	*Fleet-O-Wing*	Keel knockabout	17.75	14.50	6.00	3.00	Sloop
321	1939	Adrian R. Allan	*Westerly*	Motor-sailer	73.21	60.00	17.75	7.50	Ketch
322	1939	Various	Raceabout	Fin keel class	23.00	19.33	5.67	3.33	Sloop
327	1940	William Stetson	*Stetson*	Aux. sloop	28.17	22.67	5.69	5.00	Sloop
330	1940	Not built	*Pitcairn*	37-foot wl. cutter	52.34	37.00	12.50	5.50	Cutter
334	1940	William Strawbridge	*Escort*	Launch	39.80	39.00	9.46	2.75	Power
337	1940	W. L. Hendrickson	*Restless*	C/B sloop	37.96	27.00	10.17	4.17	Sloop
339	1940	Laurance Rockefeller	*Whirlwind*	Commuter	52.50	50.00	11.75	3.50	Power
341	1940	Avard Fuller	Runabout	V. bottom	18.00	17.00	6.46	2.08	Power
367	1940	Avard Fuller	Dinghy	Sailing dinghy	7.83	7.50	3.96	0.83	Catboat
379	1940	R. Hernandorina	*Ciclon*	34-foot wl. aux. sloop	51.00	34.00	11.50	7.02	Sloop
379.1	1947	Simms brothers	*Venture III*	34-foot wl. aux. yawl	51.67	34.00	11.50	7.00	Yawl
380	1941	H. S. Vanderbilt	*Vagrant*	Steel m/s	117.55	100.00	25.19	10.00	Ketch
381	1940	A. Howard Fuller	*Gesture*	40-foot wl. aux. sloop	57.33	40.00	12.58	8.17	Sloop
387	1940	Donald Laflin	*Windward*	26-foot wl. aux. sloop	33.14	26.00	10.04	5.00	Sloop
508	1945	Gilbert Wyland	*Windcall*	Alum. cruising sloop	35.62	27.00	10.17	5.50	Sloop
509.1	1945	Various	Brazil class	Aux. sloop	40.00	27.62	10.04	5.92	Sloop
509.2	1945	Various	Mackinac class	Aux. sloop	40.00	27.62	10.04	5.92	Sloop
539	1945	Various	Pilot class	Aux. sloop	32.92	24.00	9.50	4.75	Sloop
577	1945	John P. Wilson	*Comet*	Aux. yawl	52.84	37.00	12.46	7.50	Yawl
583	1945	Col. Edwin Chance	*Chiriqui*	52' 6" wl. m/s	59.56	52.50	13.80	4.75	Ketch
602	1945	Harvey Conover	*Revonoc*	Aux. c/b yawl	45.30	32.00	12.08	4.39	Yawl
618.B	1945	Edwin Waldvogel	Gazelle class	C/B sloop	22.63	19.00	6.58	0.60	Sloop
618.E	1945	Various	Inter-club class	Sailing dinghy	11.50	11.50	4.62	0.04	Catboat
619	1947	Gifford Pinchot	*Loki*	Cruising aux.	38.06	26.00	9.58	5.67	Yawl
621	1945	Laurance Rockefeller	*Dauntless*	Commuter	65.83	62.00	17.54	3.12	Power
622	1945	Avard Fuller	*Eroica*	Aux. yawl	48.75	33.33	10.96	7.25	Yawl
623	1945	Edward K. Warren	*Windblown*	Aux. sloop	39.58	28.00	11.16	5.80	Sloop
625	1945	Dave H. Morris	*Kawanee*	52' 6" wl. m/s	63.00	52.50	15.50	5.50	Ketch
628	1946	Simms brothers	*Argyll*	Aux. yawl	57.37	40.00	12.75	8.00	Yawl
638	1945	H. E. Bremer	*Holiday*	Aux. sloop	42.17	32.00	11.42	5.96	Sloop
639	1946	Ralph N. Isham	*Ronaele*	Motor-sailer	54.67	46.50	13.67	5.00	Ketch
642	1946	Arthur Iselin	*Courageous*	Aux. sloop	47.77	32.00	10.00	7.50	Sloop
652	1946	N.Y.C. Dept. Parks	Unknown	13-foot LOA catboat	13.00	11.98	6.03	0.47	Catboat
654	1946	William Stetson	One-design dinghy	14-foot sailing dinghy	14.00	13.75	5.19	0.54	Sloop
667	1946	Thomas S. Short	*Tasco*	Aux. yawl	49.92	34.00	11.17	7.42	Yawl
675	1946	Edgar Tolman, Jr.	*Tahltona*	Aux. ketch	45.17	33.00	10.96	6.25	Ketch
681	1946	Various	Duckling class	Sailing dinghy	11.67	10.06	4.96	0.54	Sloop
696	1946	Various	Mar-Casado class	Aux. sloop	25.20	19.00	7.50	4.04	Sloop
697	1946	Francis V. DuPont	Tech. Jr.	Power cruiser	60.00	57.10	15.00	3.75	Power
708	1946	Frank Campbell	*Rascal*	Aux. sloop	45.00	31.00	10.67	6.33	Sloop
711	1946	John N. Brown	*Bolero*	Aux. yawl	73.50	51.00	15.08	9.50	Yawl
711.6	1994	Gunter Sunkler	*Bolero*	Refit consult.	73.50	51.00	15.08	9.50	Yawl
730	1946	Ian S. Waldie	Maple Leaf class	Aux. sloops	35.17	24.00	7.83	5.50	Sloop
736	1947	Porter Schutt	*Egret*	Aux. yawl	49.42	34.00	11.00	7.00	Yawl
739	1947	Indian Harbor Y.C.	Arrow OD class	Fin-keel sloop	17.94	16.56	5.92	3.33	Sloop
757	1947	P. R. Bruce	*Oho*	Aux. keel sloop	39.08	26.00	8.00	5.75	Sloop
764	1947	Ellis Drier Co.	*Vicki*	Express cruiser	32.00	29.71	10.50	2.67	Power
773	1947	Various	Huntington class	Daycruiser	26.00	21.25	7.00	4.58	Sloop
774	1947	C.B.S.	*Columbia*	Utility launch	38.10	35.00	12.54	3.50	Power
776	1947	Robert Cox	Not built	Power cruiser	40.17	37.25	11.75	3.58	Power
790	1948	Saul Brodsky	*Kinnereth*	Express cruiser	49.71	47.00	13.33	3.48	Power
792	1947	R. Hernandorena	*Criollo*	Aux. yawl	67.08	45.50	14.04	7.75	Yawl
794	1948	Enrico Poggi	*Ciocca II*	6-meter	36.08	23.75	6.00	5.44	Sloop
805	1948	Various	Blue Jay class	Daysailer	13.50	11.25	5.17	0.50	Sloop
806	1948	Loomis/Whiton	*Lianoria*	6-meter	37.01	23.76	6.02	5.44	Sloop
809	1948	E. E. Dickinson	*Alva*	Twin-screw cruiser	60.00	57.75	16.08	4.08	Power
813	1948	Eli Lilly	*Rennjolle*	15 sq. meter boat	22.00	20.46	5.50	0.53	Sloop
819	1948	Cornelius Crane	*Maara*	Fishingboat	40.00	37.00	12.33	4.12	Power
820	1948	Carlos Oliva Paz	*Caribe*	Aux. c/b yawl	50.00	35.33	13.00	4.42	Yawl
832	1948	Wm. P. Barrows	*Chance*	Aux. yawl	38.33	26.00	9.58	5.67	Yawl
844	1948	Percy Chubb	*Laughing Gull*	Aux. yawl	44.23	30.00	10.67	6.00	Yawl
849	1949	Sound Marine Co.	Sound Marine class	Cruising sloop	31.00	23.00	9.10	3.00	Sloop
852	1949	Carl Hardeberg	*Circe*	Aux. yawl	56.71	39.00	11.75	8.00	Yawl

Design	Date	Client	Name/Class	Job Description	LOA	DWL	Beam	Draft	Type
873	1949	Harold Vanderbilt	*Versatile*	Motor-sailer	88.78	74.50	20.47	7.00	Ketch
882	1949	L. K. Jennings	*Florita*	Utility boat	26.54	25.00	8.54	2.28	Power
894	1949	John Trumpy & Sons	*Trumpy OD*	One Design class	40.17	28.00	10.00	5.75	Sloop
896	1949	Guillermo Sieburger	*Cristinita*	Commuter	53.17	50.00	14.00	3.50	Power
911	1950	G. Blunt White	*White Mist*	C/B yawl	46.58	32.00	12.08	4.39	Yawl
915	1950	K. E. Hedborg	*Anna Marina*	Aux. yawl	63.89	46.50	14.50	8.00	Yawl
917	1950	Ted Lumbard	*Gal-O-Galee*	Aux. yawl	45.17	33.00	10.96	6.25	Yawl
936	1950	Henry Wallenberg	Unknown	Aux. yawl	58.62	40.00	12.54	8.23	Yawl
955	1950	William Becker	*Helen B*	Aux. catboat	24.00	19.75	9.83	2.50	Catboat
959	1951	Curt Mattson	Unknown	5.5 meter	33.20	22.90	6.30	4.40	Sloop
976	1951	C. B. Nathorst	*Barracuda II*	Aux. yawl	64.79	45.00	13.00	8.23	Yawl
979	1951	William Horton	*Maybe VII*	6-meter	36.12	23.75	6.01	5.42	Sloop
981	1951	Philip Cole	*Hood III*	Seagoing powerboat	42.17	39.00	13.00	4.37	Power
982	1952	Edmond J. Moran	*Killara*	Aux. yawl	51.75	37.00	11.67	7.50	Yawl
991	1952	Thomas J. Watson	*Palawan*	Aux. yawl	47.25	32.50	11.25	6.67	Yawl
1001	1952	Various	Loki class	Aux. yawl	38.06	26.00	9.58	5.67	Yawl
1005	1954	Walter Rothschild	*Andante*	Motor-sailer	64.00	53.75	16.67	5.23	Ketch
1014	1953	Hugh Schaddelee	*Hilaria*	C/B yawl	55.00	40.42	14.00	5.96	Yawl
1033	1955	Arthur Horton	*Nina*	Motor-sailer	55.46	46.50	13.69	5.23	Sloop
1034	1953	Christian Fischbacher	*Cresta III*	Aux. yawl	52.10	36.00	12.12	7.42	Yawl
1044	1953	Various	Gulf Stream 36 class	Aux. yawl or sloop	36.48	26.00	10.04	5.00	Yawl
1047	1953	George Coumantaros	*Baccarat*	Aux. yawl	52.17	37.00	11.67	7.50	Yawl
1054	1954	Carleton Mitchell	*Finisterre*	C/B yawl	38.50	27.50	11.25	3.92	Yawl
1056	1954	James Farrell	*Impala*	Aux. yawl	55.97	40.00	12.50	7.56	Yawl
1059	1954	R. J. Reynolds	*Scarlett O'Hara*	Cruiser	53.27	50.00	14.42	4.00	Power
1061.2	1957	Chas. MacCulloch	*Fairwyn*	Aux. c/b yawl	42.77	29.50	11.75	4.28	Yawl
1068	1955	Various	Nevins A yawls	Aux. c/b yawl	40.00	27.50	11.17	3.92	Yawl
1089	1953	Seabrook Shipyard	Seabrook cruiser	Power cruiser	29.50	27.00	9.71	1.50	Power
1092	1954	James Moffett	*Tambo*	Express cruiser	44.50	42.00	11.67	3.00	Power
1104	1955	Jacob Wallenberg	*Refanut*	Aux. yawl	62.83	43.75	12.75	8.92	Yawl
1107	1954	William Snaith	*Figaro*	Aux. c/b yawl	47.00	32.50	12.12	4.42	Yawl
1110	1954	Sven Frisell	*Kay*	Aux. yawl	52.50	36.00	12.12	7.42	Yawl
1114	1954	Henry W. Buhl	*Njorth*	Power cruiser	52.83	49.17	13.67	3.50	Power
1115	1955	F. Trubee Davison	*Matuta*	Motor-sailer	55.17	47.00	14.17	4.00	Ketch
1131	1956	Caroline Foulkes	*Cockade*	Commuter	59.58	56.04	14.56	2.70	Power
1142	1956	W. N. H. van der Vorm	*Zwerver II*	Aux. cutter	56.77	39.00	11.17	8.04	Sloop
1144	1955	Edward S. Moore	*Zinganee*	Motor-sailer	52.00	43.33	14.17	4.25	Ketch
1147	1956	Various	Gulf Stream 30 class	Aux. sloop	29.56	21.85	8.02	4.63	Sloop
1150	1956	Henry Haskell	*Venturer*	Aux. yawl	73.25	52.50	15.42	9.50	Yawl
1151	1956	Bryan Newkirk	*Buzzy III*	6-meter sloop	37.02	23.70	6.02	5.42	Sloop
1164	1956	Carl Wikstrom	Unknown	Aux. yawl	44.48	30.00	10.67	6.00	Yawl
1170	1956	Radio Corp. of America	*Electron*	Laboratory vessel	82.00	77.00	18.50	5.00	Power
1177	1956	Clayton Ewing	*Dyna*	Aux. yawl	57.96	40.00	13.50	5.54	Yawl
1177.1	1956	George Kress	*Aria*	Aux. yawl	57.96	40.00	13.50	5.54	Yawl
1188	1956	Marvin Vale	*Fidelio*	Aux. c/b yawl	38.62	27.50	11.25	3.92	Yawl
1192	1956	Edwin Singer	*Windalier*	Aux. c/b yawl	42.75	29.50	11.75	4.33	Yawl
1195	1956	Emil Steiger	*Little Viking*	Power cruiser	47.56	44.17	13.54	3.25	Power
1197	1956	Harold Oldak	*Windborne II*	Aux. sloop	40.19	27.83	10.87	5.75	Sloop
1203	1956	E. Standish Bradford	*Windward II*	Aux. yawl	42.75	29.50	11.75	4.25	Yawl
1205.1	1957	Jose A. Mayoral	*Maruca*	Seagoing powerboat	46.50	43.33	14.58	4.08	Power
1212	1956	Ellis Drier Co.	*Aquila*	Aux. sloop	40.00	27.50	11.25	3.92	Sloop
1213	1956	John Griffith	*Mai Tai*	Aux. ketch	68.25	48.96	16.25	7.83	Ketch
1215	1956	Italo Monzino	*Mait II*	Aux. yawl	61.67	43.75	13.50	8.89	Yawl
1219	1956	H. Hinckley & Co.	New Pilot 35 class	Aux. sloop or yawl	35.11	24.00	9.56	4.75	Sloop/Yawl
1219.1	1957	Edward Greef	*Puffin*	Aux. sloop	35.13	24.25	9.50	4.75	Sloop
1221	1958	Percy Chubb	*Antilles*	Aux. ketch	45.92	32.50	12.87	4.67	Ketch
1222	1956	Harold Wilkinson	*Donchery*	Aux. cutter	38.62	27.50	11.25	3.92	Yawl
1223	1956	Winthrop Aldrich	*Wayfarer*	Aux. ketch	94.12	67.50	20.97	9.73	Ketch
1225	1956	Hinsdale Smith	*Blue Cloud*	Aux. cutter	42.77	29.50	11.75	4.28	Sloop
1226	1956	Judson Shafer	*Gray Lady*	Aux. yawl	42.77	29.50	11.75	4.28	Yawl
1228	1957	Frederick Crane	*Caution*	Aux. yawl	39.62	27.50	11.25	3.92	Yawl
1229	1958	F. M. H. Hin	*Vaer-Wel II*	Motor-sailer	70.00	60.00	16.17	6.87	Ketch
1230	1957	Austin Goodyear	*Mermaid*	Aux. ketch	45.67	32.00	11.50	6.67	Ketch
1235	1957	Ray Greene Co.	New Horizons class	Aux. c/b sloop	25.25	21.25	7.79	3.00	Sloop
1237	1956	John T. Hayward	*Winifred*	Aux. yawl	39.62	27.50	11.25	3.92	Yawl
1238	1957	Fred Adams	*Katma*	Aux. yawl	39.62	27.50	11.25	3.92	Yawl
1240	1957	Cornelius Wood	Not built	Aux. c/b yawl	54.05	38.00	13.58	4.50	Yawl
1245	1957	Mason & Wright Britton	*Delight*	Aux. yawl	39.62	27.50	11.25	3.92	Yawl
1245.2	1957	Various	Stock design	Aux. yawl	39.62	27.50	11.25	3.92	Yawl
1250	1957	John M. Dimick	*Aquarius*	Power cruiser	66.10	62.50	16.23	4.00	Power
1251	1957	Ralph Greenlee	*Simba*	Aux. c/b yawl	42.58	29.50	11.79	4.11	Yawl
1252	1957	Harvey Conover	*Revonoc II*	Aux. c/b yawl	42.58	29.50	11.79	4.45	Yawl
1254	1957	Harvey White	*White Caps*	Aux. yawl	40.44	27.83	10.87	5.75	Yawl

Design	Date	Client	Name/Class	Job Description	LOA	DWL	Beam	Draft	Type
1255	1958	R. L. Ireland	*Pandora IV*	Aux. steel c/b ketch	68.01	50.00	17.00	5.75	Ketch
1261	1957	Freeman & Merle Smith	*Mah Jong*	Aux. yawl	52.17	37.00	11.67	7.50	Yawl
1265	1958	W. L. Stewart	*Cordonazo*	Steel motor-sailer	62.59	53.00	16.29	5.83	Ketch
1269	1957	Henry Taylor	*Barunita*	Motor-sailer	59.33	50.00	16.79	5.75	Ketch
1278	1959	Irving Johnson	*Yankee*	Aux. steel c/b ketch	50.58	42.50	15.33	4.00	Ketch
1278.1	1960	Wally Byam	*Caravan*	Aux. steel c/b ketch	50.58	42.50	15.33	4.00	Ketch
1278.3	1964	Kenneth van Strum	*Argonaut*	Aux. steel c/b ketch	50.58	42.50	15.33	4.00	Ketch
1278.4	1965	Edward Noble	Unknown	Aux. steel c/b ketch	50.58	42.50	15.33	4.00	Ketch
1278.6	1969	Robert Scott	*Great Scott*	Aux. steel c/b ketch	50.58	42.50	15.33	4.00	Ketch
1278.7	1973	Cornelius de Dood	Unknown	Aux. steel c/b ketch	50.69	42.50	15.33	4.00	Ketch
1280	1957	W. H. Reynolds	*Fran*	Fishing cruiser	50.69	48.00	13.79	3.25	Power
1282	1958	Hollis Baker	*Whisper V*	Aux. c/b yawl	40.52	27.83	10.98	5.75	Yawl
1292	1957	Thomas Watson	*Palawan II*	Aux. c/b sloop	54.50	37.00	13.25	5.25	Sloop
1292.1	1959	A. Viant	*Ile de Feu*	Aux. c/b yawl	54.50	37.00	13.25	5.25	Yawl
1293	1957	Philip Miller	*Glory*	Aux. c/b yawl	42.58	29.50	11.79	4.11	Yawl
1295	1957	State of Maryland	Various	Patrol boats	40.67	38.33	12.00	3.25	Power
1305	1958	Jorge Blohm	*Hanka*	Sport fisherman	52.08	49.00	13.81	3.75	Power
1309	1958	John B. Shethar	*Valencia*	Aux. sloop	39.58	28.00	11.17	5.81	Sloop
1309.1	1958	Robt. MacCullough	*Inverness*	Aux. sloop	38.00	26.67	11.17	5.81	Sloop
1329	1959	Robt. Garland	Crusader class	Steel m/s	32.54	26.50	10.83	4.42	Sloop
1329.1	1959	Unknown	Crusader Jr.	Steel m/s	28.54	23.17	9.50	3.94	Sloop
1330	1958	Albert Boardman	*Madrigal*	Aux. yawl	46.00	32.50	11.92	6.92	Yawl
1331	1957	C. Porter Schutt	*Egret*	Motor-sailer	56.50	47.00	15.27	4.58	Ketch
1335	1957	Herman Whiton	*Goose*	6-meter sloop	37.00	23.67	6.00	5.42	Sloop
1343	1958	Sears - Cunningham synd.	*Columbia*	12-meter sloop	69.42	45.50	11.79	8.88	Sloop
1346	1958	Jakob Isbrandtsen	*Wind Rose*	Aux. yawl	47.83	32.00	11.54	6.62	Yawl
1349	1958	Cornelius Crane	*Oshidori*	Motor-sailer	52.00	43.33	14.17	4.25	Ketch
1357	1958	Edwin Thorne	*Lorna Doone*	Aux. sloop	33.00	25.00	10.50	3.00	Sloop
1358	1958	Sven Hansen	*Anitra*	Aux. yawl	48.42	33.50	12.33	6.92	Yawl
1358.3	1959	Alan Miller	*China Clipper*	Aux. yawl	48.42	33.50	12.33	6.92	Sloop
1366	1958	Henry B. DuPont	*Cyane*	Aux. sloop	46.12	32.00	10.77	6.50	Sloop
1367	1958	Ogden Reid	*Currituck*	Aux. sloop	46.21	32.00	12.83	4.81	Sloop
1380	1959	John K. Miller	*Rip Tide*	Aux. yawl	40.44	27.83	10.87	5.75	Yawl
1380.3	1959	William Buckley	*Suzy Wong*	Aux. yawl	40.44	27.83	10.87	5.75	Yawl
1380.4	1959	Graydon Smith	*Starbuck*	Aux. yawl	40.44	27.83	10.87	5.75	Yawl
1380.5	1959	Yeardley Smith	*Khira*	Aux. sloop	40.44	27.83	10.87	5.75	Sloop
1386	1959	Arthur Hughes	*Lady Linden*	Aux. sloop	41.46	29.50	10.75	6.17	Sloop
1386.3	1960	Ignacio Miro	*Almogaver*	Aux. yawl	41.46	29.50	10.73	6.23	Yawl
1397	1959	C. E. Blomgren	*Flair*	Motor-sailer	49.04	38.50	14.33	4.45	Ketch
1401	1959	Robert Flato	*Kiwi II*	Aux. sloop	37.25	25.42	10.83	4.98	Sloop
1411	1959	Peter Richmond	*Magic Carpet*	Aux. c/b yawl	55.92	38.33	13.58	5.25	Yawl
1428	1959	U. A. Whitaker	*Pavane II*	Motor-sailer	52.92	43.33	14.46	4.33	Sloop
1449	1959	James Camp	*Sea Star*	Steel aux. ketch	90.00	65.00	21.00	6.67	Ketch
1459	1959	John M. Simpson	*Awab*	Motor-sailer	55.73	46.50	15.10	5.25	Ketch
1463	1960	Jorge Geyer	*Cairu III*	Aux. c/b yawl	47.48	32.50	12.12	4.42	Yawl
1469	1959/65	George Booth	Unknown	Motor-sailer	55.56	43.33	14.50	4.59	Ketch
1474	1960	Frank Wetherill	*Jubilee*	Aux. yawl	60.42	42.50	14.39	6.00	Yawl
1476	1960	Arthur B. Homer	*Salmagal III*	Aux. yawl	46.52	33.50	11.27	6.83	Yawl
1478	1960	H. A. van Beuningen	*Hestia*	Aux. sloop	34.42	25.50	9.67	6.00	Sloop
1479	1960	Gordon Alles	*Alembic*	Aux. cutter	47.83	33.50	11.46	6.83	Cutter
1484	1960	Carl J. Gilbert	*Adventuress*	Aux. sloop	30.08	21.87	8.02	5.00	Sloop
1492	1959	Nicholas Goulandris	*Explorer*	Sportfishing boat	49.13	45.50	14.52	4.08	Power
1493	1960	Geoffry Pattinson	*Zarabanda*	Aux. sloop	38.42	28.00	10.21	5.92	Sloop
1497	1960	Various	Dolphin Class (fg)	Aux. c/b sloop	24.00	19.00	7.67	2.83	Sloop
1497.1	1960	Various	Mermaid Class (wood)	Aux. c/b sloop	24.00	19.00	7.67	2.83	Sloop
1505	1960	Italian Navy	*Corsaro II*	Aux. yawl	69.33	50.00	16.06	9.50	Yawl
1505.1	1963	Italian Navy	*Stella Polare*	Aux. yawl	70.42	50.00	16.06	9.85	Yawl
1508	1962	Columbia Yacht Corp.	Columbia 29	Aux. sloop	28.50	22.50	8.00	4.00	Sloop
1511	1960	William Boyd	*Quest*	5.5-meter sloop	32.88	22.23	6.26	4.38	Sloop
1517	1961	Frua de Angeli	*Rosina*	Motor-sailer	62.67	44.00	15.23	7.00	Yawl
1519	1959	Cecil F. Backus	*Saraband*	Aux. yawl	35.00	29.00	8.67	5.25	Sloop
1521	1959	Norwalk Yacht Club	Norwalk Y.C. launch	Wood launch	25.83	24.42	8.75	2.25	Power
1534	1959	Avard Fuller	*Diogenes*	Aux. c/b ketch	50.32	41.67	13.00	5.00	Ketch
1536	1960	J. Lakin Baldridge	*Cleopatra*	Sportfisherman	38.37	35.00	11.50	2.42	Power
1540	1960	D. R. Hooper	*Sapphire*	"K" class sloop	41.04	27.50	8.87	5.96	Sloop
1553	1960	Burmester	*Dorothee*	12-meter sloop	56.89	41.14	13.67	7.87	Sloop
1554	1959	Burmester	*Moije Bris*	7.5-meter sloop	38.92	27.33	10.96	5.58	Sloop
1557	1960	George Kiskaddon	Spirit class	One Design racer	33.42	28.50	8.39	6.00	Sloop
1567.1	1960	Etablissement Staret	*Boomerang*	Aux. yawl	64.79	45.00	13.46	9.11	Yawl
1573	1960	Francesco Tacenti	*Talent*	Aux. yawl	55.52	38.00	13.44	7.67	Yawl
1574	1960	Frank Hayford	*Day Star*	Aux. yawl	40.19	27.83	10.87	5.42	Yawl
1579	1960	Nicholas Goulandris	*Discoverer*	Fishingboat	65.00	61.33	16.50	5.00	Power
1580	1960	F. Rogers Ketcham	*Witch O the Waves*	Sportfisherman	44.12	42.00	12.75	2.94	Power

Design	Date	Client	Name/Class	Job Description	LOA	DWL	Beam	Draft	Type
1590	1960	Port Geneva, Switzerland	Unknown	5.5-meter yacht	32.08	22.20	6.27	4.38	Sloop
1595	1961	William Robinson	Mathis 33	Power cruiser	33.04	29.79	10.56	2.25	Power
1598	1961	John Griffith	*Mai Tai II*	Aux. steel ketch	75.67	54.79	18.17	9.50	Ketch
1598.1	1961	Leland Whittier	*Suvetar*	Aux. steel ketch	75.67	54.79	18.17	9.50	Ketch
1599	1961	Robert Rusk	*Salacia*	Aux. R.O.R.C. sloop	40.87	30.00	11.80	6.75	Sloop
1603	1960	Various	Lotus class	Aux. sloop	28.50	22.50	8.00	5.00	Sloop
1615	1961	Edwin Singer	*Windalier*	Aux. c/b yawl	58.29	39.00	14.21	5.50	Yawl
1617	1960	Tartan Marine	Tartan 27	Aux. c/b sloop	27.00	21.50	8.62	3.17	Sloop
1618	1960	Seafarer F. G. Yachts	Seafarer 45	Aux. sloop	45.08	30.37	11.00	6.42	Sloop
1618.1	1960	Seafarer F. G. Yachts	Seafarer 45	Aux. yawl	45.08	30.37	11.00	6.42	Yawl
1618.2	1962	Sailmasters, Inc.	Sailmaster 45	Aux. sloop	45.08	30.37	11.00	6.42	Sloop
1618.3	1962	Sailmasters, Inc.	Sailmaster 45	Aux. yawl	45.08	30.37	11.00	6.42	Yawl
1620	1960	Robert Hanann	Wayward Wind class	Aux. c/b sloop	22.58	19.00	7.71	2.83	Sloop
1621	1960	Harvey Lincoff	Knickerbocker class	Aux. racer	26.25	19.00	6.58	4.42	Sloop
1622	1960	Donald Smith	*Yare*	Aux. sloop	35.96	25.50	9.58	5.62	Sloop
1623	1960	Gifford Pinchot	*Loon*	Aux. yawl	45.44	30.25	11.00	6.42	Yawl
1624	1960	Robert Derecktor	Gulf Stream 42	Aux. yawl	41.54	29.25	11.00	6.25	Yawl
1624.1	1960	Robert Derecktor	Gulf Stream 42	Aux. sloop	41.54	29.25	11.00	6.25	Sloop
1628	1960	Gerald Driscoll	*Nova*	Aux. sloop	38.92	27.33	10.00	5.96	Sloop
1629.1	1962	Maersk M. Moller	*Klem IV*	Aux. sloop	60.67	42.00	14.27	8.00	Sloop
1631	1960	Seafarer F. G. Yachts	*Kestrel*	Aux. c/b sloop	22.02	16.50	7.06	2.35	Sloop
1631.1	1962	Sailmasters, Inc.	Sailmaster 22	Aux. c/b sloop	22.02	16.50	7.06	2.35	Sloop
1641	1960	E. Hall Taylor	*Nancy Sue*	Aux. sloop	37.37	25.42	10.00	4.98	Sloop
1642	1960	Giuseppe Vender	*Patricia II*	Aux. ketch	71.38	50.00	15.44	9.42	Ketch
1643	1960	N. F. Brooker	*Seawind*	Aux. R.O.R.C. sloop	43.06	31.75	12.00	7.00	Sloop
1645	1963	Einar Hansen	*Capricia*	Aux. yawl	73.96	54.00	16.50	10.25	Yawl
1648.1	1963	Annapolis Boat Rentals	*Mustang*	Daysailer	17.00	15.50	6.50	0.71	Sloop
1651	1963	G. R. Atterbury	*Whimsie*	Motor-sailer	46.04	39.79	13.67	4.17	Ketch
1657	1963	Chris Craft Corp.	Sail yacht	Motor-sailer	35.00	28.50	11.00	4.67	Sloop
1657.1	1969	Chris Craft Corp.	Caribbean 35	Motor-sailer	35.17	28.50	11.00	4.67	Ketch
1657.2	1969	Chris Craft Corp.	Caribbean 35	Motor-sailer	35.17	28.50	11.00	4.67	Sloop
1658.1	1961	Jay Lukens	*Sea Pigeon*	Motor-sailer	41.50	33.50	12.67	5.21	Ketch
1663	1961	Giovanni Nasi	*Tiziana*	Aux. steel ketch	116.75	80.00	24.08	10.35	Ketch
1667	1960	E. Taranger	Biscayne 27 class	C/B sloop	27.33	20.62	8.67	3.12	Sloop
1673	1961	Gaston Deferre	*Palynodie*	R.O.R.C. sloop	39.83	28.75	10.08	6.52	Sloop
1674	1961	George P. Hamlin	*Toc Toc*	Steel motor-sailer	47.00	38.00	14.25	5.60	Ketch
1674.1	1969	John B. Marlowe	Marlowe 48	FG. motor-sailer	48.00	38.00	14.25	5.60	Ketch
1674.2	1977	Sunward Yachts	Sunward 48	FG. motor-sailer	48.00	38.00	14.25	5.60	Ketch
1674.3	1985	Walter Cronkite	*Wyntje*	Sunward 48 m/s	48.00	38.00	14.25	5.60	Ketch
1679	1963	James Spear	*Sequoia*	Motor-sailer	53.08	43.33	14.50	4.25	Ketch
1685	1962	Not built	*Esquire*	Aux. yawl	42.25	29.25	11.00	6.25	Yawl
1686.3	1961	Pompeo Maresi	*Aurora*	Diesel motor yacht	114.67	108.00	22.42	6.12	Power
1687	1961	Edoardo Bianchi	Bianchi 22	Outboard cruiser	22.00	19.83	8.00	1.04	Power
1689	1963	Robert McCullough	*Inverness*	Aux. yawl	47.00	33.00	12.00	6.75	Yawl
1693	1961	Various	Sparstep 39	Aux. sloop	39.08	27.33	10.00	5.96	Sloop
1698	1961	Derek Boyer	*Clarion of Wight*	R.O.R.C. sloop	43.46	30.00	10.89	6.71	Sloop
1701	1962	Annapolis Boat Rentals	Rainbow class	Daysailer	24.21	17.25	6.25	3.50	Sloop
1703	1961	Palmer Johnson	PJ 54	Motor-sailer	54.00	41.75	12.75	5.25	Ketch
1705	1961	Angel Riveras	*Giralda*	R.O.R.C. yawl	51.94	37.00	12.50	7.83	Yawl
1705.1	1963	Norbert Schierning	*Jan Pott III*	R.O.R.C. yawl	52.69	37.00	12.50	7.83	Yawl
1706	1963	George F. Johnson	*Challenge*	Aux. sloop	63.50	45.00	14.00	8.83	Sloop
1707	1961	Ralph MacDonald	*Thunder*	Aux. yawl	45.12	30.33	11.00	6.42	Yawl
1710	1963	Cantieri Benello	Gaia class	Aux. sloop	36.04	25.50	9.67	6.00	Sloop
1710.8	1964	Cheoy Lee	Sigma 36 class	Aux. sloop	36.04	25.50	9.67	6.00	Sloop
1710.51	1965	Nautor Ky	Swan 36 class	Aux. sloop	36.04	25.50	9.67	6.00	Sloop
1711	1961	G. A. Prentice	*Jandy*	Aux. c/b sloop	48.08	32.50	12.29	5.50	Sloop
1713	1961	John B. Kilroy	*Kialoa II*	Aux. sloop	73.42	55.00	14.92	10.33	Sloop
1715	1962	E. R. Greeff	*Puffin*	Aux. yawl	39.87	27.83	10.58	6.00	Yawl
1718	1963	Grampian Marine	Classic 37	Aux. sloop	37.29	26.25	10.19	5.83	Sloop
1718.1	1963	Grampian Marine	Classic 37	Aux. yawl	37.29	26.25	10.19	5.83	Yawl
1720	1962	Cornelius Shields	Shields class	Daysailer/racer	30.21	20.00	6.44	4.75	Sloop
1724	1962	Alfred Krupp	*Germania VI*	Aux. yawl	72.63	51.89	15.56	9.79	Yawl
1727	1962	H. Hinckley & Co.	F. G. Pilot class	Aux. sloop/yawl	35.52	24.25	9.50	5.00	Sloop/Yawl
1732	1963	Edwin J. Wylie	*Nymue*	Aux. yawl	45.56	30.37	11.00	6.42	Yawl
1736	1962	Alberto Combe	*Kiwi II*	Aux. sloop	45.56	30.37	11.00	6.42	Sloop
1738	1963	Far East Yacht Builders	S&S 40 class	Aux. sloop	39.95	28.75	10.04	6.23	Sloop
1740	1965	United Aircraft Co.	*Double Eagle*	Crewboat	79.33	71.54	20.46	2.47	Power
1741	1962	Antonio Pierobon	*Al Nair II*	R.O.R.C. aux. sloop	47.46	34.50	12.10	7.42	Sloop
1742	1965	Charles Bell	*Clovelly II*	Power cruiser	68.00	64.00	17.00	4.83	Power
1743	1962	Sailmasters, Inc.	Sailmaster 22D class	Aux. c/b sloop	22.00	16.50	7.06	2.34	Sloop
1749	1963	Gale Richmond	*Heavens Above*	Daysailer	28.00	21.25	7.00	4.00	Ketch
1752	1963	John C. MacKeen	*Eskasoni*	Motor-sailer	60.00	49.58	15.58	5.54	Ketch
1754	1963	Xavier de Roux	*Stemael IV*	R.O.R.C. sloop	44.00	32.00	10.92	7.08	Sloop

Design	Date	Client	Name/Class	Job Description	LOA	DWL	Beam	Draft	Type
1755	1964	Peter Wilson	*Nan of Gare*	Cruiser/racer	39.83	27.29	9.75	6.25	Sloop
1757	1963	Wells Morss	*Carillon*	Aux. sloop	47.42	33.00	11.74	6.75	Sloop
1757.1	1966	Stephens Marine	*Alpha*	Aux. sloop	47.42	33.00	11.70	6.75	Sloop
1757.2	1967	Peter Salz	*Bohemia*	Aux. sloop	47.42	33.00	11.70	6.75	Sloop
1760	1963	Chris Craft Corp.	Capri 30 class	Aux. c/b sloop	30.00	25.00	9.67	3.75	Sloop
1761	1964	Max Boris	*Sumbra II*	R.O.R.C. aux. sloop	56.10	39.00	13.42	8.12	Sloop
1765	1964	Madison Haythe	*Poppy*	Aux. sloop	32.35	22.00	8.00	5.12	Sloop
1766	1963	George Hoffman	*Duster*	Aux. sloop	47.39	33.00	12.00	6.42	Sloop
1767	1964	Various	*Honey*, et. al.	R.O.R.C. aux. sloop	39.95	28.75	10.04	5.52	Sloop
1767.1	1965	Italian Navy	Various	R.O.R.C. aux. sloop	39.95	28.75	10.04	5.52	Sloop
1770	1963	Douglas Bremner	*Ta-Aroa*	Aux. racing sloop	59.92	45.00	12.25	8.25	Sloop
1771.1	1964	Chris Craft Corp.	Capri 26 class	Aux. sloop	26.25	19.00	8.17	4.00	Sloop
1771.2	1965	Chris Craft Corp.	Pawnee 26 class	Aux. sloop	26.14	19.98	8.00	4.00	Sloop
1773	1964	Sears – Cunningham synd.	*Constellation*	12-meter sloop	68.33	45.50	12.24	8.88	Sloop
1775	1964	Palmer Johnson	PJ 44	Aux. sloop	44.00	29.37	10.92	6.19	Sloop
1777	1963	Michael Vernon	*Assegai II*	Aux. R.O.R.C. sloop	40.79	29.00	10.67	6.54	Sloop
1777.1	1965	Thorborn Bjornefeldt	*Aja*	Aux. R.O.R.C. sloop	40.79	29.25	10.67	6.54	Sloop
1777.2	1967	A. Barbanti	*Illiria*	Aux. R.O.R.C. sloop	40.79	29.25	10.67	6.54	Sloop
1780	1965	Dennis Miller	*Firebrand*	Aux. R.O.R.C. sloop	43.21	30.00	11.25	6.71	Sloop
1780.4	1967	Pekka Herlin	*Lygaia*	Aux. R.O.R.C. sloop	43.21	30.00	11.25	6.71	Sloop
1781	1964	Arthur Slater	*Prospect of Whitby*	Aux. R.O.R.C. sloop	41.58	30.00	11.25	6.58	Ketch
1782	1965	P. E. Haggerty	*Beayondan*	Aux. c/b ketch	82.46	63.67	17.83	6.25	Sloop
1784	1963	Yngve Cassel	*Cassela*	Aux. sloop	42.58	30.00	11.25	6.71	Sloop
1784.1	1964	Philip S. Yates	*Jupiter*	Aux. sloop	42.58	30.00	11.25	6.71	Sloop
1786	1964	Eric Barker	*Deb*	Aux. c/b sloop	39.67	28.75	11.50	5.17	Sloop
1791	1964	Henry S. Morgan	*Djinn*	Motor-sailer	61.92	47.00	15.94	6.00	Sloop
1792	1964	Jose de Gamboa	*Artako*	Aux. R.O.R.C. sloop	41.58	30.00	11.25	6.71	Sloop
1797	1964	Philip Watson	*Namis*	Aux. cruiser/racer	44.71	31.50	10.77	6.54	Ketch
1801	1965	George A. Phillips	*Malu*	Motor-sailer	41.67	33.00	14.00	4.50	Ketch
1806	1964	V. A. Whitaker	*Helua*	Motor-sailer	72.46	57.25	17.14	5.60	Sloop
1812	1965	Deforest Trimingham	*Whistler of Paget*	Aux. sloop	38.33	27.50	10.25	5.87	Ketch
1813	1965	Carl Hovgard	*Circe*	Aux. c/b ketch	65.00	47.00	16.00	6.50	Power
1819	1965	Avard Fuller	*Pieces of Eight*	Twin-screw power yacht	47.56	45.83	12.08	1.75	Sloop
1821	1965	Thomas Watson, Jr.	*Palawan III*	Aux. sloop	57.98	40.00	12.35	8.10	Yawl
1826	1965	Fred Adams	*Katama II*	Aux. yawl	42.48	29.00	10.79	6.21	Yawl
1828	1965	Arthur Wull Schleger	*Elske*	Aux. yawl	47.73	33.50	11.96	6.92	Sloop
1830	1965	Milton Cross	*Windhound*	Aux. sloop	48.08	32.50	11.42	6.67	Yawl
1833	1965	Hugh Schaddelee	*Hilaria*	Aux. c/b yawl	52.83	37.00	13.50	5.67	Yawl
1833.2	1981	Parker Heinemann	Unknown	Aux. c/b yawl	52.83	37.00	13.50	5.67	Sloop
1834	1966	*Intrepid* synd.	*Intrepid*	12-meter sloop	64.25	45.50	12.00	9.00	Yawl
1836	1966	William L. Rudkin	*Kim*	Aux. yawl	54.58	37.50	13.37	7.58	Ketch
1852	1965	F. Trubee Davsion	*Matuta II*	Motor-sailer	60.00	49.58	15.58	5.54	Sloop
1856	1966	Max Aitken	*Roundabout*	Aux. sloop	36.46	26.55	9.92	6.23	Sloop
1857	1966	Derek Boyer	*Clarionet*	Aux. sloop	36.87	26.71	9.95	6.21	Sloop
1858	1966	John M. Taylor	*Toogooloowoo IV*	6-meter sloop	33.33	23.84	6.12	5.44	Sloop
1859	1966	P. R. Sandwell	*Gabrielle III*	Aux. sloop	51.75	35.00	12.58	6.87	Sloop
1860	1966	Chris Craft Corp.	Captain 26 class	Aux. sloop	26.25	19.00	8.17	4.00	Sloop
1861	1965	Chris Craft Corp.	Apache 37 class	Aux. sloop	37.00	26.25	10.21	5.75	Sloop
1862	1966	John van Voorhis	*Iroquois*	8-meter sloop	43.57	31.53	8.33	6.62	Sloop
1866	1966	Chris Craft Corp.	Cherokee 32 class	Aux. sloop	32.00	22.50	9.00	5.08	Sloop
1867	1966	Chris Craft Corp.	Comanche 42 class	Aux. sloop	42.00	30.33	10.83	6.50	Sloop
1871	1966	Mason Britton	*Sequin*	Aux. sloop	42.50	29.00	11.00	6.21	Sloop
1872	1966	Frederick Liebhardt	*Chimaera*	Aux. sloop	46.76	32.58	11.17	6.87	Sloop
1873	1966	Roger Fuller	Deb 33 class	Aux. c/b sloop	33.37	24.00	10.33	3.55	Sloop
1883	1967	Harlow Reed	*Black Jack*	Aux. sloop	44.83	31.00	11.50	6.50	Ketch
1884.1	1967	Austin H. Ross	*Big Blue*	Motor-sailer	61.92	47.00	15.27	6.00	Ketch
1884.2	1967	Maurice Perlstein	*Peloha*	Motor-sailer	61.92	47.00	15.27	6.00	Sloop
1885	1967	Giuseppe Diano	*Levantades*	R.O.R.C. aux. sloop	50.50	37.00	12.75	7.92	Sloop
1888	1967	Various	Sagitta 26 class	R.O.R.C. sloop	25.50	19.67	8.25	4.50	Ketch
1890	1967	Fairleigh Dickinson	*Cruzan*	Aux. ketch	65.46	47.00	16.00	6.50	Sloop
1891	1967	Wolfgang Denzel	*Iorana*	Aux. sloop	63.15	45.42	14.83	9.21	Sloop
1894	1967	Guy W. Bowles	*Sunmaid V*	Aux. sloop	36.83	26.71	10.12	6.21	Sloop
1894.1	1967	Ernest R. Scott	*Tina*	Aux. one-ton sloop	36.83	26.71	10.12	6.21	Sloop
1895	1967	Sven Gronblum	*Circe*	Aux. sloop	36.87	26.71	10.12	6.21	Ketch
1896	1966	William S. Stocks	*Rewa*	Aux. ketch	65.29	47.00	16.00	6.50	Schooner
1897	1967	Schaefer Brewing Co.	*America*	Aux. schooner	104.83	90.67	22.83	11.50	Sloop
1899	1967	South Hants Marine	She 31 class	Aux. sloop	30.37	22.00	8.83	5.46	Sloop
1899.1	1967	I. W. Varvet A.B.	IW 31	Aux. sloop	30.37	22.00	8.83	5.46	Sloop
1900	1967	Cheoy Lee	Sigma 38 class	Aux. sloop	38.33	27.50	10.25	5.87	Sloop
1903	1967	Hughes Boat Works	Hughes 38 class	Aux. sloop	37.58	27.00	10.12	6.00	Sloop
1904	1967	Douglas & McCleod	Tartan 34 class	Aux. c/b sloop	34.30	25.00	10.17	3.92	Yawl
1904.1	1967	Douglas & McCleod	Tartan 34 class	Aux. c/b yawl	34.30	25.00	10.17	3.92	Sloop
1905	1967	Clayton Ewing	*Dyna II*	Aux. sloop	50.88	35.00	11.96	7.33	Ketch

Design	Date	Client	Name/Class	Job Description	LOA	DWL	Beam	Draft	Type
1905.1	1968	B. W. Heineman	*Falcon*	Aux. ketch	50.88	35.00	11.96	7.33	Ketch
1906	1967	Antonio Pierobon	*Al Nair IV*	One-ton sloop	36.87	26.71	10.12	6.21	Sloop
1908	1967	Dean Brown	*Sandpiper*	Aux. sloop	50.50	34.50	11.96	7.25	Sloop
1909	1968	Serena Zaffagui	*Mabelle*	Aux. sloop	45.34	33.33	12.75	7.25	Sloop
1909.1	1968	Ron Wilkie	*Satanita II*	Aux. sloop	45.34	33.33	12.75	7.25	Sloop
1909.2	1970	J. Boardman	*Border Viking*	Aux. sloop	45.56	33.00	12.75	7.25	Sloop
1909.3	1969	Giorgio Falck	*Guia*	Aux. sloop	45.34	33.33	12.75	7.25	Sloop
1909.FG	1970	B. C. Psaltis	*Meltemi*	Aux. sloop	44.33	34.12	12.75	7.08	Sloop
1922	1967	Vittorio Treccani	*Elan*	Aux. sloop	36.87	26.71	10.12	6.21	Sloop
1925	1968	Robert Krementz	*Captiva*	Aux. steel ketch	52.83	40.00	14.05	6.75	Ketch
1925.1	1985	Frank Carruthers	*Legend*	Aux. steel ketch	52.83	40.00	14.05	6.75	Ketch
1927	1967	Wolfgang Schoenborn	*Torea*	Aux. steel ketch	58.69	47.00	16.33	7.00	Ketch
1930	1967	Cantiere Benello	Freya class	Aux. sloop	44.73	32.50	12.32	7.00	Sloop
1930.2	1968	William Ziegler	*Gem*	Aux. sloop	44.73	32.50	12.32	7.00	Sloop
1938	1967	John T. Potter	*Equation*	Aux. cutter	56.70	40.00	12.35	8.10	Cutter
1938.1	1970	Stephens Marine	*Lightnin'*	Aux. cutter	56.73	40.00	12.35	8.14	Cutter
1939	1967	P. E. Haggerty	*Bay Bea II*	Aux. sloop	49.12	35.00	11.96	7.33	Sloop
1939.3	1970	Charles Kirsch	*Scaramouche*	Aux. sloop	49.58	35.00	11.83	7.29	Sloop
1942	1968	Various	Sagitta 20 class	Aux. sloop	20.13	17.50	7.67	3.83	Sloop
1943	1968	Alfred Segers	*Trinidad II*	Aux. sloop	38.67	27.00	10.12	6.00	Sloop
1948	1968	Various	One ton cup series	Aux. sloop	36.32	26.95	10.50	6.19	Sloop
1948.1	1968	Marina Spacarelli	*Kerkyra II*	Aux. sloop	36.32	26.95	10.50	6.19	Sloop
1949	1968	Sydney Fischer	*Ragamuffin*	Aux. sloop	48.58	36.00	12.50	7.75	Sloop
1951	1968	George Coomantaris	*Baccara*	Aux. yawl	72.96	59.00	16.92	10.75	Yawl
1952	1968	Gene Trepte	*Brushfire*	Aux. sloop	51.00	36.00	12.51	7.36	Sloop
1955	1968	Philip Sharples	*Belerion*	Aux. sloop	46.46	32.58	11.50	6.58	Sloop
1956	1968	Hughes Boat Works	Hughes 48 class	Aux. yawl	48.00	33.00	11.67	6.75	Yawl
1956.1	1968	Various	Hughes 48 class	Aux. sloop	48.00	33.00	11.67	6.75	Sloop
1958	1968	Whitney Operations	Whitney 30 class	Aux. sloop	30.08	22.00	8.50	4.68	Sloop
1959	1968	Winfield & Partners, Inc.	S&S 34 class	Aux. sloop	33.53	24.17	10.08	5.83	Sloop
1959.3	1969	Palmer Johnson	PJ 34 class	Aux. sloop	33.53	24.17	10.08	5.90	Sloop
1961	1968	Alberto Rafaelli	*Tarantella*	Aux. sloop	54.60	39.50	14.50	8.33	Sloop
1963	1968	Giuseppe Vendor	*Patricia III*	Aux. sloop	55.69	41.00	13.75	8.50	Sloop
1965	1968	H. R. Hinckley	Hinckley 38	Aux. sloop	37.50	27.50	10.54	5.67	Sloop
1966	1968	Allied Boat Co. Inc.	Allied 42	Aux. c/b sloop	41.50	28.50	11.50	4.17	Sloop
1966.1	1968	Allied Boat Co. Inc.	Allied 42	Aux. c/b yawl	41.50	28.50	11.50	4.17	Yawl
1966.7	1981	International Yachts	Allied 42	Aux. sloop deep keel	41.50	28.50	11.50	5.75	Sloop
1968	1968	Emilio Bignardi	*Moby Dick III*	Aux. sloop	39.79	29.45	11.00	6.63	Sloop
1969	1969	Jakob Isbrandtsen	*Running Tide*	Aux. cutter	60.50	45.00	14.25	9.00	Cutter
1969.2	1977	Giovanni Stefani	*Marea*	Aux. cutter	60.00	45.00	14.83	9.04	Cutter
1973	1968	Nautor Ky	Swan 43 class	Aux. sloop	43.00	31.00	11.67	6.96	Sloop
1973.1	1968	Palmer Johnson	PJ 43 class	Aux. sloop	43.00	31.00	11.67	6.96	Sloop
1973W	1969	Ignacio de Aznar	Unknown	Wood version of Swan 43	43.00	31.00	11.67	6.96	Sloop
1974	1968	University of Delaware	*Skimmer*	Research vessel	41.79	38.00	13.00	3.27	Power
1976	1968	Edward Greeff	*Puffin III*	Aux. yawl	47.50	33.33	12.33	7.25	Yawl
1978	1970	McCullough synd.	*Valiant*	12-meter sloop	63.92	52.60	12.19	9.17	Sloop
1979	1968	W. R. Timken	*Kittyhawk X*	Aux. sloop	50.79	36.00	13.00	6.17	Sloop
1985	1968	Arthur Slater	*Prospect of Whitby*	Aux. sloop (steel)	42.58	32.62	12.12	7.11	Sloop
1985.2	1980	Thomas Melville	Unknown	Aux. sloop (steel)	42.58	32.25	12.25	7.10	Sloop
1986	1968	Niagara Yankee synd.	*Niagara*	Canada's Cup racer	39.32	32.23	11.42	6.50	Sloop
1986.1	1968	Armando Grandi	*Atrevido*	Racing sloop	42.42	31.00	11.50	6.50	Sloop
1988	1968	Maurice Laing	*Sasha*	Aux. sloop	41.92	30.00	11.50	6.75	Sloop
1988.1	1970	L. J. Abrahams	*Vittoria*	Aux. sloop	41.92	30.00	11.50	6.75	Sloop
1989	1968	Yankee Yachts	*Minuteman*	Sailing dinghy	11.58	11.50	4.58	0.52	Catboat
1993	1969	Carlo Aloisi	*Ulisse*	Aux. sloop	65.33	47.50	16.32	9.67	Sloop
1995	1969	George F. Johnson	*Challenge II*	Aux. sloop	49.42	36.00	13.42	7.54	Sloop
1996	1969	Thomas Watson	*Palawan IV*	Ocean cruiser	67.50	50.50	17.50	6.67	Ketch
1998	1969	Pierobon synd.	*Dida II*	Aux. sloop	41.50	30.00	11.35	6.79	Sloop
1998.1	1969	ALPA S.P.A.	ALPA 42 class	Motor-sailer	40.04	32.25	11.34	5.83	Ketch
1999	1969	Yankee Yachts	Yankee 30 class	Aux. sloop	30.04	23.00	9.00	4.83	Sloop
1999.1	1970	T. E. Swarbrick	*Ruffian*	Aux. sloop	30.00	23.00	9.00	4.83	Sloop
2006	1970	Marion O. Black	*Tortue*	Aux. sloop	43.67	33.50	13.00	5.92	Sloop
2008	1969	Royal Systems Yacht Yard	Sagitta 35 class	Aux. sloop	34.50	25.50	10.00	6.00	Sloop
2008.1	1970	Cantiere Castiglione	Impala 35 class	Aux. sloop	34.50	25.50	10.10	6.04	Sloop
2009	1969	Arthur Byrne	*Salacia II*	Aux. sloop	48.46	36.00	13.00	7.75	Sloop
2010	1969	George Schuchart	*Pemaquid*	Aux. sloop	50.25	34.00	12.50	7.33	Sloop
2011	1969	Nello Mazzaferro	*Nita*	Aux. yawl	56.28	39.50	14.50	8.33	Yawl
2012	1969	Christian Fischbacher	*Cresta IV*	Aux. yawl	55.33	38.00	14.20	8.00	Yawl
2012.1	1969	Nautor Ky	Swan 55 class	Aux. yawl (keel)	55.33	38.00	14.20	8.00	Yawl
2012.2	1970	Nautor Ky	Swan 53 class	Aux. sloop (keel)	53.00	40.00	14.20	8.00	Sloop
2012.3	1969	Nautor Ky	Swan 55 class	Aux. sloop (c/b)	55.33	38.00	14.20	6.08	Sloop
2012.4	1970	Palmer Johnson	PJ 55 class	Aux. yawl	55.33	38.00	14.20	8.00	Yawl
2012.5	1970	Palmer Johnson	PJ 53 class	Aux. sloop	53.00	38.00	14.20	8.00	Sloop

Design	Date	Client	Name/Class	Job Description	LOA	DWL	Beam	Draft	Type
2014	1969	Michael Winfield & Partners, Ltd.	S&S 30	Aux. sloop	29.87	21.00	9.00	5.42	Sloop
2016	1969	Douglass & McCleod	Tartan 30 class	Aux. sloop	30.00	24.25	10.00	4.92	Power
2021.2	1970	Aga Khan	*Kalamoun*	High-speed motor yacht	93.21	81.25	22.97	10.64	Sloop
2025	1969	Nautor/Palmer Johnson	Swan 40 class	Aux. sloop	39.52	28.50	10.83	6.37	Sloop
2025.1	1969	Nautor/Palmer Johnson	Swan 40 c/b class	Aux. sloop	39.52	28.50	10.83	4.87	Yawl
2028	1970	Bruce Dalling	*Jacaranda*	Aux. yawl	56.83	40.00	14.37	8.31	Sloop
2031	1970	David Steere	*Yankee Girl*	Aux. sloop	55.64	40.00	14.37	8.31	Cutter
2031.1	1970	Jesse Philips	*Charisma*	Aux. cutter	55.94	40.00	14.37	8.31	Sloop
2032	1970	John M. Taylor	*Toogie V*	6-meter sloop	33.14	24.40	6.12	5.56	Sloop
2035	1969	Nautor Ky	Swan 37 class	Aux. sloop	36.44	27.33	10.83	6.12	Sloop
2035.1	1969	Palmer Johnson	PJ 37 class	Aux. sloop	36.44	27.33	10.83	6.12	Yawl
2040	1970	Richard Vogt	*Mischief III*	Aux. yawl (c/b)	42.58	32.00	13.00	4.25	Sloop
2040.1	1983	Thomsen/Christiansen	*Passport*	Aux. sloop (keel)	46.37	32.00	13.33	6.00	Sloop
2042	1970	South Hants Marine	She 31 class	Aux. half-ton sloop	30.00	22.39	9.29	5.33	Sloop
2042.1	1970	Eino Antinoja	S&S 6.6 class	Aux. half-ton sloop	30.00	22.37	9.29	5.47	Sloop
2047	1970	Northern Yachts	Northern 29 class	Aux. sloop	29.00	21.25	9.00	4.50	Yawl
2055	1970	A. Lee Loomis	*Northern Light*	Aux. yawl	61.25	42.50	15.61	8.63	Sloop
2056	1970	Derek J. Boyer	*Carillion*	Aux. sloop	45.00	33.00	13.00	7.00	Sloop
2057	1970	Arthur Slater	*Prospect of Whitby III*	Aux. sloop	45.15	33.33	13.00	7.08	Sloop
2058	1970	Edward Heath	*Morning Cloud II*	Aux. sloop	40.67	32.00	12.50	6.75	Sloop
2058.1	1971	Georgio Carriero	*Sagittarius*	Aux. sloop	40.67	31.62	12.58	6.75	Sloop
2058.2	1971	J. Martens	*Easy Rider*	Aux. sloop	40.67	31.62	12.58	6.75	Sloop
2058.3	1971	Willi Illbruck	*Pinta*	Aux. sloop	40.65	31.60	12.64	6.75	Sloop
2058.9	1978	Huisman Shipyard	Huisman 41 class	Aux. sloop	41.07	31.63	12.56	6.50	Sloop
2058.10	1978	Jacinto Viladomiu	Unknown	Aux. sloop	41.07	31.03	12.56	6.50	Sloop
2058.11	1981	John Kerkvliet	Unknown	Aux. sloop	41.05	31.62	12.58	6.75	Sloop
2058.14	1983	Terence Conklin	Unknown	Aux. sloop	40.67	31.62	12.58	6.75	Sloop
2060	1971	Tartan Marine	Tartan 46 class	Aux. sloop	46.67	36.00	14.00	7.54	Sloop
2061	1971	R. C. Watson	*Cervantes IV*	Aux. sloop	40.18	30.00	12.00	6.62	Sloop
2062	1970	Marina Spacarelli	*Kerkyra IV*	Aux. one-ton sloop	38.58	29.63	11.42	6.50	Sloop
2062.1	1971	Endo Corp.	*Sun Bird II*	Aux. one-ton sloop	38.58	29.63	11.75	6.50	Sloop
2062.2	1971	Brin Wilson	*Pathfinder*	Aux. sloop	38.58	29.63	11.75	6.50	Sloop
2062.3	1971	Jorge de Churruca	*Machichaco*	Aux. one-ton sloop	38.58	29.63	11.75	6.50	Sloop
2062.4	1971	Aydin Kent	Unknown	Aux. sloop	38.58	29.63	11.75	6.50	Sloop
2062.6	1978	Prestige Yachts	Superstar 339	Aux. cruiser/racer	38.58	29.63	11.75	6.50	Sloop
2062.FG1	1971	R. J. Langman	*Mark Twain*	Aux. sloop	38.63	29.63	11.75	6.50	Sloop
2062.FG3	1971	A. le Conte Co.	Admiral's Cup class	Aux. sloop	39.62	29.63	11.75	6.50	Sloop
2062.FG4	1971	Graham Evans	*Pilgrim*	Aux. sloop	39.62	29.63	11.75	6.50	Sloop
2065	1970	South Hants Marine	She 27 class	One-quarter-ton sloop	26.00	19.25	8.50	4.75	Sloop
2065.1	1971	Yankee Yachts	Yankee 26 class	One-quarter-ton sloop	26.00	20.67	8.96	4.75	Sloop
2069	1971	M. R. L. Dowling	*Queequeg*	Aux. sloop	46.00	35.30	13.31	7.25	Sloop
2070	1970	E. A. Maxwell	*Gosling*	6-meter sloop	33.07	24.59	6.62	5.52	Yawl
2074	1971	G. F. Jewett	*Zaida*	Aux. yawl	52.87	37.83	13.17	7.25	Yawl
2074.1	1979	Frank Warburton	Unknown	Aux. yawl	52.87	37.83	13.17	6.50	Yawl
2077	1971	Philip F. Miller	*Arcadia*	Aux. yawl (c/b)	48.50	36.17	13.50	6.00	Sloop
2079	1971	Nautor Ky	Swan 48 class	Aux. sloop	48.08	39.00	13.60	7.75	Yawl
2079.1	1971	Nautor Ky	Swan 50 class	Aux. yawl	50.17	39.00	13.60	7.75	Yawl
2079.2	1971	Palmer Johnson	PJ 50	Aux. yawl	50.17	39.00	13.60	7.75	Ketch
2081	1972	Paul Nicholson, Inc.	*Shohola*	Motor-sailer	58.83	43.50	15.50	5.75	Sloop
2082	1971	E. S. Lorentzen	*Saga*	Aux. sloop	57.63	42.75	14.80	8.83	Yawl
2084	1971	John B. Goulandris	*Amazon*	Aux. yawl	73.05	55.00	18.00	10.50	Sloop
2085	1971	*Courageous* synd.	*Courageous*	12-meter sloop	65.50	51.43	11.94	8.94	Sloop
2088	1971	Ernst Rohner	*Bolle V*	6-meter sloop	32.74	24.38	6.12	5.47	Sloop
2089	1971	Lynn Williams	*Dora*	Aux. sloop	61.42	46.00	15.67	8.95	Sloop
2089.1	1973	R. T. Veale	*Santervea*	Aux. sloop	61.42	46.00	15.78	8.94	Sloop
2090	1971	Douglas & McCleod	D&M 22 class	Quarter-ton sloop	21.96	18.75	8.42	2.75	Sloop
2091	1971	Finn Craft Co.	Finn-Craft class	Aux. sloop	38.00	30.00	12.00	5.42	Sloop
2094.1	1971	Ed Jussen	*Lightnin'*	One-ton sloop	38.48	28.71	11.72	6.25	Sloop
2094.2	1972	Yankee Yachts	Yankee 38	One-ton sloop	38.48	28.71	11.72	6.25	Sloop
2095	1972	Tartan Marine	Tartan 41 class	Aux. sloop	40.67	32.62	12.25	6.33	Sloop
2095.2	1972	Tartan Marine	Tartan 42 class	Aux. sloop	42.00	32.00	12.25	6.17	Sloop
2098	1971	Palmer Johnson	PJ 30 class	Half-ton sloop	29.92	22.50	9.50	5.25	Sloop
2098.1	1972	Hans Edward Reith	*Hobbytry*	Half-ton sloop	29.92	22.50	9.50	5.25	Sloop
2098.6	1972	North Star Yachts	Northstar 1000 class	Half-ton sloop	29.92	22.50	9.50	5.25	Ketch
2100	1971	Burt H. Keenan	*Southerly*	Aux. ketch	55.42	42.25	14.00	5.00	Ketch
2100.1	1985	Dave Schmidt	Unknown	Aux. ketch	56.54	42.72	14.00	5.00	Sloop
2102	1972	Hans Otto Schumann	*Rubin*	Aux. sloop	49.55	37.00	13.50	7.58	Sloop
2103	1972	Arthur K. Watson	*Anjacaa*	Aux. sloop	52.67	40.00	16.00	5.75	Sloop
2104	1972	T. C. Chadwick	*Green Highlander*	Aux. sloop	41.46	32.50	12.25	6.92	Sloop
2106	1972	Sandell & Mantymaki	*Indigo*	One-quarter-ton sloop	24.61	20.23	9.00	4.81	Ketch
2110	1972	Nautor Ky	Swan 65 class	Aux. ketch	64.87	47.00	16.33	9.25	Sloop
2112	1972	Nautor Ky	Swan 44 class	Aux. sloop	44.00	35.22	12.58	7.15	Sloop
2112.1	1972	Palmer Johnson	PJ 44	Aux. sloop	44.00	35.22	12.58	7.15	Sloop

Design	Date	Client	Name/Class	Job Description	LOA	DWL	Beam	Draft	Type
2114	1972	Maurice Laing	*Lou Jaine*	Aux. sloop	41.79	32.50	12.83	6.92	Sloop
2116	1972	Bruce Eissner	*Columbine*	One-ton sloop	35.28	29.00	12.25	6.34	Sloop
2117	1972	Malcom Kinnaird	*Chaos*	One-ton sloop	38.70	28.96	11.72	6.25	Sloop
2119	1972	Marina Spaccarelli	*Paxos*	One-ton sloop	36.87	29.00	12.25	6.33	Sloop
2120	1972	Robert Jones	*Gunfleet of Hamble*	Aux. sloop	41.00	30.25	11.96	6.50	Sloop
2121	1972	David May	*Winsome IV*	Aux. sloop	41.79	32.42	12.83	6.92	Sloop
2122	1972	Chris Dunning	*Marionette IV*	Aux. sloop	41.21	30.00	12.00	6.75	Sloop
2126	1972	Roy Disney	*Shamrock*	Aux. yawl	52.00	37.00	14.50	6.00	Yawl
2130	1972	D. W. Johnstone	*Barnacle Bill*	Aux. sloop	41.79	32.50	12.83	6.92	Sloop
2131	1972	Evan Julian	*Inca*	Aux. sloop	45.00	34.50	13.00	7.04	Sloop
2134	1972	North Star Yachts	Northstar 80/20 class	Motor-sailer	40.00	31.00	13.33	4.75	Ketch
2134.2	1978	Swallowcraft Yachts	Swift 40 class	Motor-sailer	39.00	31.00	13.33	5.31	Ketch
2135	1972	North Star Yachts	Northstar 500 class	One-quarter-ton sloop	24.98	20.23	9.00	5.00	Sloop
2135.2	1972	North Star Yachts	Northstar 600 class	Aux. sloop	25.98	20.23	9.00	4.00	Sloop
2136	1972	Bruno Calandriello	*Dida III*	Aux. sloop	41.79	32.50	12.83	6.92	Sloop
2137	1972	Peter Kurtz	*Love & War*	Aux. sloop	47.00	34.58	13.42	7.33	Sloop
2137.1	1972	Dennis Doyle	*Moon Duster*	Aux. sloop	47.00	34.58	13.42	7.33	Sloop
2140	1972	Albert Buell	*Saudade*	Aux. sloop	47.00	36.31	13.44	7.58	Sloop
2142	1973	Eric Ridder	*Tempest*	Aux. ketch	79.50	63.00	16.88	11.73	Ketch
2143	1972	Charles Holland	*Ojala II*	Aux. sloop	37.92	28.25	11.50	6.25	Sloop
2146	1972	D. M. Powell	*Oyster*	Aux. sloop	49.29	37.50	14.92	7.62	Sloop
2147	1972	Percy Chubb	*Bird-O-Passage*	Seagoing powerboat	48.42	41.25	15.33	5.00	Ketch
2148	1972	Ron Amey	*Noryema IX*	Aux. sloop	52.33	40.00	14.08	7.92	Sloop
2149	1972	Arthur Slater	*Prospect of Whitby IV*	I.O.R. racer	47.00	36.31	13.44	7.58	Sloop
2149.1	1973	Gunter Havermann	*Struntje*	Aux. sloop	47.00	36.31	13.41	7.50	Sloop
2149.2	1973	John Prentice	*Battlecry*	I.O.R. racer	46.83	36.31	13.44	7.58	Sloop
2150	1972	Nautor Ky	Swan 41 class	Aux. sloop	41.00	30.25	11.96	6.50	Sloop
2150.1	1975	Nautor Ky	Swan 411	Aux. sloop	41.06	31.00	11.96	6.83	Sloop
2151	1972	Kenneth Murray	*Bardoo*	Aux. ketch	51.75	37.50	14.92	6.37	Ketch
2153	1974	D. R. Hooper	*Corinthian*	Aux. sloop	50.00	38.17	13.67	7.67	Sloop
2155	1973	Derek Pitt-Pitts	*Thunder*	Aux. sloop	38.46	28.75	11.50	6.25	Sloop
2157	1972	Edward Heath	*Morning Cloud III*	Admiral's Cup yacht	44.76	34.08	13.47	7.09	Sloop
2158	1972	Brin Wilson	*Quicksilver*	Admiral's Cup yacht	41.00	30.25	11.96	6.50	Sloop
2159	1973	Max Boris	*Sumbra III*	One-ton sloop	38.48	28.70	11.74	6.20	Sloop
2159.1	1973	Alessandro Rasini	*Ornella*	One-ton sloop	38.48	28.72	11.72	6.25	Sloop
2160	1973	George Tooby	*America Jane*	Aux. sloop	38.67	29.25	11.71	6.50	Sloop
2161.1	1973	Neth.-American Yachts	*Avante II*	Diesel cruiser	85.83	77.00	20.25	5.83	Power
2161.2	1976	Neth.-American Yachts	Unknown	Diesel cruiser	89.83	80.67	20.25	5.83	Power
2162.1	1974	Carlos & Alfredo Behrens	*Beagle II*	Offshore motor yacht	65.48	58.50	18.50	5.00	Power
2164	1973	Paul Hoffmann	*Thunderhead*	Aux. cutter	58.33	42.33	14.85	8.33	Cutter
2165	1973	Joseph Wright	*Siren Song*	Aux. sloop	58.04	40.58	13.87	8.05	Sloop
2166	1973	North Star Yachts	Northstar 1500 class	Aux. sloop	35.50	26.00	10.32	5.83	Sloop
2166.1	1976	South Hants Marine	She 36 class	Aux. sloop	35.60	26.00	10.40	6.00	Sloop
2167	1973	Nautor Ky	Swan 38 class	Aux. sloop	38.00	28.71	11.58	6.33	Sloop
2169	1973	Ron Rawson, Inc.	Rawson 40 class	Aux. sloop	40.58	31.00	12.00	6.67	Sloop
2171	1973	John B. Kilroy	*Kialoa III*	I.O.R. maxi ketch	79.00	62.50	17.42	11.62	Ketch
2172	1973	ALPA S.P.A.	ALPA 36 class	Motor-sailer	37.29	27.25	11.21	5.00	Ketch
2173	1973	Nick Kinyeres	*Clavileno*	Aux. sloop	31.92	23.42	9.50	5.43	Sloop
2174	1973	Howard L. Smith	*Quickstep*	One-ton sloop	38.00	28.71	11.58	6.33	Sloop
2174.1	1973	D. G. Beck	*Riptide*	One-ton sloop	38.00	28.71	11.58	6.33	Sloop
2175	1973	H. H. Behnke	*Nicola V*	Aux. sloop	42.00	32.00	12.29	6.92	Sloop
2176	1973	Earl Birdzell	*Tantara*	Aux. sloop	43.94	33.33	12.50	7.98	Sloop
2182	1973	Giorgio Carriero	*Mandrake*	Aux. sloop	48.17	36.50	12.79	7.50	Sloop
2182.1	1974	Gaston Defferre	*Palynodie VI*	Aux. sloop	48.17	36.50	12.79	7.50	Sloop
2183	1973	David O. May	*Wanton*	Aux. sloop	38.25	28.25	11.46	6.25	Sloop
2184	1973	Tartan Marine	*Tock*	Aux. c/b ketch	41.33	32.33	13.25	4.83	Ketch
2186	1974	I. W. Varvet	I. W. 40 class	Aux. sloop	39.50	28.50	11.42	6.25	Sloop
2187	1973	Alcort Div. AMF	Weekender	Trailerable sailboat	24.08	19.25	7.92	3.00	Sloop
2189	1974	Edmond de Rothschild	*Gitana VI*	Aux. sloop	65.62	48.00	15.64	9.52	Sloop
2190	1974	Arne Frissell	*Kay*	Aux. yawl	51.33	37.50	13.50	7.75	Yawl
2192	1974	George Clowes	*Peregrine*	Aux. ketch c/b	45.50	37.75	12.17	5.00	Ketch
2193	1973	Cantiere Castiglioni	Impala 41	Aux. sloop	41.81	31.76	12.10	6.70	Sloop
2195	1974	Chris Dunning	*Marionette V*	I.O.R. sloop	44.25	32.30	12.29	7.17	Sloop
2196	1974	Richard Steele	*Jubilee*	Motor-sailer	60.00	49.58	16.00	7.00	Sloop
2201	1974	Nautor Ky	Swan 47 class	Aux. sloop	47.80	34.50	13.76	7.80	Sloop
2202	1974	Raymond Kirby	*Patrice III*	Aux. sloop	46.83	36.31	13.44	7.58	Sloop
2203	1974	Thomas J. Watson	*Come On Daddy*	Utility boat	37.83	34.00	11.87	3.67	Power
2204	1974	ALPA S.P.A.	ALPA 21 class	Aux. sloop	21.25	18.50	8.12	4.00	Sloop
2206	1974	Yvon Plisson	*Chrismuir*	Aux. sloop	61.45	46.00	15.75	8.96	Sloop
2207	1974	Nautor Ky	Nautor 50 class	Motor-sailer	48.85	37.00	15.08	5.50	Ketch
2207.1	1980	Siltala Yachts	Nauticat 52	Motor-sailer	51.17	39.58	15.00	7.17	Ketch
2210	1975	Giacomo Benello	*Smack*	Aux. sloop	46.83	34.88	13.33	7.50	Sloop
2213	1975	Jesse Philips	*Charisma II*	Aux. sloop	54.13	39.37	14.04	8.25	Sloop

Design	Date	Client	Name/Class	Job Description	LOA	DWL	Beam	Draft	Type
2218	1974	Peter Spencer	*Cotton Blossom*	Half-ton sloop	31.17	22.50	10.00	5.33	Sloop
2221	1975	Virginia Moister	*Sankaty III*	Cruising cutter	32.25	24.00	9.92	4.83	Cutter
2222	1975	Arthur Slater	*Prospect of Whitby V*	Aux. sloop	44.33	32.08	12.20	7.17	Sloop
2222.1	1975	W. C. Petersen	*Dorothea*	Aux. sloop	44.33	33.00	12.17	7.14	Sloop
2222.2	1975	Torquato Gennari	*Tramp*	Aux. sloop	44.36	34.00	12.25	7.17	Sloop
2223	1975	Tatsumitsu Yamasaki	*Sun Bird V*	Admiral's Cup yacht	54.17	39.30	14.00	8.17	Sloop
2223.1	1975	Hiroshi Okasaki	*Miyakadori*	Admiral's Cup yacht	54.17	39.30	14.00	8.17	Sloop
2226	1975	Charles Owens	*Caribe Owl*	Aux. c/b ketch	50.00	44.00	14.08	4.83	Ketch
2227.1	1975	Eino Antinoja	Antilla 36	Three-quarter-ton yacht	34.87	27.50	10.67	5.83	Sloop
2228	1975	Albert Buell	*Saudade II*	Aux. sloop	51.17	36.83	13.82	7.58	Sloop
2228.1	1975	Willi Illbruck	*Pinta II*	Aux. sloop	51.17	36.83	13.82	7.58	Sloop
2232	1975	Jose Laport	*Mach II*	One ton class	38.25	28.00	11.25	6.25	Sloop
2232.5	1975	Miles Jaffe	*Leonore*	One ton class	38.23	27.11	11.25	6.25	Sloop
2234.4	1975	N. Goulandris	*Mania Two*	Fishing yacht	92.00	84.00	21.26	7.10	Power
2235.1	1975	M. Demeyer	*C & She*	One-quarter-ton yacht	27.06	19.67	9.27	4.87	Sloop
2236	1975	Edward Heath	*Morning Cloud IV*	Aux. sloop	44.96	34.29	13.25	7.33	Sloop
2237	1975	Mr. Coal	*Lady Sail*	Aux. cruising ketch	84.00	68.42	19.17	10.83	Ketch
2238	1975	Nautor Ky	Swan 431 class	Aux. sloop (keel)	43.36	33.33	13.39	7.29	Sloop
2238.1	1975	Nautor Ky	Swan 431 class	Aux. sloop (c/b)	43.50	33.33	13.33	4.79	Sloop
2239	1976	Nautor Ky	Nautor 43 class	Motor-sailer	43.00	31.50	13.67	5.50	Ketch
2239.1	1984	Siltala Yachts	Nauticat 43	Motor-sailer	42.72	32.83	13.10	6.30	Ketch
2241	1976	ALPA S.P.A.	ALPA 27 class	Aux. cruiser/racer	26.79	23.23	9.62	5.25	Sloop
2242	1976	ALPA S.P.A.	ALPA 33 class	Aux. cruiser/racer	33.00	25.00	10.50	5.25	Sloop
2244	1975	Rolly Tasker	*Siska*	Aux. sloop	51.39	38.10	13.56	9.00	Sloop
2245	1975	Rodney Basil	*Evrika*	Aux. cutter	47.25	35.25	13.75	7.42	Cutter
2248	1975	Michael Swerdlow	*Aries*	Aux. cutter	49.13	37.33	13.50	7.87	Cutter
2249	1975	Bruno Calandriello	*Dida*	Aux. sloop	42.92	31.75	12.29	7.00	Sloop
2250	1975	Bruce McPherson	*Maltese Cat*	One-half-ton yacht	31.46	23.46	10.02	5.58	Sloop
2253.1	1976	Tartan Marine	Tartan 38	Aux. sloop (keel)	37.29	28.50	11.75	6.75	Sloop
2253.2	1976	Tartan Marine	Tartan 37	Aux. sloop (c/b)	37.29	28.50	11.75	4.17	Sloop
2253.3	1977	John Wright	Condor 37	Aux. sloop	37.29	28.50	11.75	6.75	Sloop
2254	1976	Robert Beck	*Pirana*	Aux. sloop	45.62	33.75	12.31	7.60	Sloop
2261	1976	Arturo Parenti	Unknown	Two-ton yacht	42.92	31.75	12.29	7.00	Sloop
2268	1976	W. T. Pascoe	*Scandalous*	Aux. sloop	50.46	36.60	14.00	8.00	Sloop
2269	1977	James Michael	*Sirona*	Aux. sloop	58.40	46.00	17.08	8.00	Sloop
2270	1976	*Enterprise* synd.	*Enterprise*	12-meter yacht	67.00	48.00	12.50	9.00	Sloop
2273	1976	C. van Rietschoten	*Flyer*	Round-the-world racer	65.19	49.79	16.33	10.00	Ketch
2276	1976	Center Amusements, Inc.	Pari 34 class	Three-quarter-ton yacht	34.50	25.00	10.86	6.00	Sloop
2276.1	1977	S. Gordon Demetre	Orion 35 class	Three-quarter-ton yacht	34.50	28.75	10.86	6.04	Sloop
2278	1977	Ardell Nelson	*Su Shan*	Aux. c/b cutter	50.58	40.00	14.67	5.75	Cutter
2279	1977	Jack Carter	*Agena*	Aux. c/b sloop	47.00	35.96	12.70	5.00	Sloop
2281	1976	New York Yacht Club	N.Y.Y.C. 50 class	Aux. c/b sloop	49.25	36.25	14.25	5.50	Sloop
2281.1	1977	New York Yacht Club	N.Y.Y.C. 48 class	Aux. c/b sloop	47.90	34.50	13.76	5.50	Sloop
2281.2	1978	Rabeux & Bombart	*St. Jean*	Aux. c/b sloop	49.25	36.00	14.25	5.17	Sloop
2281.3	1983	Brain Folbigg	*Centrefold*	Aux. c/b sloop	47.90	34.50	13.70	5.60	Sloop
2282	1976	Eugene Sydnor	*Zephyr*	Aux. sloop	45.92	33.75	12.31	7.60	Sloop
2283	1976	ALPA S.P.A.	ALPA 40 class	Aux. sloop	39.50	32.14	12.94	6.42	Sloop
2284	1977	Peter Fazer	*Quartet*	One-quarter-ton yacht	26.04	19.50	9.14	5.00	Sloop
2286	1977	Swarbrick Bros.	*Morning Star*	Three-quarter-ton yacht	34.00	25.83	11.33	6.00	Sloop
2288	1976	Bianca Yacht I/S	*Riviera*	Aux. sloop	32.00	26.00	10.83	5.75	Sloop
2289	1976	Pedro Valero	*Andoval*	Aux. ketch	55.33	39.00	14.00	7.33	Ketch
2289.1	1977	Antonio Coch	*Scorpio*	Aux. ketch	55.33	39.00	14.00	7.33	Ketch
2291	1977	South Hants Marine	She 33 class	Half-ton yacht	32.11	23.97	10.54	5.50	Sloop
2292	1977	Fuji Yacht Builders	Fuji 40 class	Aux. sloop	39.17	30.00	12.67	6.00	Sloop
2297	1977	Nautor Ky	Swan 57 class	Racer/cruiser sloop/ketch	57.36	43.19	15.79	9.00	Sloop/Ketch
2299	1977	Ake Lindquist	Unknown	Half-ton yacht	31.50	22.37	11.00	5.50	Sloop
2301	1977	Nautor Ky	Nautor 39 class	Motor-sailer	39.21	31.00	13.26	5.50	Sloop/Ketch
2301.1	1983	Siltala Yachts	Nauticat 40	Motor-sailer	39.33	32.79	13.08	5.75	Ketch
2302	1977	Tartan Marine	Tartan 10	One Design racer	33.14	27.00	9.25	5.87	Sloop
2323	1977	Osman Ozdemiroglu	*World of Love*	Aux. sloop	49.42	37.33	15.96	8.33	Sloop
2326	1977	Gunther Schulz	*Gotz von Berlichingen*	Aux. ketch	66.50	49.00	18.00	7.25	Ketch
2331	1978	Nautor Ky	Swan 76 class	Deckhouse version	76.40	60.00	19.04	7.50	Sloop/Ketch
2331	1978	Nautor Ky	Swan 76 class	Flushdeck version	76.40	60.00	19.04	11.17	Sloop/Ketch
2332	1978	Calixto Valenti	Unknown	Aux. motor-sailer	44.75	31.50	13.67	5.83	Ketch
2333	1978	Stephen Nichols	*Obsession*	Aux. sloop	45.70	34.81	14.29	8.08	Sloop
2334	1978	Leonard Yablon	Not built	Three-masted bark	157.00	130.00	27.00	10.50	Bark
2335	1978	Don Brown	Not built	Schooner yacht	183.67	136.67	36.00	6.00	Schooner
2348	1978	Tartan Marine	Tartan 33 class	Cruiser/racer	33.67	28.83	10.99	4.50	Sloop
2348.1	1983	Tartan Marine	Tartan 34 class	Cruiser/racer	34.50	28.10	10.99	4.50	Sloop
2349	1978	Howmar Boats	Designer's Choice class	C/B One Design	14.87	12.75	6.08	0.42	Sloop
2351	1978	David Burn	*Abraxas/Aquarius*	Aux. sloop	45.70	34.81	14.32	8.12	Sloop
2362	1978	Eino Antinoja	*Antilla*	Aux. sloop	39.40	32.54	12.25	7.50	Sloop
2365	1979	Lawson Reid	*Zimba*	Aux. sloop	50.83	40.75	15.00	8.50	Sloop

Design	Date	Client	Name/Class	Job Description	LOA	DWL	Beam	Draft	Type
2368	1980	Ft. Schuyler Fndn.	*Freedom*	12-meter yacht	62.21	44.79	12.15	8.80	Sloop
2371	1980	Anonymous	*Rose Marie*	Diesel motor yacht	87.50	79.00	20.65	5.83	Power
2373	1980	Thomas Watson	*Palawan V*	Aux. ketch	50.00	36.00	14.17	6.75	Ketch
2377	1979	Westsail, Inc.	Westsail 63 class	Aux. ketch	62.50	48.00	17.33	7.00	Ketch
2378	1979	Peter de Jong	*Yonder*	Aux. ketch	56.00	41.92	15.37	6.17	Ketch
2381	1979	Lou Abrahams	*Challenge*	I.O.R. racer	45.60	36.54	14.32	8.00	Sloop
2381.1	1980	Brian King	Unknown	I.O.R. racer	46.17	36.54	14.32	8.00	Sloop
2381.2	1980	Brian Millar	*Ngaruru*	I.O.R. racer	45.60	36.54	14.32	8.00	Sloop
2382	1979	Robert Hurst	*Fly*	Aux. ketch	59.00	45.00	14.74	9.00	Ketch
2383	1979	Sigismundo Cortes	0.28 class	Offshore One Design	28.40	22.00	8.00	5.10	Sloop
2386	1979	Ocean Cruising Yachts	O.C. 48 class	Cruising c/b sloop	47.58	36.00	13.75	4.83	Sloop
2390	1980	Queen Long Marine	Hylas 47	Aux. sloop	46.83	37.75	14.33	6.00	Sloop
2390.1	1980	Stevens Yachts	Stevens 47 class	Aux. sloop	46.83	37.75	14.33	6.00	Sloop
2390.3	1983	Stevens Yachts	Stevens 50 class	(Aft cockpit) aux. sloop	50.00	37.75	14.33	6.00	Sloop
2390.5	1984	Renata Vesely	*Ananda*	Cruising sloop	49.87	37.75	14.33	7.00	Sloop
2390.8	1984	Stevens Yachts	Stevens 50 cl.	Aux. sloop (pilot house)	50.00	37.75	14.33	6.00	Sloop
2391	1983	James P. Baldwin	*Osprey*	Motor-sailer	95.95	76.00	23.00	10.00	Sloop
2392	1980	S.I.P. Industries	SIP 51 class	Aux. cruising yawl	50.97	41.83	16.07	2.73	Yawl
2394	1979	J. R. Schmidt	Unknown	Single-handed cutter	39.42	31.00	11.50	6.25	Cutter
2396	1980	Lyman - Morse	Seguin 44 class	Aux. cruiser	44.52	33.54	12.83	6.25	Sloop
2396	1981	Robert Schmidt	*Hobnob*	Aux. cruiser	45.00	33.54	12.83	6.25	Sloop
2396.01	1981	L. Simon	Not built	Aux. cruiser	45.00	33.54	12.83	6.25	Sloop
2396.02	1981	D. Jackson	Not built	Aux. cruiser	45.50	33.54	12.83	7.75	Sloop
2396.03	1982	M. L. Bond	Not built	Aux. cruiser	45.00	33.54	12.83	6.25	Sloop
2396.04	1982	D. W. Trimingham	Not built	Aux. cruiser	45.50	33.54	12.83	7.75	Sloop
2309.05	1982	Duane Strawn	*Windwalker*	Aux. cruiser	46.29	33.54	12.83	6.25	Sloop
2396.06	1982	Louis Cabot	*Yonder*	Aux. cruiser	45.00	33.54	12.83	6.25	Sloop
2396.07	1981	Russel Goldsmith	*Holimar*	Aux. cruiser	45.00	33.54	12.83	6.25	Sloop
2396.10	1981	Robt. Armstrong	*Alert*	Aux. cruiser	45.54	33.54	12.83	5.25	Sloop
2396.11	1983	James House	*Scrimshaw*	Aux. cruiser	46.29	33.54	12.83	6.25	Sloop
2396.12	1983	John Maynard	*Magic*	Aux. cruiser	45.00	33.54	12.83	6.25	Sloop
2396.13	1983	James Pitney	*First Light*	Aux. cruiser	45.50	33.54	12.83	7.75	Sloop
2396.14	1983	F. R. Nelson	*Galivant*	Aux. cruiser	46.31	33.54	12.83	6.25	Sloop
2396.15	1984	Fred Gilman	*Butterfly*	Aux. cruiser	45.83	33.54	12.83	6.25	Sloop
2396.16	1984	Hugh Tullos	*Envy*	Aux. cruiser	45.83	33.54	12.83	5.25	Sloop
2396.17	1984	Peter Lind	*Rainbow*	Aux. cruiser	45.83	33.54	12.83	6.25	Sloop
2396.18	1984	Gifford Pinchot	*Lark*	Aux. cruiser	46.29	33.54	12.83	5.25	Yawl
2396.20	1987	Richard Davis	*Cherub*	Aux. cruiser	44.52	33.54	12.83	6.25	Sloop
2397	1981	Tartan Marine	Tartan 3000	Aux. sloop	30.00	25.25	10.08	5.15	Sloop
2405	1981	Howmar Boats, Inc.	Howmar 12	One Design daysailer	12.00	10.39	5.00	2.54	Sloop
2407	1981	Evan Julian	*Marac*	I.O.R. racer	46.11	37.00	14.29	8.00	Sloop
2407.1	1981	Lemmington Marine	Unknown	I.O.R. racer	46.11	37.00	14.29	7.54	Sloop
2409	1981	Edmond de Rothschild	*Gitana, Sr.*	6-meter yacht	33.27	24.00	6.17	5.50	Sloop
2410	1981	Rodney Basil	Unknown	Aux. ketch	84.75	60.00	20.00	11.50	Ketch
2413	1981	Stevens Yachts	Stevens 40 class	Cruising sloop (keel)	40.57	31.33	12.25	6.00	Sloop
2413.1	1981	Stevens Yachts	Stevens 40 class	Cruising yacht (c/b)	40.57	31.33	12.54	4.50	Sloop
2413.3	1984	Stevens Yachts	Stevens 32 class	Cruising sloop	42.17	31.33	12.50	6.00	Sloop
2415	1981	Eugene Sydnor	*Dancer*	IOR racer	42.58	33.60	12.97	7.56	Sloop
2418	1981	W. D. Bremner	*Harrier*	Seagoing power yacht	61.00	56.75	16.33	4.58	Power
2420	1981	F. T. Schuyler Fdn.	*Spirit of America*	12-meter yacht	64.67	51.07	12.33	8.58	Sloop
2429	1982	Jose L. Ugarte	*Orion Iru*	Aux. sloop	44.80	39.00	12.04	9.00	Sloop
2432	1982	Prestige Yachts	Prestige 36 class	Cruiser/racer	35.50	29.25	11.50	6.67	Sloop
2432.2	1983	Holiday Boats, Inc.	S&S 36 class	Cruiser/racer	35.50	29.25	11.50	6.67	Sloop
2434	1981	George Nicholson	*Geo. Nicholson*	Three-masted schooner	170.00	140.00	31.00	12.00	Schooner
2436	1982	Avance Yachts	Avance 40 class	Aux. sloop	40.00	32.00	12.58	7.00	Sloop
2436.1	1982	Kai Granholm	Unknown	Aux. sloop	40.00	32.00	12.58	7.00	Sloop
2436.2	1982	Heiki Siren	Unknown	Aux. sloop	40.00	32.00	12.58	7.00	Sloop
2437	1982	Peggy Nichols	*Golden Eagle*	Cruiser/racer	51.45	40.00	15.45	8.75	Sloop
2441	1982	Walsteds Baadewerft	Walsted 42 class	Aux. sloop	42.00	32.80	12.14	7.09	Sloop
2447	1982	George Herrdum	*Cyclos*	Aux. ketch	92.30	74.00	21.20	12.00	Ketch
2450	1982	Anonymous	Unknown	Aux. ketch	82.02	65.03	20.01	8.20	Ketch
2455	1983	Edward King	*Sea Angel*	Aux. ketch	88.25	68.54	20.50	8.00	Ketch
2458	1983	Thomas Watson	*Palawan VI*	Aux. ketch	60.31	43.64	14.76	7.40	Ketch
2459	1983	Thomas Hsueth	Not built	Motor-sailer	66.18	58.00	19.33	5.67	Ketch
2460	1983	Jaime Torres	Not built	Aux. sloop	40.60	32.50	11.77	7.00	Sloop
2467	1983	Henry Hinckley Co.	Not built	Aux. sloop	36.98	26.00	10.58	5.00	Sloop
2468	1983	Dale Denning	*Esprit*	Trawler	53.62	46.67	15.85	4.62	Power
2470	1983	Dennis O'Brien	Not built	Cruising ketch	101.50	77.50	23.00	8.00	Ketch
2475	1983	Christos Kritikos	*Karyatis*	Aux. sloop	69.57	54.00	17.85	10.00	Sloop
2476	1983	Fisher's Island Ferry District	*M/V Race Point*	Auto/passenger ferry	132.00	115.00	33.50	7.42	Power
2477	1984	Coates Shipping Co.	*Queen Nefertiti*	Aux. schooner	126.67	96.00	27.58	11.00	Schooner
2480	1984	Helmut Keller	*Ebb Tide*	Aux. ketch	85.00	68.70	19.68	9.84	Ketch
2481	1984	Tartan Marine	Tartan 40 class	Aux. sloop (keel)	40.25	30.75	12.70	7.00	Sloop

Design	Date	Client	Name/Class	Job Description	LOA	DWL	Beam	Draft	Type
2481	1984	Tartan Marine	Tartan 40 class	Aux. sloop (c/b)	40.25	30.75	12.70	4.75	Sloop
2481.1	1985	Cantiere Zuanelli	Zuanelli 40 class	Aux. sloop	40.25	33.96	12.80	6.40	Sloop
2482	1984	Yachting France	Lacoste 42 class	Aux. sloop	42.17	35.75	13.00	7.50	Sloop
2483	1984	William Simon	*Freedom*	Cruising ketch	123.75	98.00	26.00	10.00	Ketch
2485	1984	Stevens Yachts	Stevens 59 class	Motor yacht	58.50	51.46	17.10	4.75	Power
2487	1984	Yachting France	Lacoste 36 class	Aux. sloop	36.50	30.00	12.19	6.46	Sloop
2490	1984	Poul Pappalardo	Not built	Aux. sloop	64.20	48.50	16.70	7.00	Sloop
2493	1985	Charles Butt	*Ranger*	Aux. ketch	107.00	82.00	23.43	11.93	Ketch
2494	1985	C.I.M. Shipyard	Maxi 88 class	World cruiser	88.56	68.57	20.47	10.24	Sloop
2499	1985	Sunward Yachts Corp.	Sunward 63 class	Aux. cruising sloop	62.50	48.00	16.56	7.00	Sloop
2500	1984	*America II* synd.	*America II*	12-meter yacht	65.00	45.00	12.00	9.00	Sloop
2500.1	1984	*America II* synd.	*America II* US42	12-meter yacht	65.00	45.00	12.00	9.00	Sloop
2500.2	1985	*America II* synd.	*America II* US44	12-meter yacht	65.00	45.00	12.00	9.00	Sloop
2500.3	1985	*America II* synd.	*America II* US46	12-meter yacht	65.00	45.00	12.00	9.00	Sloop
2501	1985	Baltic Yachts	Baltic 83 class	Aux. cruising yacht	83.00	68.50	20.24	10.67	Sloop
2502	1985	George Armadoros	Not built	Sport fisherman	88.42	78.88	27.50	6.00	Power
2504	1986	Steve Nichols	*Obsession*	Mini-maxi racer	69.67	56.67	17.50	12.17	Sloop
2505	1986	Eric Ridder	*Tempest*	6-meter yacht	32.90	22.90	6.20	5.30	Sloop
2510	1986	Howard Keck	*Galileo*	Aux. cruising ketch	123.30	96.00	26.10	11.50	Ketch
2511	1986	Holiday Yachts	Holiday 47 class	Cruiser/racer	46.95	37.75	13.95	7.60	Sloop
2512	1986	Dereckor's	*Lady Frances*	Motor yacht	105.00	90.75	23.00	4.00	Power
2515	1988	Concordia Yachts	Concordia 52 class	Racer/cruiser	52.60	42.00	15.35	7.30	Sloop
2515.2	1988	Concordia Yachts	Concordia 52 class	Center cockpit version	52.60	42.00	15.35	7.30	Sloop
2516	1988	Eldon Trimingham	Bermuda dinghy	Racing daysailer	14.37	14.11	5.02	0.92	Sloop
2517	1987	Baltic Yachts	Baltic 64 class	Racer/cruiser	64.00	51.50	17.30	7.60	Sloop
2527	1987	Charles Dolan	*Encore*	Racer/cruiser	73.00	58.00	18.50	12.67	Sloop
2529	1988	Raymond Tublitz	*Venturosa*	Cruising yacht	109.50	84.00	24.50	12.70	Ketch
2536	1988	Charles Cella	*Astral*	Cruising yacht	114.00	88.00	25.42	10.00	Ketch
2544	1988	Baltic Yachts	Baltic 52 class	Racer/cruiser	51.50	41.90	15.42	9.17	Sloop
2546	1989	Robert Day	Not built	Motor yacht	93.00	91.00	21.00	6.42	Power
2546.4	1993	Robert Day	*Keldi*	Motor yacht–refit of *Petite Ruth*	88.67	78.71	18.36	4.90	Power
2550	1988	Paolo Perotti	*Maysylph*	Cruising ketch	123.50	96.00	26.50	12.00	Ketch
2551	1989	Alastair Dunn	*Victoria*	Cruising yacht	90.62	71.85	20.67	10.05	Ketch
2553	1989	Arnold Meier	Not named	Aux. sloop	131.25	108.00	27.92	11.50	Sloop
2555	1989	Tecnomarine	T-boat	High-speed mega-yacht	163.00	129.50	33.50	4.92	Power
2560	1989	Bennet brothers	*Jam Session*	Racer/cruiser	48.25	38.75	14.38	6.25	Sloop
2560.1	1991	Bennet brothers	S&S 48 class	Racer/cruiser	48.02	39.00	14.33	6.25	Sloop
2561	1991	Anonymous	*Luja*	Racer/cruiser	82.00	67.26	20.18	11.22	Sloop
2568	1989	J. Lefrak	Not named	Motor yacht - not built	67.00	58.79	19.00	6.00	Power
2575	1990	Charles Gosnell	*Timoneer*	Cruising yacht	117.27	88.00	25.04	9.70	Ketch
2579	1991	Leo Leibowitz	*Mit-sea-Ah*	114-foot motor yacht	114.00	96.00	23.33	6.42	Power
2580	1991	Baltic Yachts	Baltic 58	Racer/cruiser	58.50	47.57	16.62	10.50	Sloop
2583	1992	Silvano Boroli	*Quarta Santa Maria*	Cruising yacht	82.28	67.26	20.18	9.38	Sloop
2584	1991	La Esperanza de Puerto Rico, Inc.	*La Esperanza*	Steel aux. (refit consult.)	100.00	88.00	17.50	6.25	Schooner
2585	1991	Anthony Seibert	Hylas 49	Offshore cruiser	48.83	37.75	14.25	6.00	Sloop
2587	1991	Isam K. Kabban	*Sariyah*	World-cruising ketch	140.00	95.00	27.17	11.00	Ketch
2596	1992	Fred Callahan	*Stealth*	15-foot sailing dinghy	15.06	15.00	6.33	0.62	Sloop
2596.1	1994	J. Gubelmann	*Hot Tomato*	15-foot sailing dinghy	15.06	15.00	6.33	0.62	Sloop
2598	1992	John White	Bermuda dinghy	Racing daysailer	14.37	14.37	5.10	0.82	Sloop
2601	1992	Atlantic Boat Group	A.B.G. 2549	Riverine assault craft	26.50	22.50	9.42	2.00	Power
2604	1993	John Watts	*Bandera*	59-foot cruising yawl	58.50	42.50	15.50	7.42	Yawl
2608	1993	William Simon	*Itasca*	Motor yacht - ice mod.	175.00	155.00	35.00	16.00	Power
2614	1993	James Dolan	*Sagamore*	78-foot I.M.S. race boat	81.17	68.92	18.11	14.08	Sloop
2615	1993	Annapolis Boat Rentals	Pending	90-foot cruising sloop	95.67	73.00	22.50	8.00	Sloop

Winners of Major Races

Design	Name	Race	Year	Postition
7	*Dorade*	Transatlantic	1931	1st overall
7	*Dorade*	Fastnet	1931	1st overall
7	*Dorade*	Bermuda	1932	1st overall
7	*Dorade*	San Francisco - Honolulu	1936	1st overall
27	*Stormy Weather*	Transatlantic	1935	1st overall
27	*Stormy Weather*	Fastnet	1935	1st overall
77	*Ranger*	America's Cup	1937	1st overall
222	*Baruna*	Bermuda Race	1938	1st overall
222	*Baruna*	Bermuda Race	1948	1st overall
381	*Gesture*	Bermuda Race	1946	1st overall
628	*Argyll*	Bermuda Race	1950	1st overall
1054	*Finisterre*	Bermuda Race	1956	1st overall
1054	*Finisterre*	Bermuda Race	1958	1st overall
1054	*Finisterre*	Bermuda Race	1960	1st overall
1343	*Columbia*	America's Cup	1958	1st overall
1773	*Constellation*	America's Cup	1964	1st overall
1834	*Intrepid*	America's Cup	1967	1st overall
1834	*Intrepid*	America's Cup	1970	1st overall
1969	*Running Tide*	Bermuda Race	1976	1st overall
2085	*Courageous*	America's Cup	1974	1st overall
2085	*Courageous*	America's Cup	1977	1st overall
2110	*Sayula II*	Whitbread	1973	1st overall
2148	*Noryema IV*	Bermuda Race	1972	1st overall
2368	*Freedom*	America's Cup	1980	1st overall
2527	*Encore*	Fastnet	1993	1st overall

Index